PARADIGMS OF REGIONAL PLANNING AND DEVELOPMENT

PARADIGMS OF REGIONAL PLANNING AND DEVELOPMENT

AMITABH SHUKLA
M.A. (Eco.) Ph.D.

DEEP & DEEP PUBLICATIONS PVT. LTD.
F-159, Rajouri Garden, New Delhi - 110027

PARADIGMS OF REGIONAL PLANNING
AND DEVELOPMENT

ISBN 978-81-8450-388-3

Typeset by THE LASER PRINTERS, 8/15, 3rd Floor, Subhash Nagar, New Delhi-110027.

Printed in India at MAYUR ENTERPRISES, WZ Plot No. 3, Gujjar Market, Tihar Village, New Delhi - 110 018

Published by DEEP & DEEP PUBLICATIONS PVT. LTD.,
F-159, Rajouri Garden, New Delhi-110027. Phones: 25435369, 25440916.
E-mail: ddpubs@yahoo.com • ddpubs@gmail.com
Sales Showroom: 2/13, Ansari Road, Daryaganj, New Delhi-110002
Phone/Fax: 23245122

CONTENTS

PART B

LIST OF CONTRIBUTORS

Amitabh Shukla, Faculty, Department of Post-graduate Studies and Research in Economics, Rani Durgawati University, Jabalpur (M.P.).

Amitava Mukherjee, Professor, Rajeev Gandhi Foundation, New Delhi.

B. Choudhury, Assistant Director, T & CP, Government of Assam, Karimganj.

B. Satyanarayan, Co-ordinator, Special Asst. Programme (UGC), Department of Economics, O.U., Hyderabad.

B.N. Yugandhar, Member (Ex), Planning Commission, Government of India.

Inderpal Kaur, Punjab School of Economics, Guru Nanak Dev University, Amritsar (Punjab).

Kamta Prasad, Chairman, Institute for Resource Management and Economic Development, Karkardooma, New Delhi.

Kanchan Chopra, Professor, Delhi School of Economics, Delhi University, New Delhi.

M.L. Patel, Director, Tribal Resource Cell, Bhopal (M.P.).

Md. Abdus Salam, Department of Economics, AMU, Aligarh (U.P.).

N. Roy, Department of Economics, Karimganj College, Karimganj, Assam.

Naseem A. Zaidi, Department of Economics, AMU, Aligarh (U.P.).

P.C. Dutta, Department of Statistics, S.S. College, Hailakandi, Assam.

P.G. Marvania, Professor of Economics, Saurashtra University, Rajkot (Gujarat).

R.N. Prasad, Professor, Indian Institute of Public Administration (I.I.P.A.), I.P. Estate, New Delhi.

Rahul Singh, School of Planning and Architecture, New Delhi.

S.K. Sharma, Department of Geography, Dr. H.S. Gaur University, Sagar (M.P.).

Shri Prakash, Director, Birla Institute of Management and Technology (BIMTEC), Noida (U.P.).

Surendra Singh, Department of Geography, North-Eastern Hill University, Shillong.

PART A

Regional Dimensions of Agricultural Development and Poverty*

Surendra Singh

INTRODUCTION

There are several poverty alleviation and rural development programmes initiated by the central as well as state governments since 1952. In these programmes, the main emphesis has been laid specially to generate the income of the individual families. The strategies prepared under these programmes do not serve the purpose of self-sustained growth and well-balanced development, so that the problems of low productivity and poverty in rural areas are still existant. Poverty persisting in the rural areas of the country, if it is attributed in its relative term, is dependent upon two basic factors: income inequalities and the conditions of under-

*This paper was presented in the International Conference of Regional Science Association at I.I.T., Kharagpur and published with kind permission of the Secretary, Regional Science Association, India.

development. The variation in the operational size of landholdings (which reflects the uneven distribution of resources in rural areas) is the major factor of income inequalities in the society. In spite of higher agricultural productivity in the smaller and marginal size of landholdings (below 2.0 ha), the income of the peasants of India is recorded very low because of low magnitude of their total income (Minhas, 1970).

The second factor of rural poverty, the under-development of agricultural phenomena and slow processes of agricultural production increase, which have been dealt with many agricultural scientists by correlating the level of poverty with agricultural growth and productivity, is found stronger and significant factor for poverty alleviation in the rural areas. Infact, productive processes has a direct bearings on poverty. It has been proved by many studies that there is an inverse relationship between the proportion of poor persons below poverty line and per capita income. Higher productivity per male agricultural worker has led to reduction in the incidence of poverty (Ahluwalia, 1978; Bhalla, 1980, Singhal and Gill, 1991). The study of the regional inequalities of agricultural development and its optimal patterns may be useful for understanding the causes and reducing the incidences of poverty in rural areas. Infact, labour productivity index (agricultural output per worker) appears to be more meaningful for searching out the causes of poverty. But, labour productivity is directly related to and dependent upon the index of agricultural productivity (output per land unit) particularly in India where the agriculture is characterised as labour intensive and food-grain dominated. In such conditions, the causes of rural poverty may be studied and the areas of its severity may be identified to emphasize the regional dimensions of agricultural development. In the present paper, the attention is therefore focussed on (a) the evaluation of underlaying agricultural development processes by correlating the regional patterns of its two main attributes, namely agricultural growth and productivity, and (b) the identification of the areas of severe incidence of rural poverty in order to suggest the optimal patterns of agricultural development by comparing actual and potential productivity levels.

The objectives of the present study is worthwhile to state the techniques over emphasizing the causes of regional inequalities persisting in the patterns of agricultural growth for which the a real features of existing productivity and agricultural growth potential are essentially to be studied. The comparison of existing (or actual) productivity pattern with potential productivity pattern would be able to give the answer of the important question where and upto what extent the production processes can be speeded up to get the optimal growth and productivity of agricultural activities.

It is widely recognised that Indian agricultural production processes which are food-grain dominated, has been operating through the application of green revolution technology. Of course, it is complementary to boost up the production and productivity. But its effects have been marginalised because of its improper use without consideration of environmental conditions of agricultural production possibilities. The production processes have their own limitations and they are accelerated within the limits of various agro-ecological conditions which can be and/or have been slightly relaxed by human effects to employ technological factors (Mc Carty and Lindbarg, 1967). The effects of these factors on production structure may be seen to assess and compare the pattern of agricultural growth potential. It would also lead to the solution of the problem of the use of appropriate technology for self-sustained growth.

So far as the assessment of agricultural growth potential intensity which is directly related to the maximum expected production level (A) and is defined here as 'potential productivity index' (maximum expected agricultural output per land unit) is concerned, there are a number of studies which assess potential productivity on the basis of agro-ecological conditions of land for instance, the assessment of agricultural growth potential was made by food and Agriculture Organisation in 1976 to develop a model in which land resources and physiographic constraints for their utilisation were considered (FAO/UNFPA/IIASA, 1982; Grosjean and Messerli, 1988). This idea of integrated approach of productivity assessment was mooted first by Stamp (1962), and he produced land suitability classification for England. Infact, potential yield of various crops in the various agro-ecological conditions have also been assessed in India by the Indian Council of Agricultural Research, New Delhi under its All India Coordinating Project on National Demonstration (Prasad, *et. al.*

1987). The results of this project were utilised later on by the Planning Commission for demarcating the agro-climatic regions of the country (Alagh, 1987).

METHODS AND DATA BASE

The district-wise informations regarding area, yield production and farm production prices are collected from the various volumes of Agricultural Situation in India published by Directorate of Economics and Statistics, Ministry of Agriculture, New Delhi. For calculating annual agricultural growth, three years averages (1979-80 to 1981-82) for early 1980s and two years average (1988-89 to 1989-90) for early 1990s have been worked out and used for proper reliability of results interpretation by eliminating annual data fluctuations due to climatic variations. Further, to prepare potential productivity index, the data of maximum expected yield of the various crops is required. District-wise data of maximum expected yield for various crops have been completed from the Annual Reports of All India Coordinating Project on National Demonstration published by Indian Council of Agriculture Research, New Delhi (Mathur and Gupta, 1985).

District-wise total agricultural output for early 1980s and 1990s have been calculated by in its aggregated form by converting production of each crop into the money value and then average annual agricultural growth which is the differentiation of total agricultural output between two points of times has been calculated. Agricultural productivity index has been compiled for early 1980s and 1990s. But the potential productivity index (that in maximum expected output per hectare) is compiled only for early 1990s. The coefficient of productivity improvement which is ratio between existing productivity (Y) and potential productivity (A) has been calculatéd district-wise and the a real Pattern was show for suggesting the proper acceleration of production processes for self-sustained growth in its a real perspective.

AGRICULTURAL GROWTH BY PRODUCTIVITY CLASSES

The regional pattern of agricultural growth-productivity relationship are infact the result of intensification of output augmenting practices (increasing use of modern technology). The application of technological factors increases level of productivity and rate of agricultural output (Binswanger & Ryan, 1977). As a result, it can conceptually be generalised that the areas of high product should follow fast growth rate with strong growth-producting relations. To test the validity of the fact, a cross-classification of total number of districts has been made on the basis of considering five categories of average annual growth rate of agricultural output (1979-82 to 1988-90) and seven categorics of agricultural producting levels (1979-32). It would help in understanding the obliterated pattern/of agricultural output growth in relation to production pattern. Bi-variate frequency distribution (35 cell of 5x7) shows the statistical significance of the areal extent of growth-productivity relationship. The average area under each cell must be 2.86% to total area. The cells which have percentage share of its areal extent about 2.86% have been chosen for the interpretation of the regional patterns. Bi-variate frequency Table 1 reveals that 10 cells out of total 35 are significant to note. Out of these 10 cells, 9 fall into the categories ranging low to extremely low levels of land product (below Rs. 750) which have high and very high average annual rate of agricultural output growth (above 8.0%). It accounts for more than one-fifth (21.37%, 48 districts) part of the country which includes Thar desert of Rajasthan, interior parts of Karnataka, most of the Telangana part of Andhra Pradesh and Coastal Orissa. In addition, nearly one-sixth part of the country, (17.01%, 6 districts) which includes Malwa and Bundekhard plateau of Madhya Pradesh, Vidharwa of Maharashtra, Arawali Ranges and interior part of Orissa, have low level of agricultural products with medium rate of agricultural growth (8-4%). Further, the areas of terai foot hills of Himalayas specially situated in Uttar Pradesh and Bihar and Konkan coastal areas of Karnataka which include one-tenth part of the country (10.11% area, 43 districts) are marked fast growth (8% above) at low level of agricultural productivity (Rs. 250 to Rs. 750 per ha).

In fact, the positive relationship between agricultural growth and productivity as Binswanger and Ryan (1977) hypothesized, evolves concentrated patterns of agricultural growth, while negative relationship of these attributes would evolve diversified pattern of agricultural development. Concentrated patterns may be of two types as the areas of low growth rate with low agricultural productivity and secondly, the areas of high and very high growth rate with high productivity level. In India, the obliterated patterns of agricultural development reveals that the areas of high concentration (higher growth rate at high productivity level) are found in the surroundings of three metropolitan centres of the country (Delhi, Calcutta and Madras). The centre-oriented fast growth in these areas may be because of increasing food demands of fast increasing population pressure at those centres (urbanisation), intensive operation of diffusion of agricultural innovations and yield-augmenting practices through these urban centres and better transport facilities. Thus, the centre-approach of agricultural development is found valid in India.

In general, there are the evidences of weakening the growth-productivity relationship over time. The coefficient of correlation between agricultural growth and productivity has been recorded very high (r = .671) in the 1960s, low (r = .325) in the 1970s and very low and insignificant (r = .109) in the 1980s. Decreasing coefficient of growth-productivity relationship leads to the conclusion that there is a transformation of areal patterns of agricultural development from concentrated pattern to diversified ones. The effects of green revolution technology has been 'area specific' during 1970s and now its effects has been transmitting to the remote areas of low productivity (Raza, 1935). Now, questions arises whether agricultural development patterns are optimal or not? The answer of this question may be given to correlate the actual and optimal productivity patterns.

IMPROVEMENT IN AGRICULTURE PRODUCTIVITY

The strategic points for agricultural extension services can be suggested by identifying the optimal pattern of agricultural development. For the same, comparison of actual productivity (Y) pattern with potential productivity pattern (A) can be made to calculate its ratio (A/Y) which is defined here as 'agricultural growth potential intensity' (for further details, see Singh, 1982). It reflects the coefficient of improvement of agricultural conditions of the area.

The regional inequalities and areal comparison of these two main attributions of agricultural growth potential intensity would explain the causes of its variability. The basic characteristics of the distribution of these attributes are given below.

(a) The national average of potential productivity index is Rs. 3228 per hectare which is more than double (2.06 times) than that of the national level of actual agricultural productivity, i.e., Rs. 1577 per hactare. It implies that there is enough agricultural growth potential to intensify agricultural practices.

TABLE 1

Bivariate Frequencies of Percentage Share of Area and Number of Districts by Productivity Level (1979-82) and Output Growth (1979-82 to 1988-90).

Productivity Classes (Rs./ha)	*Average Annual Growth Rate (in %)*					*Total 12<*
	(VH)	*12-8 (H)*	*8-4 (M)*	*4-0 (L)*	*neg.*	
1750 and above (E.H.)	1.98 (10)	1.26 (9)	3.26 (16)	2.58 (13)	1.66 (13)	10.74 (61)
1750-1500 (V.H.)	1.30 (5)	.08 (1)	1.52 (5)	1.08 (4)	.94 (6)	4.92 (21)
1500-1250 (H)	.62 (5)	1.51 (8)	1.70 (9)	.82 (4)	1.87 (11)	6.52 (37)
1250-1000 (M)	2.45 (11)	2.47 (14)	2.63 (12)	1.01 (4)	2.55 (9)	11.11 (50)
1000-750 (L)	2.76 (9)	2.43 (9)	3.51 (12)	2.53 (10)	2.80 (10)	14.02 (50)
750-500 (VL)	5.89 (13)	5.98 (17)	9.02 (24)	7.06 (22)	3.12 (9)	31.08 (85)
500 and below (EL)	9.50 (18)	1.23 (2)	4.46 (10)	4.40 (10)	2.01 (6)	21.60 (46)
Total	24.50 (71)	14.96 (60)	26.09 (88)	19.48 (67)	14.96 (64)	99.99 (350)

N.B.: Figures in Parentheses denote number of districts in each category.

Abbreviations: EH = Extremely High; VH = Very High; H = High; M = Medium; L = Low; VL = Very Low; EL = Extremely Low, and neg = negative.

(b) In spite of higher coefficient of variations in the distribution of actual/productivity (CV = 80.92%) than the areal variation of potential productivity (CV = 73.58%) in India in the early 1990s, the value of class interval showing the regional variations is lesser (Rs. 250 within the class variation) in the case of actual productivity distribution than the class-interval of potential productivity distribution. It is because of very high national average and wider range of potential productivity index.

(c) There is equal distribution of areal extent of actual and potential agricultural productivity in all their categories except extremely high under which nearly one-fourth part of the country falls. However, the areal extent of potential productivity is recorded larger particularly in the categories of high and very high magnitudes than the areal extent of actual productivity. On the other hand, the very low potential productivity areas account for only 8.22% while the areal extent under this category is much larger as more than 18.0% of the entire country. It means the areas of high and very high agricultural products may be proposed for further extension of agricultural activities in the areas of very low agricultural productivity.

(d) There is significantly positive relationship between actual and potential productivity indexes (r = .6414), which reflects co-existing and inter-dependent pattern of agricultural productivity with agricultural growth potential of the country. Comparing the regional pattern of these two attributes of agricultural growth potential intensity, it is obvious that the entire areas of Northern Great Plains of India including Brahmaputra Valley of Assam and the Koromandal Coasts of Krishna, Kavery and Godawari deltas, where the fertile alluvial soils with favourable humid climatic conditions prevail, are noticeable for very high and extremely high index values of potential as well as of actual productivity levels. Contrastingly, the areas of arid climate conditions covering the most of the parts of southern plateau including the Thar areas of Rajasthan have the low and

TABLE 2

Percentage Share of Area under Various Categories of Actual and Potential Productivity Indexes (1988-90)

Categories	*Actual Productivity*		*Potential Productivity*	
	Classes (Rs./ha)	*Area* (&)	*Classes* (Rs./ha)	*Area* (%)
Extremely High	1750 and above	25.30	4000 above	25.86
Very High	1750-1500	7.85	4000-3500	11.58
High	1500-1250	8.14	3500-3000	11.82
Medium	1250-1000	12.28	3000-2500	13.85
Low	1000-750	15.01	2500-2000	14.38
Very Low	750-500	18.13	2000-1500	8.22
Extremely Low	500 and below	13.29	1500-below	14.28
National Average	Rs. 1577	—	Rs. 3228	—

N.B.: Class interval is Rs. 250 for Actual Productivity and Rs. 500 for Potential Productivity Index.

very low values of both the productivity indexes. It means the productivity patterns of existing agricultural conditions are considing the patterns of potential productivity, which is the symbol of balanced agricultural development within the limits of optimal growth potential conditions of the country, although the regression coefficient value of actual productivity (dependent variable) on potential productivity (considered as independent variable) has been recorded very low (b = .345) but significant as .01 level with high degree of determinant (R^2 = .4115). It proves the significance of spatial variance of areal patterns of agricultural productivity in relation of agricultural potential productivity.

(e) There are two different agro-ecological conditions prevailing in the areas of high and extremely high coefficients of agricultural growth potential intensity (above 2.5). First, the areas of fertile alluvial soils with better humid climatic conditions of the middle Ganga plains and of the Brahmaputra valley (northern parts of

Bihar and entire Assam) where growth potential intensity is recorded very high. Secondly, the most of the parts of Deccan plateau where undulating topography and arid climatic conditions are affecting the agricultural activities and, hence the values of potential productivity index in these areas have been recorded low and very low. However, the coefficients of productivity improvement are marked very high. It may be because of very low level of existing productivity. It appears that these areas of high growth potential intensity are in great needs of modern package of agricultural technology.

On the other hand, the fertile lands of the country—the entire part of great northern plains including coastal areas of high productivity have very low coefficient of productivity improvement (below 2.0), despite of very high values of potential productivity. In these areas of favourable agro-ecological conditions where application of green revolution technology appears to be more effective, the agricultural intensification might not be much profitable although there are possibility for agricultural extension services.

CONCLUSION

The main causes of rural poverty are the less income and the conditions of under-development particularly of primary sectors of the economy. Poverty alleviation programmes would, therefore, be made and implemented in the light of agricultural development. The present study concludes that our agricultural growth processes are so slow and area specific, and the farmers frustation with the new system of agricultural innovation's diffusion is so high (because of system's inefficiency) that we predict beyond our expectations at the time of plans preparation which fail in real sense at the tine of its implementation. As a result, the problems of rural poverty, major nutritional deficiency diseases and diguised employment in agriculture sector can be seen every where in the country. The areas of low level of agricultural productivity and slow growth, where agricultural growth potential intensity is enough to use, have been identified for delimiting the areas of severe rural poverty. They include (i) the entire interior parts of the Deccan plateau (the Vidharbha of Maharashtra; Malva, Bundelkhand and Beghelkhand of Madhya Pradesh; entire parts of Chhotanagpur plateau; interior Karnataka and Andhra Pradesh) (ii) the Thar areas of Rajasthan, (iii) the Northern Bihar of middle Ganga plains, and (iv) the entire Brahmaputra valley of Assam. What is truly striking is that the spatial features of rural poverty follow the diversified patterns in its regional context because of evolving diversified pattern of agricultural development which is 'Centre-oriented' and hance, Binswanger and Ryan (1977) hypothesis of appropriate technological enhancement is still found valid in Indian conditions. Through implementing agricultural extension programmes of appropriate technology specially in the high growth potential areas of the country, the rural poverty can be minimised.

Notes and References

Ahluwalia, M.S. (1978): Rural Poverty and Agricultural Performance in India, *Journal of Developmental Studies*, Vol. XIV, pp. 298-323.

Alagh, Y.K. (1987): *Guidelines for Planning at the Agro-climatic Regional Level*, Planning Commission, New Delhi.

Bhalla, G.S. (1980): *National and Regional Economic Development in India during 1961-71* (Mimeo), C.S.R.D., Jawaharlal Nehru University, New Delhi. pp. 11-16.

Binswanger, H.P. and J.G. Ryan (1977): Efficiency. and Equity Issues in *ex ante* Allocation of Research Resources, *Indian Journal of Agricultural Economics*, Vol. 32 (No. 3).

FAO/UNFPA/IIASA (1982): Potential Population Supporting Capacity of Land in the Developing World, *Tech. Report*, FPA/INT/513, Rome.

Grosjean, M. and B. Messerli (1988): African Mountains and Highlands-Potential and Constraints, *Mountain Research and Development*, Vol. 8 (Nos. 2/3), pp. 111-22.

Mathur, P.N. and M.P. Gupta (1985): *National Demonstration Project*, Pub. and Information Division, I.C.A.R., New Delhi.

McCarty, H.H. and J. Lindbarg (1967): *A Preface to Economic Geography*, Englewood Cliffs, Prentice-Hall, New Jersey.

Minhas, B.S. (1970): Rural Poverty, Land Distribution and Development Strategy, *Indian Economic Review*, Vol. VI, pp. 97-128.

Prasad, C., *et. al.* (1987): *First Line Transfer of Technology Projects*, Pub. and Information, I.C.A.R., New Delhi.

Raza, M. (1981): Regional Disparities in India—A Preliminary Exploration of the Regional Dimension of Agricultural Development, in Noor Mohammad (ed): *Perspectives in Agricultural Geography*, Vol. IV, Concept Pub. Coy., New Delhi, pp. 103-44.

Singh, S. (1982): Identification and Phasing of Agricultural Development in Rohilkhand, *National Geographical Journal of India*, Vol. XXVIII (Nos. 1&2), pp. 28-36.

Singhal, K.C. and H.S. Gill (1991): Poverty, Per capita Income and Per Worker Sectoral Incomes, *Indian Journal of Regional Science*, Vol. XXIII, (No. 2), pp. 1-10.

Stamp, L.D. (1962): *The Land of Britain—Its use and Misuse*, IIIrd edn., Longmans, Green & Co. Ltd., London, p. 351.

Regional Planning for Sustainable Agriculture Development—A Case Study of Assam

P.C. Dutta, N. Roy and B. Choudhury

INTRODUCTION

Productivity has become the buzzword of our times. Few agree upon the definition of productivity, but every one is certain of one thing—the more productivity the better. The term productivity is beset with numerous definitional problems. After a prolonged deliberation in debate, it has been generally agreed upon that productivity is a measure of the ratio between output and combined input, both taken together in real terms. And it is held that there is no rise in productivity if the production function runs under constant returns to scale. In earlier accounts of the history of economic thought, the term "Productivity" was hardly used, instead the classical economists spoke of production and the rate of production which essentially meant more or less what is now referred to as productivity. The "Productivity" is one of the most elusive concepts in economic literature. Productivity indices can be awfully misleading if it is misinterpreted. A rising productivity does not necessarily reflect a gain in the well-being of the people. Even in the period of declining economic activity, the trend in productivity seems to be moving in upward direction. It is thus imperative that in interpreting productivity, one must take cognizance of physical changes in output.

The Earth's growing population raising antropogenic pressures and concern for the capacity of life supporting systems to continue assimilating them. But the period also coincide with era of less frequent famines, draughts, etc. on one hand technological development raising further possibilities of producing more food and other agricultural product from relatively lesser land on the other. Both agricultural resources and their sustainability have ecological, social and economic dimensions. Technology in general, biotechnology and genetic engineering in particular, providing opportunity for converting biodiversity into ecological-*cum*-economic assets can help in promoting sustainable agriculture. These refer to inefficient and irrational management of soil, land and water, crops and farm animals and hords of other related aspects of agriculture systems as much as the needed support of basic and applied research as an element of R & D input.

2. THE ISSUE

Coming to productivity aspect of the agricultural production in the state of Assam, what perplexes, one is not only the gross difference in the productivity level between the state and the country as a whole, but also the wide intra-state variation as well.

Although in keeping in the SDP of the state has been declining over the years, the primacy of the agrarian sector has been more or less stable in the state when viewed in terms of its support base for the vast rural populace. Agriculture can still provide Assam with on "bargain sector" and by any account, is still remains the *sine-qua-non* of the economic emancipation of the state of Assam.

But before injecting the growth stimulant into the artery of this vital sector, of the economy of Assam, we must address to the major issue confronts the growth of this vital sector. And this major issue is nothing but the wide variation in the productivity levels across the spatial units (the districts) of the state and it is this issue around which the present paper revolves.

With the knowledge that all the districts of Assam are primarily agricultural, that there is no widespread diversity in the distribution of natural resources in the state and with inapplicability of the famous Nurksian view that "A state is poor because it is poor"—the conclusion that naturally crops up is that nothing but, the wide variation of the productivity level primarily across the districts which ails the sickly agrarian sector of the state economy.

Wide variation in the level of agricultural development has been a historical fact since the dawn of planned economic development. Economists have long recognised the existence and the stubborn persistence of regional dualism at all levels of national development and throughout the historical experience of almost all presently developed countries (Williamson, 1968).

M. Shafi (1972) made an elaborate analysis of spatial differential in the level of agriculture productivity in the U.P. state. Using some seven productivity indices, like standard nutrition unit, output per agriculture worker. Shafi identified the level of development of the U.P. districts on productivity differentials. M.N. Pal (1975) examined the regional imbalance for the country as a whole using the principal component on the basis of productivity differential using several indicators of development. Choudhury (1994) also identified the development differential across the agro-climatic zones of Assam on the basis of agricultural productivity.

Daberkow and Reichelderfer (1988) conceptualised the Sustainability in economic sense and emphasised that alternate farming system, can decrease or optimise the use of purchased inputs and this can increase the net cash returns, through decreased cost of production. This may effectively improve the competitive position of the farmer and decreased the potential for adverse environmental impacts.

Dobbs *et al.* (1988) calculated economic potential for alternative (low input sustainable) farming systems in a small grain row crop region of northern plain. They considered two sets of alternative cropping systems, in which no chemical fertilisers or herbicides were used, which were compared with various conventional and reduced tillage systems. Results of basic line economic analysis showed that alternative farming systems can be competitive with more conventional in atleast some situations.

Gupta and Singh (1991) concluded that the productivity index of agricultural inputs in India has declined over the last two decades. One of the most important factors contributing to this decline was the lack of research on sustainable agriculture.

Gangower and Sen (1993) examined the changes in cropping pattern and their impact on sustainability of resources use in Tarai region of Uttar Pradesh. The study reveals that there had been wide shirt in the area from course grains, oil seeds and pulses to paddy wheat and sugarcane. Continuous monoculture cropping pattern led to the emergence of soil borne disease and the problems of weed management in paddy and wheat. This resulted in increased use of plant protection chemicals which have adverse impact on the environment and health. The present study, however, examines the productivity differential in the agricultural sector across the different districts of Assam.

The Objectives

Following the foregoing discussion, the present study revolves round the following broad objectives:

(i) to establish the existence of spatial variation in the level of agricultural productivity in Assam;

(ii) to examine the reasons behind such spatial variation; and

(iii) to identity the backward districts of Assam for regional sustainable agricultural development.

The Methodology

In order to examine the aforesaid objectives, the following methodology sequences have been followed in the present study:

(1) Examining the variation with the dependent as well as independent variables using standard variation and co-efficient of variation.

(2) Examining the degree of relation between the dependent and each of the independent variables separately using rank correlation.

(3) Establishing the causal relation between the dependent

and each of the independent variables separately using linear regression) and between the dependent and the independent variables combined using log linear regression method).

(4) Identification of backward districts by using widely used Principal component method.

THE DATA BASE

The dependent as well as the independent variables used in the present study are:

Dependent variable:

Y = Average yield of rice per hectare.

Independent variables:

X_1 = Rural literacy rate as per 1991 census.

X_2 = Irrigation intensity, i.e. Ratio of Gross Irrigated area to Gross cropped area. And the irrigation data takes care of both major and minor irrigation.

X_3 = Consumption of fertiliser (the summation of the three nutrients of fertiliser, i.e. N.P. and K) per hectre.

X_4 = HYV intensity, i.e. the ratio of gross areas under HYV to gross cropped area.

The aforesaid data have either been complied directly or calculated wherever necessary and these data have been collected from the following sources:

(a) The Directorate of Economics and Statistics, Assam;
(b) The Directorate of Agriculture, Assam; and
(c) The Chief Engineer, Irrigation, Assam.

INTRODUCING THE STUDY AREA

Assam, the second largest of the seven north eastern states of India extends from lat. N 24° 0′ 0″ to N 28° 0′ 0″ and long. 89° 45′ 0″ E to 96° 0′ 0″ E. Nestling between the eastern Himalayan foot hills and the Patkai range, Assam occupies roughly a triangular area of 78438 sq. km.

Physiographically, the state is comprised of three broad zones: (a) The Brahmaputra Valley, (b) The Central Assam Range Comprising, the hill districts of Karbi-Anlong and N.C. Hills, and (c) the Barak Valley. Geographically, the location of the state is highly humid as the mean annual rainfall of the State is estimated at 2252 mm. However, the variation of annual rainfall in different districts is between 3500 to 1225 mm.

In general, the Barak Valley and the eastern and western regions of the Brahmaputra Valley are more humid. Rainfall is considerably low in the central Brahmaputra Valley region, while the lowest rainfall is recorded in the rain shadow regions comprising the south of Nagaon district, Diphu sub-division of Karbi-anglong district and the South-West part of Golaghat district. Temperature in Assam is moderate.

The mean minimum temperature ranges between 31°C to 37°C while the mean minimum ranges between 3°C to 7°C. Humidity is considerable high not only during monsoon, but also during the winter months. The wind velocity in the State is considered to be low, but it is comparatively higher towards the western region of the Brahmaputra valley.

THE CROPPING PATTERN

Since long past, Assam has been predominantly an monocropped state with rice as its principal crop. In some pockets, however, double cropping was being followed in rice-based cropping systems which resulted in 116% cropping intensity in 1951-52 with the increase in the creation of irrigation potential, increased use of fertiliser and agricultural implements (mechanisation), inclusion of more area under HYV extension of bank loan and extension services - the practice of multiple cropping is slowly picking up which has resulted in a cropping intensity of 145% in 1990-91.

With the rest of the country, Assam too has got two crop seasons—the Kharif or the season of summer crops; and the Rabi or the season of winter crops.

The cropping pattern (the proportion of area under different crops at a point of time) for the state as a whole in case of foodgrains reveals that rice occupies the major share, about 90% (89.84% to be more precise) in the gross cropped area under foodgrain product. Next to rice comes pulses with a negligible 4.82% and wheat with a scanty 4.33% of the gross cropped area.

The cropping pattern for the different spatial units (the districts) of the state conforms to the State pattern, and it has been more or less uniform across the districts.

ANALYSIS OF THE RESULTS

A reference of Table 1 dearly reflects the variation with the dependent as well as independent variables as has been confirmed by the respective standard deviation (S.D.) and co-efficient of variation (C.V.) The C.V. has been estimated since we have to compare the variability of the variables having different units of measurements, it is observed that C.V. is the highest (100.00) with irrigation followed by fertiliser (55.55) thereby substantiating the varying degree in the level of irrigation potential used and the volume of fertiliser consumed across the different districts of Assam. C.V. with the rural literacy rate is significantly lower (16.99%) thereby establishing a relatively uniform impact of the governmental policy towards the rural literacy. The C.V. with area under HYV is relatively significant and the possible argument behind it might be the minor differences in the cropping pattern (thereby limiting the scope of bringing more area under HYV) and the inequitable potential of irrigation facilities created across the districts during Kadi crop. No. 1. Generalisation should however be made towards a high C.V. associated with each of the independent variables on the dependent variables is not uniform either individually or collectively. For instance, the use of irrigation potential might be fluctuating significantly across the districts but the impact of such a variation gets neutralised effectively since it does not work in isolation.

TABLE 1

	Y	X_1	X_2	X_3	X_4
Mean	1376.96	40.20	0.08	0.009	0.44
S.D.	24.437	6.83	0.08	0.005	0.14
C.V.	17.75	16.99	100.0	55.55	31.99

A close look at the Table 2 confirms that the rank correlation between the dependent and each of the independent variables are significant. It is observed that the rank correlation between the yield rate and the rural literacy rate is highest (0.79) and it is reasonably higher between the former and irrigation (0.59), fertiliser (0.61) and HYV area (0.53) respectively. The high degree of correlation between the yield rate and the rural literacy rate speaks for the direct impact of literacy on the agricultural work force in securing high growth rate. The degree of relationship between the yield rate and the irrigation confirms the fact that while the former takes care of the entire production of paddy, the later takes care of mainly Rabi crops and also the variation in the level of irrigation facilities across the districts, the degree of relationship between the yield rate and fertiliser as well as HYV are also reflects similar pattern of variation with the latter of two variables across the districts, we can thus safely infer from the aforesaid correlationship that each of the independent variables does have a contributory role towards increasing the yield rate. And such an inference can be tested econometrically with the help of a production function analysis. Before taking up production function analysis, let us first identify the backward districts of the state in terms of differences in agricultural production.

TABLE 2

Rank Correlation

	X_1	X_2	X_3	X_4
Y	0.79	0 59	0.61	0.53

INDICATION OF BACKWARD DISTRICTS

Using the principal component method, the backward districts of the state can be identified for regional agricultural development. The index of agricultural development 'P_1', can be estimated with the variables under study. For the purpose the required correlation matrix as computed has been depicted in Table 3.

TABLE 3

Correlation Matrix for Agricultural Group

	X_1	X_2	X_3	X_4
X_1	1			
X_2	-0.29	1		
X_3	0.49	0.48	1	
X_4	0.58	0.47	0.69	1

The index of agricultural development 'P_1' which is the first principal component of variables x_1, x_2, x_3, and x_4 has been estimated as below with the help of above correlation values (Table 3.).

$$P_1 = 0.60\ x_1 + 0.56\ x_2 + 0.89\ x_3 + 0.92\ x_4$$

After putting the values of the respective variables in the above equations, the value of the index of development of agriculture has been found out and tabulated (Table 5) with their respective classes of occurrence. The classification of index has been done in the way as given in Table 4.

TABLE 4

Classification of Index

Class interval of index	*Class symbols*
Below 600	VL
600-800	L
800-1000	M
1000-1200	M
Above 1200	VH

In the light of the above results, two points are to be noted, (i) Negative correlation co-efficient (as found between two important indicators) has been retained in the analysis in order to maintain the live fact, (ii) Second Principal component is not being calculated in this study for two reasons—

(a) The specific indicators of economic development need not be independent while principal components must by very assumption, be orthogonal.

(b) Computational load is much reduced in this approach. With this identification of the level of backwardness across the districts of Assam in the level of agricultural development, the next step will be the examination of the parameters can be best done with the help of a production Function Analysis.

TABLE 5

Values of Index and Classes of their Occurance

	Districts	*Value of Index*	*Classes*
1.	Hailakandi	1188.648	H
2.	Dibrugarh	782.574	L
3.	Cachar	992.073	M
4.	Morigoan	1108.861	H
5.	Golaghat	897.372	M
6	Sibsagar	871.730	M
7.	Nagoan	1160.683	H
8.	N.C. Hills	588384	VL
9.	Jorhat	797.338	L
10.	Goalpara	1272.334	NH
11.	Kamrup	1035621	H
12.	Tinsukia	874.569	M
13.	Darrang	1102.436	M
14.	Karbi-Anglong	683 962	L
15.	Karimganj	1026 374	H
16.	Lakhimpur	823.394	M
17.	Barpeta	1263.589	VH
18.	Demaji	843.351	M
19.	Kokrajhar	949 956	M
20	Bongaigoan	903 481	M
21.	Dhubri	1203.281	VH
22.	Sonitpur	1108.976	H
23.	Nalbari	809 576	M

Although a variety of model has been available in the literature of applied economics to capture the dynamic input-output relationship, the Cobb-Douglas production function has been used in the present study. Despite its function has been chosen since being an homogenous function, it provides a scale and to interpret the elasticity coefficients with relative case.

The Cobb-Douglas production function generally takes the following form:

$$Y = K \prod_{j=1}^{n} x_j . L_j . e^u$$

$$==> \text{Log } y = \text{Log } k + \sum_{j=1}^{n} L_j \text{ Log } x_j + u$$

where the variables are defined in section 5.

TABLE 6

Cobb-Douglas Production Function

Variable	*Co-efficient*	*STD error*	*T-Value*
X_1	0.36	028	1.28
X_2	0 15	0.14	1.07
X_3	0.25	0.17	1.47
X_4	0 18	0 17	1.05
constant	0.85	0.15	5.72
R^2	0.74		
Degrees of freedom	18		

From the estimated results (Table 6) of the production function, it is found that, out of four variables under consideration, the rural literacy rate plays the most significant role in the production of paddy. Although neither total labour force is employed in the agricultural field nor effectively hours of works by labour force are considered, the estimates for the rural literacy rate comes out to be very significant. It shows that, keeping other variables constants, if there is an increase in the literacy percentage by 1%, we can anticipate an increase in the food grain production by 0.36%. It is quite justifiable that the rural folk becomes more and more literate, they will be more and more encourage to practice the modern method of farming and shall be in a position to thwart the attempt of the middle man and the rich agriculturist in the design to exploit them (the agricultural labourer), coming to irrigation, it is found that its contribution is negligible, such theoritically unexpected result might be that effect of the continuing night mare caused by the endless fury of flood. Such a negligible co-efficient for irrigation does out mean that irrigation was not a contributory factor for agricultural development. What this means is that, during the year 1992-93, this variable was a non-issue as the overall agricultural scenario was determined by the recurrence of flood visiting the state as many as three times during the year. Contribution of fertiliser come to be much better in relation to irrigation. The reason behind the relatively better contribution of fertiliser in comparison with irrigation may be that although flood washed away the fertilisers in the rainy season, in winter months during the Rabi crop the impact of fertiliser is positive since it is not affected by floods during that period. In the case of irrigation, however, the same conclusion can not be drawn since during the Rabi crop, the volume of irrigation comes down. Regarding HYV seeds it is found that that its contribution is relatively better than irrigation but smaller than fertiliser. The probable reason may be that more and more area are brought under HYV seeds during Rabi crop and that HYV growing areas are usually in these pockets which are relatively less affected by floods.

It has been founded that the sum of production elasticities is smaller than unity which means that the agricultural production throughout the state is on diminishing returns to scale. It means that if all the inputs are increased by 100%, the output of paddy will go up by 94%. The value of R^2 is 0.74 which indicates that the four variables included in the study together explain 74% variation in the paddy output level. The S.E. associated with each input is found to be significant at 5% probability level of significance.

CONCLUSION

The present exercises thus established the existence of spatial variation in the level of agricultural productivity in Assam. Productivity varies substantially across the districts of Assam and such a variation is explained by the infrastructural factors like irrigation, literacy fertiliser, etc. Although the present analysis could not cover all the variables associated with the agricultural production, it can be safely demand that a reasonable wider domain of the agricultural production function has been take care of. It is presumed that has this analysis been made taking in consideration the institutional managerial and technological parameters, a more rational inference could be drawn:

(i) Faulty irrigation practices coupled with poor drainage have made many areas less productive. Indiscriminate use of fertilisers and pesticides has led to serious unforeseen problems adversely affecting the stability of crops. Economic and environmental concerns have raised the question of agricultural sustainability in the long-run.

(ii) It may be emphasised that crop rotation can be profitable and contribute to sustainable agriculture.

(iii) It is necessary that to maintain the tempo of green revolution and also to strengthen it, the state government must take immediate step to stop further degradation of soil and damage created by flood and subsequent irrigation facilities to reduce the dependence on monsoon for farming. Moreover, some other steps that also needed special attention for sustainable agricultural development in this region, includes:

(a) Development of cropping systems that are less dependent on costly inputs.

(b) Soil fertility maintenance through various cultural practices and balanced fertilisation.

(c) Short duration varieties resistant to economic pests and environmental stress.

(d) Use of bio-fertilisers for attainment of sustainable agriculture.

References

1. Choudhuiy, B. (1994): Spatio-Temporal Dynamism in the Level of Agricultural Development in Assam—An Econometric Approach, Unpublished Ph.D. Thesis (G.U.).
2. Daberkow, S.G. and Reichelder, K.H. (1988): "Low Input Agriculture: Trends, Goals and Prospects for Input Use", *American Journal of Agricultural Economics*, 70 (12), 1159-66.

3. Dobbs, T.L., Leddy, M.G. and Smolik, J.D. (1988): "Factors Influencing the Economic Potential for Alternative Farming Systems: Case Analysis in South Dakota", *American Journal of Alternative Agriculture*, 3 (1), 26-34.
4. Gangwar, L.S. and Sen, C. (1993): Impact of Conventional Farming Long-term Sustainability of Agricultural Production in Nainital Tarai of Uttar Pradesh, *Indian Journal of Agricultural Economics*, 48 (3): 596.
5. Gupta, A.K. and Singh, R. (1991): Corporate Investment in Agricultural Research Issues in Sustainable Development, *Working Paper No. 132*, Indian Institute of Management, Ahmedabad, p. 21.
6. Pal, M.N. (1975): "Disparities in the levels of Development in India", *IJRS*, Vol. VII, No. l.
7. Shafi, M. (1972): "The Measurement of Agricultural Productivity of the Great Indian Plains", *The Geographer*, 19 (1), 1972.
8. Williamson, J.G (1968): "Regional Inequality and the Process of National Development: A Description of the Patterns", in Needleman, L. (ed.) *Regional Analysis*, Penguin Book Ltd, Middlesex, England.

Disparities in Agricultural Development in Madhya Pradesh:

A Study of Rates, Pattern and Production Relations

Shri Prakash

Importance attached to agriculture and its role in growth process has received differential degrees of emphasis both in literature and policy through time. Three distinct thought streams can be distinguished in the literature (Streeten, P., Ref. 6). During the post-war period upto the mid-fifties, agriculture was supposed to play a secondary role of providing labour, raw materials and other resources to develop industries and other secondary and tertiary activities. During the next decade, emphasis shifted from industrialisation to balanced growth. But recently, role of agriculture in the growth of developing economies as a generator of employment for ever rising number of job seekers and as the single largest contributor to the national output is greatly highlighted. This swing in favour of agriculture has been accompanied by a shift in policy of allocation of investible resources between agricultural and non-agricultural sectors of the economy.

Like other sectors of the national economies of developing

countries, their agriculture is also characterised by dualism. Progressive farm production for the market is surrounded by traditional subsistence cultivation. Besides, different regions differ sharply in resource endowments. Differential resources endowments and/or differential rates of growth account for the major share of the existing regional inequalities of agricultural development. These inequalities have been further accentuated by the developmental efforts that have remained concentrated mainly to the regions, which are richly endowed with the natural resources like more fertile soil, better assured irrigational facilities, more enterprising and literate/educated farmers, etc.. Though agriculture and household industries have been assumed to take care of regional inequalities through spatially dispersed development in the planned programmes, scarcity of resources and considerations of productivity of investment have caused an extension of the principle of selectivity in the choice of growth centres from industries to agriculture. Such an approach to development has created rural regional inequalities in general and inequalities of agricultural development in particular, which are similar to those created by the concentration of industries in few urban regions (Prakash and Mohapatra, 1980; Prakash and Rajan, 1977; Prakash, 1977).

Regional inequalities of agricultural development can be reduced only if the backward regions develop more rapidly than the developed ones (For impact of such growth on regional inequalities, see Prakash and Goel, 1986). Besides, a vast and agricultural country like India can attain an appreciable degree of agricultural development only if the process of growth spreads throughout and it embraces all the major crops of different regions of the country. Attainment of this objective necessitates a detailed examination of the problems, processes, trends and patterns of agricultural development in each individual region of the country. This study attempts to analyse the rates and pattern of agricultural development and the relationships between output and the modern factor inputs in the state of Madhya Pradesh. The State of M.P. is almost as varied in agro-climatic conditions as the country taken as a whole.

Broad outlines of the ensuing analysis are as follows: Section I develops model of decomposition of growth, while Section II analyses the rates and pattern of agricultural development. Section III is devoted to the determination of the relationship between output and factor inputs on the basis of time series data. Section IV analyses input-output production relations on the basis of cross-section data. Last section contains conclusions and resume. Sources of data and assumptions relating to them are discussed in the appendix.

I. DECOMPOSITION OF RATE OF AGRICULTURAL GROWTH

Recent experience in India has highlighted the importance of agriculture in the growth of the economy. Empirical evidence shows that, whenever agricultural sector records a substantial increase in its production, it is accompanied by an all-round prosperity in the economy as a whole. As against this, whenever agricultural sector performs poorly in terms of output and its growth, it lowers over all performance of the entire economy. In fact, the growth of Indian economy in the post-liberalisation period since 1991 has been sustained mainly by agricultural development (Prakash and Dutta, 1996, Prakash, Sharma & Singh, 1996). But agricultural development is sustained mainly by the growth of yield, which needs continuous investment in yield raising inputs, on the one hand, and the evolution of new strategy, whenever a new trough is reached in agricultural cycle, since each strategy seems generally to be exhausted in a period of about 3-4 years (Prakash, Buragohain and Sharma, 1997). This is true about the state of Madhya Pradesh also where agriculture has led the rest of the sectors of the economy in the generation of additional income (Prakash & Rajan, 1977a, 1977b). the growth of real agricultural income has been twice as fast as that of total income (Prakash & Rajan, 1977a, 1977b).

Agricultural development may be defined in terms of rates of growth of output per unit of time. The OLS estimates of the following equation has been used to determine the growth rates:

$$Y = A\,e^{bT}\,u, \quad \text{or} \quad \log Y = \log A + bT + u \qquad \text{... (1)}$$

where Y is the variable whose growth is to be measured, T is time, A and b are the constants of the equation, b gives the rate of growth of Y per unit of time T. Year is taken as the unit of time in the study and u is error term.

Total output (Oi) of i-th crop is identically equal to the product of area under cultivation, A (i) and yield per unit of cultivated area, y (i): O (i) = A (i) y (i), or

$$\log O(i) = \log A(i) + \log y(i) \qquad \text{... (2)}$$

Differentiating with respect to time T and dividing both sides by O (i), we get

$$\frac{dO(i)}{dt} \cdot \frac{1}{O(i)} = \frac{dA(i)}{dt} \cdot \frac{1}{A(i)} + \frac{dy(i)}{dt} \cdot \frac{1}{y(i)}, \text{ or}$$

$$= \frac{dO(i)}{O(i)} = \frac{dA(i)}{A(i)} + \frac{dy(i)}{y(i)}, \text{ or}$$

$$g(O) = g(A) + g(y) \qquad \text{... (3)}$$

where g (O), g (A) and g (y) are rates of growth of output, area and yield respectively (Prakash and Goel, 1978).

Production per acre, area and intensity of cropping are the major determinants of growth of agricultural output, while the prices determine the monetary income of the farmers. Area under cultivation of all crops can not increase simultaneously beyond a limit for reasons that are obvious. Cropping intensity depends mainly upon the availability of quick maturing crops, that are suited to the agro-climatic conditions of a region. Naturally, growth of yield per acre emerges as the leading factor of agricultural development. Yield per acre is mainly a function of modern inputs like high yielding varieties of seeds, irrigation, fertilisers, management of farm operations, soil-climatic conditions and pesticides. As data for cropping intensity are not available for most of the years covered by this study, only other two factors of agricultural development have been examined. Rates of growth of output, area and the yield per acre have been estimated by equation 1. Estimated growth curves for output, area and yield per acre for 27 different crops raised in the state of Madhya Pradesh. The period covered is from 1950-51 to 1983-84.

II. EMPIRICAL RESULTS: ANALYSIS OF RATES OF GROWTH OF OUTPUT

The production of pulses has increased at a rate of 1.52 per cent per annum, output of cereals and millets has increased at a slightly lower rate of 1.32 per cent per annum and the production of oil-seeds has expanded at a rate of even less than 1 per cent per annum. Both area and yield per hectare of cereals have increased at 0.91 per cent per annum, while area under pulses has grown twice as fast as their yield per hectare. Area under oil-seeds has increased at a rate five times greater than the rate at which yield per hectare has increased. Thus, growth of area and yield per hectare share the growth of output of cereals and millets equally, whereas growth of area under pulses has contributed the major share to the growth of their output. But the growth of output of oil-seeds is almost entirely accounted by the growth of area under these crops.

The following are the important features of the estimated curves:

(1) Barley, ground-nut, castor-seed, sun-hemp and tobacco are five crops that show negative growth of area under cultivation. Four out of these five crops are cash crops. Barley is the only cereal crop that shows negative growth of area under cultivation. It seems that the increasing profitability of cereals, pulses and other cash crops has made the cultivation of these crops less attractive to the farmers of the state. The profitability or the attractiveness of a crop depends largely upon its yield and price relative to the yields and prices of other crops. We find that while yield per hectare of sun-hemp and castor-seed has remained stagnant, yield per hectare of ground-nut and tobacco has increased by 0.76 per cent per annum. This must have induced farmers to transfer area from these low yield crops to crops with higher yields. The movement of relative prices might have further decreased the attractiveness of these crops. For example, price of barley relative to that of rice decreased from 0.83 in 1965 to 0.61 in 1972, relative price of groundnut decreased from 1.56 in 1965 to 1.43 in 1972

and relative price of tobacco decreased from 6.14 in 1965 to 4.73 in 1973. These trends have continued thereafter also. These facts support our hypothesis.

(2) The highest rate of growth of area under cultivation is 2.84 per cent per annum for mesta, while the lowest rate of growth is 0.14 per cent per annum for cotton. Thus, both the highest and the lowest rates of growth of area under cultivation are recorded by commercial crops other than oil-seeds. The area under mesta shows such high growth despite the fact that its yield per hectare has been decreasing at as high a rate as 2.62 per cent per annum. Such decrease in yield must have reduced the profitability, and hence, the attractiveness of the crop to the farmers. The fact that this crop became more attractive to the farmers can be explained only in terms of the movements of relative price of mesta rising to a level which must have more than compensated for the loss in its yield. The higher relative price of mesta must have induced the farmers to increase area under mesta, and in the process even those lands might have been put under mesta which were not suitable for its cultivation with the result that the yield per hectare declined at such a high rate through time.

The negligible rate of growth of area under cotton implies that the total area under this crop has remained, more or less, stagnant. It is not surprising in view of the fact that, on the one hand, yield per hectare of cotton has been decreasing at a negligible rate of 0.17 per cent per annum, and on the other hand, its price relative to that of rice declined from 2.49 in 1961 to 1.92 in 1973-74. Both these trends continued to remain in operation thereafter also. These two factors must have made this crop less attractive to the farmers. Introduction of high yielding varieties of seeds of wheat, rice, maize, etc. might have further reduced the profitability and attractiveness of crops like cotton.

(3) The highest rate of growth of output is 5.62 per cent for maize, while the lowest rate of growth of output is 0.60 per cent per annum for kodokutki. Thus, both the highest and the lowest growth rates are recorded by the

cereal crops. The highest rate of growth of output of maize is accounted by the fact that both the area and yield of maize show relatively high growth rates. Increasing yield made possible by the use of HYV seeds and other modern inputs and the increasing price which rose from Rs. 27.93 per quintal in 1961 to Rs. 68.76 in 1972-73, an increase of more than 100 per cent, must have induced the farmers to raise the output of maize. But kodokutki shows a growth rate of 0.30 per cent per annum both for area and yield. This implies near stagnancy of both these factors of growth of output. But it is a minor crop of the state.

(4) Five out of 27 crops show negative growth of output, and all these crops happen to be the cash crops. Decrease in area under sun-hemp and tobacco account for the decrease in their output, while the decrease in yield accounts for the decrease in output of sesamum, mesta and cotton. This suggests that M.P. has kept pace with progressive states like Punjab and Haryana, where the traditional subsistence cereal crops have emerged as the main crops in the post-green revolution era due to revolutionary rise in yield, and hence, output, on the one hand, and the prices, on the other, while the customary cash crops have been pushed into the background.

(5) The number of crops that show negative growth of yield is also five. Two of them are oil-seeds and the other three are also commercial crops other than oil-seeds: mustard-seeds, sesamum seeds, mesta, cotton and sugarcane. But area under all these five crops has increased during the same period. The rising prices of these crops must have induced the farmers to increase area under these crops. The absolute price level of sesamum in 1972-73 is more than three times its level in 1961, that of mustard seeds is nearly 2.5 times its price in 1961, while the prices of cotton and sugarcane in 1973 are more than double and four times their prices in 1961 respectively. Such movements of relative prices have continued throughout the eighties and nineties. The fact is that the prices of different crops have been changing in India in such a manner as has maintained the parity between the prices

of foodgrains and non-food crops. This has facilitated the maintenance of relative stability of acreage allocation between these crop groups at 4:1 (Prakash *et. al.* 1997). It is interesting to note that not only the yield but the total output of sesamum, mesta and cotton also decreased, while the total output of sugarcane and mustard show some increase during the same period. The opposite trends shown by the growth of area, on the one hand, and the growth of output and yield, on the other, may perhaps be explained in terms of the changes in relative prices. Despite the phenomenal rise in prices of these crops, their relative prices have not changed much in favour of cash crops of this group. For example, the price of mustard-seeds relative to that of rice decreased from 1.8 in 1961 to 1.5 in 1973, price of cotton decreased from 2.49 in 1961 to 1.92 in 1973, while prices of sesamum and sugarcane have remained unchanged, more or less. Such price trends have not been reversed in the subsequent period. Besides the attractive relative prices, availability of HYV seeds and other complementary inputs for cereal crops like wheat, paddy, jowar and maize might have induced farmers to reserve more fertile land for cereal crops and transfer less fertile land to the cultivation of these cash crops. But the steep rise in absolute prices of the crops with declining yields might have more than compensated the farmers' loss caused by decrease in yield.

(6) The proportion of growth of output accounted by growth of area under 'other cereals', tur, urad, moong/moth, masoor, sesamum, rape/mustard, lin-seeds, potato, mesta, cotton, and sugarcane is larger than the proportion of growth of output accounted by the growth of yield. Thus, almost all the pulses fall under this category. Unlike cereals, area under all pulses, except lakh, has expanded faster than the yield. The growth of output of pulses has resulted largely from the growth of area under them. While wheat and paddy replaced most of the other crops in Punjab and Haryana, making those states major producers of these two cereal crops in the country, pulses have found favour with the

farmers of Madhya Pradesh. The increase in prices of pulses seems to have acted as the chief motivating factor. In 1973, the price of gram was 3.5 time higher than its price in 1961, the price of tur was 4.2 times more, whereas the price of masoor was 3.5 times higher than its price in 1961. The relative prices have further moved in favour of pulses in the subsequent period. Besides, the relative prices of pulses have also been highly attractive. For example, the price of gram relative to that of rice rose from 0.97 in 1961 to 1.05, the relative price of tur increased from 0.97 to 1.3 and that of masoor rose from 0.90 to 1.01 during the same period. The attractiveness of the prices of pulses must have induced the farmers to increase the area under pulses. Consequently, the state of Madhya Pradesh emerges as one of the major producers of pulses in the country. Whereas the share of M.P. in the production of gram rose from 15.44 to 24.36 per cent of the total output in the country, its share in the production of total pulses increased from 7.47 per cent in 1951 to 21.85 per cent in 1983. Thus, nearly one-fifth of the total production of pulses in the country is accounted by the state of Madhya Pradesh.

For other crops, the growth of yield accounts for a larger proportion of the growth of output than that accounted by the growth of area under cultivation. The growth of yield of all the cereals, except 'other cereals', had grown faster than the area under them. But the contribution of the growth of yield to the growth of output of rice, wheat, gram, kodokutki, lakh and 'other oil-seeds' is only negligibly higher than the contribution of the growth of area under cultivation. But for other remaining crops, the growth of yield is largely responsible for the growth of output.

(7) Within the cereals and millets, maize, jowar, bajra and wheat, in that order, led the rest of the crops in the growth of output and yield. It may be noted that HYV seeds have been evolved for all these four crops. Another interesting point is that the growth of output of wheat, which has been mainly responsible for agricultural

development in the states of Punjab and Haryana, trailed behind the growth of output of course grains in Madhya Pradesh. One of the reasons for this facet of growth seems to be that Madhya Pradesh has got much less irrigational facilities than Haryana and Punjab. Due to the quality of soil and agro-climatic and other conditions, larger proportion of irrigated area is under the cultivation of rice than wheat. The growth of area under wheat has also trailed behind the growth of area under maize, but the growth of area under wheat has been faster than the growth of area under jowar and bajra. The relatively more rapid growth of area under maize might have been due to its small value both in absolute and relative terms in the base year.

The above analysis shows that (i) agricultural development in Madhya Pradesh had proceeded slowly but steadily. Production, area and yield of all but five crops increased at varying annual rates of growth. In fact, the production of cereals and millets and pulses has grown faster than their production in the country as a whole. The state's share in the production of cereals in the country increased from 6.99 in 1951 to 9.04 per cent in 1973-74. Similarly, the state's share in the production of pulses in the country increased from 7.47 in 1951 to 19.83 per cent in 1974. Crop-wise, share of the state in the production of jowar, bajra, maize, gram and groundnut increased during the same period. The highest increase in the state's share in the country's output is for gram; (ii) the process of agricultural development in M.P., unlike that in Punjab, has been mainly led by the growth of output, yield and area under course grains and pulses. Both wheat and rice have trailed behind these crops. The state's share in the production of jowar, bajra, maize and gram in the country has gone up, but its share in the production of rice and wheat has decreased. The growth of output of course grains in M.P. has been faster than their growth in the country as a whole, while the growth of output of wheat and rice in the state has been slower than the growth of their output in the country; and (iii) another interesting feature of the process of agricultural development in M.P. is that the (growth of area rather than the growth of yield accounts for a major proportion of growth of output of several important crops.

III. PRODUCTIONS RELATIONS OF AGRICULTURE

Agricultural output is generally a function of investment in farm inputs, adoption of improved cultural practices, governmental programmes of agricultural development, quality of soil, farm technology and agro-climatic conditions. Of all these, new farm technology has been found to be the single most important factor in agricultural development of several countries/ regions. In fact, it is new farm technology that has been responsible for taking the agriculture of some developing economies out of the low level equilibrium trap (Mudhar, M.S., 1974, p. 1). The diffusion and adoption of new farm technology hinges, among other things, upon the availability of modern inputs like high yielding crop varieties, fertilisers, pesticides, irrigational facilities, rural credit, new tools and machines for farming operations, evolution of new strategy of agricultural development, and above all, an appropriate policy frame.

In case of Madhya Pradesh, growth of area has been an important determinant of agricultural development. Irrigation is also likely to play an important role in the process of agricultural development. It is, therefore, assumed that a very high proportion of systematic variation in agricultural output can be explained in terms of changes in area cultivated and area under irrigation. But agricultural production has also got a strong trend relationship (See, for example, Prakash, S. and Rajan, P., 1976). Even if production data are corrected for changes in technology and area under cultivation, the growth of output may still contain effects of other factors such as policies, prices, crop rotations, etc. Some of these factors might even be completely unknown or immeasurable, and/or they may change slowly and smoothly with time. Therefore, it has been assumed that time can be taken as an index of all other factors. Consequently, output depends not only upon area and irrigation but also upon time. Step-wise correlation/regression analysis is used to study inter-relations among above mentioned variables as the determinants of agricultural output from the year 1950-51 to 1983-84. We postulate a Cobb-Douglas type of production function for the transformation of agricultural inputs into output:

$$X(1) = a + b\,X(2) + c\,X(3) + dT + U \qquad \ldots (3)$$

where X (1), X (2) and X (3) are the logs of output, unirrigated and irrigated area respectively, all in physical units, T is time variable with origin in 1950-51, and U is random error (Cf. Tintner, 1952, pp. 30-34). As data relating to water used for irrigation are not available, proportion of area irrigated is used as its proxy. Total area cultivated is thus divided into its two components: irrigated and unirrigated area. Data for irrigated area are available for 8 crops separately for the period covered by this study.

The correlation between output and area is statistically not significant for rice, maize and barley. But it is significant for other five crops at 5 per cent probability level, which is used for testing the statistical significance of all coefficients. The coefficient of correlation between output and irrigation is also not significant for three crops: rice, cotton and sugarcane. In view of the fact that two of these crops require generally very high doses of water, the result is surprising. It might be due to the fixity of irrigated area under these crops over the period under study. The thesis is supported by the fact that the rate of growth of irrigated area under crops has been as negligible as 0.25, 0.80 and 0.17 per cent per annum. It is as if the irrigated area under rice, cotton and sugarcane were fixed. Besides, rice and sugarcane crops are grown mainly in those regions of the state which receive adequate rainfall in normal years. Naturally, cultivation is carried in the traditional ways. Want of assured irrigational facilities in most parts of the state accounts for the dominance of growth of output by acreage growth.

Above two factors may explain the non-significance of the coefficient. But the correlation between output and time is not significant only in case of rice and barley. Thus, time emerges as an important factor of growth in 6 out of 8 crops. For rice, all three coefficients of correlation between output, on the one hand, and area, irrigation and time, on the other, are not significant. The inter-correlations among the explanatory variables are significant in 14 and not significant in 10 cases. Thus, as is usually the case in production function studies, we have the problem of multi-collinearity in 6 out of 8 crops.

The combined influence of area, irrigation and time, taken as a group of two and three factors at a time, is examined by means of multiple correlation coefficients. All multiple correlation coefficients of second order, except two for rice, are statistically significant. A comparison of values of the total correlation coefficients with the values of second order multiple correlation coefficients show that the introduction of second variable in the regression improves the proportion of variation explained by the regression appreciably in all the cases. But replacement of area or irrigation in the regression by time variable does not improve the value of multiple correlation coefficient of second order in these cases, and even in those cases in which values of the second order coefficients increase due to replacement of variable 2 or 3 by time in the regression, this increase is negligible. In fact, results show that in case of wheat and pulses, it is irrigated area which is the most dominant factor in the growth of output, whereas it is unirrigated area which accounts for the major share of growth of output of rice, maize, cotton and sugarcane. But in case of gram and barley, both irrigated and unirrigated area are important factors of growth.

All multiple correlation coefficients of third order are significant at 5 per cent probability level. The proportion of variation due to regression ranges from 46 to 91 per cent. But the introduction of the third explanatory variable in the regression raises the value of the coefficients of determination only marginally in most of the cases. Another point to be noted is that, it is the introduction of time variable into the regression along with area and irrigation, which raises the value of the coefficient of determination only negligibly except in case of rice, maize and cotton. Besides, the partial regression/correlation coefficients of second order attached to time variable are not only not significant but they also have negative sign attached to them in 5 out of 8 cases. If the dependent or the explanatory variable does not vary sufficiently between observations, one may find either an inappropriate sign attached to the regression coefficient (s), or the coefficient may turn to be non-significant. Inappropriate sign or non-significance may also be caused by multi-collinearity. Kamiya obtained negative regression coefficients attached to labour in his study of paddy farms in Tokoku and Seinan districts of Japan due to fixity of family labour engaged on these farms and the fixed size of the farms in Japan (Heady, E.). However, time variable is dropped from the regression in the analysis of production relations as the superfluous explanatory variable. It implies that the production function has not been shifting temporally at significant rates. This might be due to tardy pace of the diffusion of green revolution technology.

The partial first order coefficients of regression of output on area and irrigation are tabulated below:

Crop b	*Wheat*	*Rice*	*Maize*	*Barley*	*Gram*	*Cotton*	*Sugarane*	*Pulses*
b12.3	.3010	-.3408	-.1898	-1.7357	1.0095	1.0588	0.8632	-.1877
b13.2	1.2825	1.6464	1.7707	13.9825	-1.6000	0.2432	-0.0044	3.2332
Sum	1.5835	1.3056	1.5809	12.2468	-0.5905	1.3020	0.8588	3.0455

The sign of regression coefficients attached to area is negative for rice, maize, barley and pulses. This might be due to the fixity of unirrigated area under these crops during the period of study. In fact, even total area under two of these crops had remained stagnant, while the area under barley declined. The sign of regression coefficient attached to irrigated area is negative only in case of gram and sugarcane. While negative sign of regression coefficient, attached to irrigated area under sugarcane, can be explained by the fixity of irrigation over time; irrigated area under sugarcane has expanded at the negligible rate of 0.17 per cent per annum, the negative sign of regression coefficient attached to irrigated area under gram can not be explained in similar terms, since the rate of growth of irrigated area under gram has been 2.72 per cent per annum all through the period covered by this study.

An important point to be noted is that numerical value of elasticity of output with respect to irrigation is several times the value of elasticity of output with respect to unirrigated area for all crops except cotton, gram and sugarcane. Another feature of these coefficients is that their sum is greater than unity in all cases except gram and sugarcane. It implies that there are increasing returns to scale with respect to the inputs of irrigated and unirrigated area. But one cannot be very sure about it as almost all other important inputs of agricultural production have been excluded from the regression (See, Heady, 1961, p. 69).

New Technology and Production Relations

The success of modern agricultural technology hinges largely upon ever increasing use of high yielding crop varieties. But use of high yielding crop varieties becomes effective only if all modern inputs are used as a package. The package involves mainly the use of improved seeds, chemical fertilizers, irrigation water and pesticides as essential inputs (Mudhar, p. 12). High yielding seed varieties mainly of wheat, paddy, maize, bajra, and jowar have been introduced in Madhya Pradesh since 1966-67. If we take all modern inputs of agricultural production into account, their number will be quite large. In view of the fact that we have only 8 observations relating to the use of inputs like high yielding seed varieties, fertilizers, irrigation and pesticides, etc., it would be advisable to restrict the number of explanatory variables in the regression to study production relations. For time series data, fertilizers and high yielding seed varieties along with area and irrigation have been taken as explanatory variables. But we have many more observations for cross-section data for which some other variables have also been taken into consideration as explanatory factors.

The growth of output and use of modern inputs has not been uniform for all five crops. Compound annual growth rates of output and the inputs of these crops over the period. The output of paddy has increased, on an average, by 1.5 per cent per annum. This has resulted from the growth of area, irrigation, high yielding seed varieties and fertilizers. The use of HYV seeds has increased at as high a rate as 48.4 per cent per annum, but the use of fertilizers has increased only at a rate of 5.7 per cent per annum. Area and irrigation also show nominal growth at rates of 1.1 and 0.2 per cent per annum respectively. The disparity between the growth rates of different inputs seems to have been the result of the fact that, whereas the HYV seeds were introduced for the first time in 1966-67, other inputs like fertilizers and irrigation were already in use for quite some time. Consequently, growth rates for the supporting inputs are much lower than that of the HYV seeds. Output of wheat has increased at 4.7, per cent per annum, while the use of HYV seeds and fertilisers increased at such high rates as of 47.8 and 42.2 per cent per annum. In case of wheat, use of HYV seeds and fertilizers have increased at, more or less, similar rates. Irrigated area also show a comparatively high annual growth rate of 9.6 per cent. But the highest rate of growth of output is for bajra. For bajra also, the use of HYV seeds and fertilisers increases at high rates of 27 and 61 per cent per annum. But the disparity between the growth of these two inputs for jowar show negative growth of output during the same period. Negative growth of output of maize might have been the result of the negative growth of irrigation and fertilizers, whereas the output of jowar has decreased despite the growth of use of HYV seeds and fertilizers. Either the proportionate shares of different inputs in the package might have violated the technical norms, or cultural practices might have deviated from those warranted by new technology. The above analysis shows that the use of HYV seeds and other supporting inputs like fertilizers has not increased at rates commensurate with each other except in case of wheat. The growth of irrigation has also lagged behind that of HYV seeds and fertilizers. The new agricultural technology has been so far introduced mainly in those areas which have a certain minimum amount of assured irrigational facilities. This large base, besides other factors, might explain the slow growth of irrigation in comparison to HYV seeds and fertilisers.

IV. ANALYSIS OF TIME-SERIES DATA

Cobb-Douglas production function has been fitted to the data for the years from 1951 to 1974 by the method of least squares. The estimated equations are given below:

$$\text{(Wheat)}\ X(1) = 94.159 + 0.4687\,X(2) - 3.6432\,X(3) + 0.0893\,X(4) + 0.6126\,X(5) \qquad (R^2 = .9437)$$

$$\text{(Paddy)}\ X(1) = -2200.25 - 0.0188\,X(2) - 78.4856\,X(3) + 0.0851\,X(4) + 0.3674\,X(5) \qquad (R^2 = .8094)$$

$$\text{(Maize)}\ X(1) = -6820 - 0.3908\,X(2) - 4.2059\,X(3) + 0.0219\,X(4) + 0.1397\,X(5) \qquad (R^2 = .5710)$$

(Bajra) X (1) = –37.91 – 2.5647 X (2) – 0.2778 X (4) + 0.4067 X (5)
(R^2 = .8472)

(Jowar) X (1) = 1106.37 – 40.3850 X (2) – 0.0838 X (4) + 0.0887 X (5)
(R^2 = .8038)

where X (1) is output, X (2) is irrigated area, X (3) is unirrigated area, X (4) stands for HYV seeds and X (5) denotes fertilizers, all variables are measured in logarithmic terms.

The coefficient of multiple correlation is significant in case of wheat; but the coefficient is non-significant for all other crops, even though its value is greater than 0.8 for all crops except maize. The partial regression coefficients attached to irrigated area are negative both in case of paddy and maize. It is not surprising in view of the fact that irrigation has grown negatively in case of maize, while its rate of growth for paddy has been very tardy. But the partial regression coefficient attached to unirrigated area is negative only in case of wheat. The coefficient attached to HYV seeds is negative in case of paddy, bajra and jowar. The negative sign of this coefficient is surprising in view of the fact that annual compound growth rate of HYV seeds for all three crops has been very high. The coefficient attached to fertilizers is also negative in case of paddy and maize. It might be due to the negative growth of the use of fertilizers in the production of paddy and maize. In fact, reduced supplies of fertilisers and the steep rise in their prices towards the last years covered by the study have greatly affected the use of fertilizers in the state. The partial regression coefficient attached to total area is negative in case of jowar for which total area under cultivation has grown negatively. Thus, we find that 3 out of 4 partial regression coefficients in case of paddy, 2 out of 3 coefficients in case of jowar, and 2 out of 4 coefficients in case of maize have negative signs attached to them. Inputs of irrigated area, HYV seeds and fertilizers in case of wheat, unirrigated area and HYV seeds in the production of maize, total area and fertilizers in the production of bajra, and fertilizers in case of jowar make a positive contribution to the growth of their respective output.

An important point to be noted is that the sum of regression coefficients is positive and greater than unity in case of paddy, maize and bajra, while it is negative for wheat and jowar. Negative contribution of unirrigated area to the output of wheat makes the total returns negative. Similarly, negative contribution of area and HYV seeds to the output of jowar makes total returns to scale negative. But increasing returns to scale in the production of paddy, maize and bajra are indicated.

The marginal productivities of factor inputs have been calculated at their respective geometric means which are given below:

Crop/Input	*X (2)*	*X (3)*	*X (4)*	*X (5)*
Wheat	0.577	–3.527	0.140	0.475
Paddy	–0.023	76.660	–0.128	–0.288
Maize	–2.310	4.080	0.043	–0.179
Bajra	2.340		–0.774	0.343
Jowar	–1666.79		–0.177	0.089

Some of the elasticities or the marginal productivities of factor inputs are negative. It is hardly conceivable that total output would decrease as a result of an increase in the quantities of anyone of the essential inputs. But only two of the negative coefficients are statistically significant. In case of maize, output, irrigation and fertilizers grow negatively, while HYV seeds grow positively. Thus, the violation of use of modern inputs in the recommended package may account for negative productivities of irrigation and fertilizers. Similarly, negative growth of irrigation in case of bajra might be responsible for negative productivity of one of the inputs, while in case of jowar, negative growth of both output and irrigation may similarly explain the odd results. But in case of wheat, absence of HYV seeds, suitable for dry farming, and unsuitability of unirrigated lands for the existent technology may account for odd results. Some of the odd results might also be due to the limited number of observations from which we have to estimate the functions.

V. PRODUCTION FUNCTIONS ESTIMATED FROM CROSS-SECTION DATA

Cross section data relate to the year 1983-84 and district is the unit to which it is related. As all crops are not cultivated in each district of the state, number of observations differ from crop to crop. Districts, where new crop varieties and other complementary inputs for the production of a crop (s) have not been introduced so far, have also been left out of the analysis. The following are estimated equations of the production functions:

(Wheat) X (1) = 0.923 – 1.733 X (2) – 0.715 X (3) + 0.241 X (4) + 0.684 X (5) (R^2 = .9694)

(Paddy) X (1) = 2.139 – 1.362 X (2) – 0.521 X (3) + 0.356 X (4) + 0.066 X (5) (R^2 = .9618)

(Maize) X (1) = 1.237 – 0.977 X (2) – 0.199 X (3) + 0.106 X (4) + 0.395 X (5) (R^2 = .9995)

(Jowar) X (1) = 1.141 – 0.185 X (2) – 0.152 X (3) + 0.001 X (4) + 0.049 X (5) (R^2 = .5813)

where X (1) denotes output, X (2) is irrigated area, X (3) stands for unirrigated area, X (4) is area under HYV seeds and X (5) is the amount of chemical fertilizers used, all measured in logarithmic units.

Tractors were also tried as one more explanatory variable. But the increase in value of correlation coefficient (multiple) is nearly zero and the presence of additional variable makes regression coefficients attached to other explanatory variables negative in two crops. Besides, partial regression coefficient attached to tractors themselves is negative in all cases. This indicates the presence of multi-collinearity, and the superfluousness of the tractors as the determinants of the growth of output. Therefore, results are not reported here. If, however, the state experiences the full impact of green revolution, making multiple cropping a regular feature of the agricultural economy of the state, then the timely preparation of the fields for sowing, harvesting of bumper crops, etc. may make the introduction of mechanisation necessary, which may make tractors significantly to the growth of yield and output, as has been the case in Punjab.

The marginal productivities of factor inputs at geometric means are as follows:

Crop/Input	*X (2)*	*X (3)*	*X (4)*	*X (5)*
Wheat	–0.816	0.259	0.111	0.308
Paddy	2.366	0.321	0.330	0.048
Maize	0.464	–0.196	0.051	1.130
Jowar	0.138	0.219	0.0006	0.077

All four coefficients of multiple correlation are statistically significant, whereas for the production functions estimated from time-series data coefficient for wheat alone is significant. Naturally, values of all coefficients, except one for jowar, are greater than the values of these coefficients for the functions estimated from time-series data. In view of the above results, it seems that non-significance of coefficients of multiple correlation for time-series data is due to limited number of observations in relation to the number of explanatory variables included in the function. The partial regression coefficient (and therefore, the marginally productivities) attached to irrigation in the production of wheat and that attached to HYV seeds in case of maize alone are negative. The marginal productivities estimated from the production functions indicate the direction in which the pattern of allocating the scarce inputs should change in order to achieve optimum output. For example, fertilizers have the highest marginal yield in the production of maize, while irrigation yields the best results in the production of paddy. Therefore, diversion of fertilizers from other crops to maize and transfer of irrigated area from other crops to paddy is likely to raise the overall output in the state.

The results indicate that, as in case of time series analysis, the sum of partial regression coefficients for wheat is negative for cross-section analysis also. It means that the returns to scale in case of wheat are decreasing. The sum of partial regression coefficients for jowar is positive but less than one. Whereas the time-series analysis indicated negative returns to scale for jowar, cross-section analysis indicates positive but diminishing returns to scale. For paddy and maize, the cross-section results, like the time-series analysis, show increasing returns to scale.

VI. CONCLUSIONS AND RESUME

Results of the study show that agricultural production in Madhya Pradesh has increased slowly but steadily ever since 1950-51. While the state achieved faster development than that in the country as a whole in the production of course grains and pulses, it has lagged behind the country in the production of wheat, paddy, oil-seeds and other commercial crops. Another important point is that the growth of output of several crops has depended more upon the growth of area than upon the growth of yield. It highlights the need for the widespread diffusion of green revolution technology in the state.

These results indicate that market forces as reflected by changes in absolute and relative prices of various crops have played a decisive role in the allocation of land among competing crops. Introduction of high yielding varieties of seeds have supplemented the influence of price changes.

An important policy implication of these results is that Punjab and Haryana model of agricultural development may not be appropriate for all the regions of the country. But different regions should be encouraged to concentrate developmental efforts on those crops for which their agro-climatic conditions are most suitable. This will facilitate specialisation in different crops by different regions. Madhya Pradesh has already revealed its comparative advantage in the production of pulses and course grains. In the short-run, it will be an appropriate strategy to encourage these crops. In the long-run, when irrigation becomes more widespread, this strategy might be changed.

Irrigated area emerges as an important factor of growth of output in stepwise regression analysis. The sum of regression coefficients attached to irrigated and unirrigated area under all the crops, except gram and sugarcane, indicate increasing returns to scale.

There seems to be a lack of package approach in the use of modern inputs like HYV seeds, chemical fertilizers and irrigation as a result of which the use of these inputs in the production of most of the crops increases at vastly different rates. Increasing returns to scale obtain in the production of paddy, maize and bajra, while the total returns to scale are negative in the production of wheat and jowar. But the results obtained from cross-section data seem to be better than those furnished by time series data. The estimated marginal productivities of the factor inputs indicate the desirability of reallocation of inputs among the competing crops for obtaining optimum production. These results indicate decreasing returns in the production of wheat, increasing returns in the production of paddy and decreasing returns in the production of maize and jowar.

Note

Barewald distinguishes between two types of growth processes: (i) growth initiated and sustained by factor multiplication, and (ii) growth initiated and sustained by factor transformation. Yield increase through the process of factor transformation (Also see, Prakash, Buragohain and Sharma, 1997).

REFERENCES

Barewald, F. (1969), History and Structure of Economic Development, India Book House.

Heady, E.O. and Dillon, J.L. (1961), Agricultural Production Functions, IOWA.

Mudhar, M.S. (1974), Dynamic Analysis of Direct and Indirect Implications of Technological Change in Agriculture—The Case of Punjab, India, Department of Agricultural Economics, Cornell University, Dec.

Prakash, S., and Rajan, P. (1979), Regional Inequalities of Rural Development in Madhya Pradesh, *The Indian Journal of Regional Science*, Vol. XI, No. 1.

Prakash, S. and Rajan, P. (1977), Economic Development and Structural Changes in the Economy of Madhya Pradesh, *The Indian Journal of Economics*, Vol. LVIII.

Prakash S. and Goel, V. (1986), Regional Inequalities of Agricultural Development in India with special reference to Growth of Output of Foodgrains. Published in *The Economic Journal of Nepal*, Vol. IX, No. 3.

Prakash, S., Buragohain T. and Sharma, Amit (1997) Determinants of Allocation of Land Among Different Crops Under Conditions of Dynamic Growth. Published in *Scandinavian Journal of Development Alternatives and Area Studies*, Vol. XVI, No. 1, March.

Prakash, S. and Sharma, A. (1996), Effect of Liberalisation on Industry-Agriculture Interrelations and Terms of Trade. Published in *The Indian Journal of Economics*, Vol. LXXVII, No. 304, July.

Prakash, S. and Dutta, R. (1996), New Economic Policy: Analysis of Actual and Perceived Impacts on Indian Economy. Published in Jauhri, B.M. (Ed.) *New Economic Policy: A Critical Appraisal*, Commonwealth Publishers, New Delhi.

Prakash, S. and Mohapatra, A.C. (1980), Economic Development in the State of Madhya Pradesh: A Study of Inter-Temporal and Intra-Regional Variations. Published in *Third World Planning Review*, Vol. II, No. 1, Liverpool.

Prakash, S. (1977), Regional Inequalities of Economic Development with reference to Infrastructural Facilities. Published in *The Indian Journal of Regional Science*, Vol. IV, No. 2.

Prakash, S. and Goel, N.P. (1978), A New Algorithm of Decomposition of Growth of Agricultural Output into its Component Parts. Published in Datta Ray, B. (Editor) *Agriculture in the Hills—A Case Study of Meghalaya*, North-East India Council of Social Science Research, Shillong.

Streeten, P. (1971), The Frontiers of Development Studies: Some Issues of Development Policy. Published in Livingstone, I. (Ed.) *Economic Policy for Development*, Penguin Modern Economic Readings.

Tintner, G. (1952), *Econometrics*.

APPENDIX

Data Sources and Assumptions

All data have been taken from Agricultural Statistics 1969-70, 1970-71, 1971-72, 1973-74, 1983-84, Directorate of Agriculture, Bhopal and Agriculture and Animal Husbandry, Part I, 1967-68, Directorate of Economics and Statistics, Bhopal. Land area is measured in thousand hectares and output is measured in thousand tonnes. All other inputs are also measured in physical units. Crop-wise use of fertilisers is not available. Therefore, total amount of fertilizers consumed in the state in a year is allocated to different crops in proportion to the area covered by the High Yielding Seed Varieties (HYV)/area irrigated. Other methods of allocating fertilisers among different crops were also tried, but the results were not satisfactory. One such method, which was tried, is to allocate 50/60 per cent of the recommended doze of fertiliser for each major crop. But the sum total of fertilisers thus allocated to all major crops far exceeds the amount of total fertilisers consumed in the state. Quantity of water used for irrigation is also not available. Therefore, area irrigated under each crop is assumed to measure the degree of irrigation.

Inter-State Disparities and Policy Measures

B. Satyanarayan

INTRODUCTION

The problem of regional inequalities in development within nations (apart from between nations) is increasingly engaging the attention of social scientists all over the world. The issue assumes special significance in India where the overwhelming majority of the people live below the poverty line. This is all the more so because India's Constitutional structure is somewhat federal in nature and considerable heterogeneity exists in terms of language and culture among the people of the different regions of India.

The main focus of Indian Planning has been on economic growth with social justice. All along, our capital-centred and urban-oriented approach has not been able to make us either self-reliant or it could solve the main problems of poverty and unemployment. Many a people are of the view that inter-state and inter-regional disparities are a product of our planning process. The remedial problems could be the optimum utilisation of available natural resources, dispersal of industries for balanced regional development and establishment of employment-oriented industries.

The degree of economic development of a nation/region depends upon the integration and inter-relationship of industrial and agricultural sectors. Various studies point out that the modern industries which have sprung up both at the national and regional level are not properly integrated and dovetailed with the rest of the economy. Reports about industrialisation in Independent India say that the industrialisation is concentrated in and around established metropolitan and industrial centres. The most unhappy aspect of this kind industrialisation has been the negligible share of the rural masses in the fruits of nearly five decades of Industrial Planning.

REGIONAL DISPARITIES IN INDIA

Regional disparities exist in all developed and underdeveloped countries of the world. The task of regional planning in UDCs is far more complex. Because of widespread poverty and below-subsistence level of existence of the vast majority of people in many backward regions of these countries, the task is two-fold:

(i) Reduction of regional disparities; and
(ii) Ensuring atleast a minimum level of subsistence to the majority of people inhabiting the backward areas and living below the level of subsistence.

The strategy of deliberate promotion of "Growth Centres" can go a long way in accomplishing the former. Table 1 gives estimates of per capita income for different states of India at current prices.

DISPARITIES IN INDUSTRIAL GROWTH

The initial distribution of industries was determined by the historical processes of growth reflected in the interests of the British Rulers. As a result, most of the industries got concentrated at a few centres. This pattern continued in the post-Independence period as well. For instance, a study of (28) large-scale industries in 1950 showed the dominance of the Western region and West Bengal in the regional distribution of industries. Thus, 35% of total productive capital was concentrated in Western region, while 25% was concentrated in West Bengal. Taken together, the Western region and West Bengal accounted for 63% of total persons employed, 60.5% of gross ex-factory value of output, and 64% of value added by manufacture.

TABLE 1

Per Capita State Net Domestic Product in (15) Major States (At current prices) in Rupees

S. No.	*State*	*1960-61*	*1980-81*	*1992-93*
1.	Andhra Pradesh	314	1380	5802
2.	Assam	349	1200	5056
3.	Bihar	216	868	3280
4.	Gujarat	380	1951	7586
5.	Haryana	359	2370	9609
6.	Karnataka	292	1623	6313
7.	Kerala	278	1513	5065
8.	Madhya Pradesh	274	1183	4725
9.	Maharashtra	419	2427	9270
10.	Orissa	226	1231	3963
11.	Punjab	383	2690	10857
12.	Rajasthan	271	1222	5035
13.	Tamil Nadu	344	1498	6205
14.	Uttar Pradesh	244	1278	4280
15.	West Bengal	386	1580	5901
	Average	305	1630	6929

Source: Indian Economy (1995), Misra & Puri.

DISPARITIES IN AGRICULTURAL DEVELOPMENT

Regional disparities have increased over time with the States of Punjab, Haryana and parts of Uttar Pradesh pushing well ahead of others. This is due to the HYV etc. For example, in 1990-91, per capita output of foodgrains, was 968 kgs. in Punjab which was (5) times the national per capita output (197 kgs).

OTHER INDICATORS OF DISPARITIES

(a) Urban population;
(b) Domestic Electricity consumption per capita;
(c) Road length per 100 km. of area;
(d) Percentage of villages connected with all-weather roads;
(e) Per capita bank deposit;
(f) Infant mortality rate;
(g) Literacy rate; and
(h) Population below poverty line.

POPULATION BELOW POVERTY LINE

Table 2 shows the population below the poverty line in various states in India.

TABLE 2

Population Below Poverty Line in various States

Sl. No.	*State*	*1983-84*
1.	Bihar	49.5%
2.	Madhya Pradesh	46.2%
3.	Uttar Pradesh	45.3%
4.	Orissa	42.8%
5.	Tamil Nadu	39.6%
6.	West Bengal	39.2%
7.	Andhra Pradesh	36.4%
8.	Karnataka	35.0%
9.	Maharashtra	34.9%
10.	Rajasthan	34.3%
11.	Kerala	26.8%
12.	Gujarat	24.3%
13.	Assam	23.5%
14.	Haryana	15.6%
15.	Punjab	13.8%

Source: CMIE, Sepr. 1988 & 1994.

As far as poverty is concerned, in 1983-84 the proportion of the poor was the highest in Bihar (49.5%) and the lowest in Punjab (13.8%). May be, this is due to the higher level of per capita land

and percentage of irrigation in Punjab. Inversely, Bihar has the lowest per capita income while Punjab has the highest.

So far as Kerala is concerned, the poverty ratio has declined from 47% in 1977-78 to 26.8% in 1983-84. People attribute this steep fall to three reasons:

(i) Due to remittances from migrants to the Middle-East Countries;
(ii) Due to the extensive Welfare Programmes; and
(iii) Due to relatively lower population growth.

Likewise, Assam seems to have recorded a noticeable fall in the proportion of population below the poverty line. On the other hand, Punjab has the lowest poverty ratio and is not particularly known for having adopted any welfare programmes as is done in Kerala and some other states. But Punjab has consciously or unconsciously set to provide a firm production base which has helped to maintain the lowest poverty ratio. If this is so, it holds a lesson to others.

Given the socio-economic structure, the decline in the poverty ratio is generally the result of growth achieved, especially in agriculture and the effective implementation of various poverty alleviation programmes like NREP, RLEGP, JRY, etc. These anti-poverty programmes have to be area and community specific, in order that their benefits may be wide-spread. They have to off-set the uneven effects of economic progress on the poorer sections in different areas. Generally, the tendency is to select the easily accessible areas and politically dominant groups. The numerical targets may thus be attained but the basic purpose of the programme will not be served. Planning at the block, district and region within the State level has been devised to counteract this tendency.

It is very often expected that the fruits of "development" will percolate to the weakest sections of the society. It is a fact that in India the poverty ratio has no direct relationship with the existing per capita income level. While per capita income is rising, poverty ratio is more or less constant. It is time that the overall economic, agricultural, industrial and technological development is a condition necessary but not sufficient to eradicate poverty and undernutrition. There is a reason to believe that the very momentum of the developmental process has served to accentuate socio-economic disparities. Therefore, the challenge of development, for countries like India, which have chosen democratic political system, lies in devising ways and means of ensuring equitable distribution of the benefits of economic growth not only among various sections of population but also in various states and regions across the country. Only then the development could be properly sustained.

Data from country-wide diet surveys carried out by the National Nutrition Monitoring Bureau (NNMB) shows that diet in more than half of the households surveyed in Kerala are inadequate, while the percentage of these households is in the range of 40% in Andhra Pradesh and Orissa. The position of Karnataka looks far better, in the sense, that only 13% of the surveyed households are suffering from inadequate diets. Table 3 shows the proportion of households with inadequate calorie intake.

TABLE 3

Distribution of Households According to Dieting Inadequacy

Sl. No.	*State*	*% of HHS with inadequate Diets in Calorie and Proteins*
1.	Punjab	N.A.
2.	Kerala	53%
3.	Maharashtra	N.A.
4.	Andhra Pradesh	38%
5.	Orissa	42%
6.	West Bengal	29%
7.	Karnataka	13%

Source: *EPW*, Dated 17-12-1983.

All these exercises boil down to one important point. If the pace of development in most of the States which are below the All-India Average Per Capita State Income is not accelerated, there is every possibility of their sliding down still further. Thereby, the sustainability of a balanced development in the country as a whole becomes very difficult. This process could be combated to a very great extent by means of effective industrialisation.

Some broad policy issues are:

1. Optimum utilisation of natural resources with emphasis on conversion of raw-materials into value-added products within the State;
2. Dispersal of industries to get balanced regional development.
3. Encouraging employment-oriented industries.

POLICY FOR SUSTAINABLE DEVELOPMENT

The move towards liberalised economic policies in the recent past arising out of the logic of competition has led (given the pattern of income distribution in the context of a mixed economy), to profit-seeking investment in consumer's durables and luxury consumables demanded by the upper and middle income groups. It has resulted in the import of repetitive technology and adverse balance of payments including an abnormal increase in external debt. The liberalisation policies are encouraging capital and energy intensive techniques leading to depletion of natural resources and degradition of environments.

Environmentalists fear that the thrust of the New Economic Policy will result in greater pollution as the authorities will be tempted to be lenient towards industries in the interest of economic growth. They also apprehend that given the lax implementation of environmental laws, this country may attract "dirty" industries from the West. Added to this, growth of consumerism, particularly in urban areas, will lead to a spurt to urban pollution, unless higher pollution control standards are introduced and implemented strictly. On the other hand, industrialists fear that if environmental laws are made too strict, investment in the country including foreign investment may decline. They argue that voluntary environmental audits will be better than statutory ones, as the latter may bring about a mere mechanical compliance. They want pollution control standards established through a dialogue between the industry and the government, rather than unilaterally. It is clear that environmental protection cannot be looked upon as an after thought. It needs to be integrated into planning and costing of all industries. Once, this is accepted, the change in economic policies need not spell environmental disaster, thereby paving the way for a better development sustainability.

REFERENCES

Michael, P. Thodaro, "Economic Development in the Third World," Longman, New York (1981).

Gunnar Myrdal, "The Challenge of World Poverty," New York, Pantheon (1970).

Hollis B. Chenery (Ed.), "Studies in Development Planning," Cambridge, Mass; Harvard University Press (1971).

Gautam Mathur, "Planning for steady growth," Bail Blackwell, Oxford (1965).

B. Satyanarayan, "India's Trade with Asia and the Far East Countries," BR Publishing Corporation, New Delhi (1986).

B. Satyanarayan, "A Comparative Study of Foreign Direct Investment in China and India," (Edited) Himalaya Publishing House, Bombay (1996).

B. Satyanarayan, "Social Sciences and Planning for Sustainable Development" (Edited) Himalaya Publishing House, Bombay (1997) (In Press).

H. Myint, "The Economics of the Developing Countries" (1965).

B. Satyanarayan, "An Analysis of Inter-State Disparities in India," *Economic Growth and Social Change*, New Delhi, March 1994.

H.B. Chenery, "Pattern of Industrial Growth," *American Economic Review*, Sept. 1960.

Regional Balance and Resource Transfer from Centre to States*

Kamta Prasad

Regional disparities in our country are widening. These disparities are likely to widen still further due to increasing reliance on market forces in recent years since private capital has a tendency to gravitate towards the already developed regions and to be hesitant to go to backward ones. Promotion of regional balance, therefore, would require government to play a more active part in this respect. One important way in which the government of India can promote the cause of regional balance is through fiscal transfers, e.g. by ensuring larger flow of central resources to backward states. Faster development of backward states/regions would require a substantial rise in the level of their investment if we believe in the dictum that investment creates income. Backward states, however, have limited capacity to

* The facts and ideas presented in this paper are taken from the author's report entitled 'Financial Restructuring of Bihar' prepared under the auspices of Council for Research and Development of Bihar, Delhi and sponsored by Ministry of Finance, Government of India.

generate surplus for investment from their own sources. Experience tells us that some of them are not in a position even to provide matching funds for the so-called centrally sponsored schemes. An increase in resource transfer from the centre to them can be of considerable help. Hence the important question that arises is one of identifying the manner in which this can be done within the prevailing institutional framework of the country. The present paper deals with the aspect. This is not to deny the role of several other facts which may be equally or even more important for promoting regional balance. But given the constraint of space, I propose to confine myself only the aspects related to resource transfer from the centre to the states.

In what follows, the discussion is further confined to the state of Bihar which has the lowest per capita income, highest concentration of poverty and lowest per capita consumption of electricity. Bihar can, therefore, be treated as a typical backward state in the country. Hence we depend mainly on facts and data related to Bihar in discussing the alternative approaches and criteria.

Resource transfer from the centre to states in India takes place through Planning Commission, Finance Commission and other agencies. We may examine each of them.

A. TRANSFER THROUGH PLANNING COMMISSION

Planning Commission allocates resources to States by two methods: (i) formula-based plan assistance, and (ii) discretionary plan assistance. The first one, known originally as Gadgil formula and modified subsequently, provides a mechanism for horizontal transfer only and not vertical. As such, the total amount to be devolved to the states lies outside its scope. There has been a gradual decline in the share of states during the last twenty years. As a result, Bihar has been one of the sufferers. Allocation of resources is guided by the category of states: Special category states (HP, J&K, Sikkim and 7 N.E. States including Assam) and Non-special category states which include Bihar. The states in the second category receive 30 per cent of the plan assistance as grant and 70 per cent as loan (whereas those in the first category receive 90 percent as grant and only 10 percent as loan). This has added to the debt burden of Bihar. The interest payment on central loan has been a major cause of revenue deficit of the state. An increase in grant component in plan assistance to say 50 per cent, would provide considerable relief to the state government.

Considering the economic backwardness of Bihar, there is an overiding need to re-examine the criteria for plan assistance to this State. Two steps are needed here. First weightage to backwardness must be increased and that too substantially say above 50 per cent, if these transfers are to promote faster growth of more backward areas. And second, backwardness should be measured in terms causative factors in development like infrastructural and human capital development. Preparing a composite index of infrastructural development, however, is beset with difficulties on account of the familiar weightage problem. Moreover, in the case of a component like transport and communication, mere physical indicator in terms of length of roads is not enough, the quality of the road is equally important. But its measurement is not easy. Such a problem, however, does not arise in the case of power for which per capita electricity consumption provides a sufficiently reliable index of power development. However, availability of power is now recognised as the most critical factor in the development process affecting other sectors, i.e. agriculture, industry as well as services. This factor also affects amenities of life in both homes and offices. Hence, an index of power development as measured by per capita electricity consumption should receive adequate attention while allocating resources for development.

In a study conducted under auspices of Delhi-based Council for Research and Development of Bihar, I made an attempt to quantify the impact of three alternative models based on the above approach. Model I gave 100 per cent weight to per capita electricity consumption for 1992-93. Model II gave 50 per cent weight to per capita electricity consumption (1992-93) and 50 per cent to distance formula (distance of a state's per capita SDP during 1987-90 from that of Punjab). Model III gave 30 per cent weight to per capita electricity consumption (1992-93), 50 per cent to distance formula as explained above and 50 percent weight to IATP. The exercise was concerned with non-special category states only. The share of Bihar which was 12.74 per cent as per modified Gadgil Formula and 13.70 per cent as per Revised Gadgil

Formula*, increased to 16.03 under Model I, 15.9 under Model II and 16.1 under Model III. Thus giving more weightage to backwardness in the allocation of plan funds would have resulted in much larger flow of resources to Bihar. During the 8th Plan it would have amounted to about Rs. 200 crores per annum. The level of discretionary plan assistance has increased over the years and has become more important than the formula-based plan assistance. This assistance is channelled through Central Sector and Centrally Sponsored Schemes; States do not have much say in this. The Centrally Sponsored Schemes require matching resource contribution from States. Bihar, being very poor in domestic resource mobilisation has been unable to provide required matching funds and hence has not much benefitted from this mechanism. In this connection figures pertaining to Cental and Centrally Sponsored Schemes of the Department of Agriculture and Cooperation given below are quite revealing. Agricultural development is crucial for Bihar's overall development. But its share in all India total was only 1.29 percent while that of Maharashtra was 11.82 per cent, of Uttar Pradesh 12.13 per cent, Andhra Pradesh 8.54 per cent, Karnataka 8.55 per cent and Tamil Nadu 7.62 per cent. (Table 1)

TABLE 1

State-wise Expenditure on Central/Centrally Sponsored Schemes of the Department of Agriculture and Cooperation, Government of India

Sl. No.	*Name of State*	*Expenditure from 1992-93 to 1995-96*	*Percentage to Total*
1	2	3	4
1.	Andhra Pradesh	22,032.36	8.54
2.	Assam	1,910.08	0.74
3.	Bihar	3,331.93	1.29
4.	Gujarat	12,099.37	4.69
5.	Haryana	9,110.97	3.53

(Contd.)

* Plan Transfer to States: Revised Gadgil Formula and Analysis, R. Ramalingam and K.N. Kurup, *Economic and Political Weekly*, March 2-9, 1991 (based on Planning Commission's Working Papers).

1	2	3	4
6.	Karnataka	22,063.00	8.55
7.	Kerala	12,873.55	4.99
8.	Madhya Pradesh	23,163.61	8.98
9.	Maharashtra	30,486.00	11.82
10.	Orissa	13,340.10	5.17
11.	Punjab	10,597.94	4.11
12.	Rajasthan	25,115.69	9.73
13.	Tamil Nadu	19,653.47	7.62
14.	Uttar Pradesh	31,294.85	12.13
15.	West Bengal	5.720.89	2.22
16.	Others	15,206.82	5.89
	Total	2.58,000.63	100.00

Source: Government of India, Ministry of Agriculture.

There is, therefore, a need for re-examination of the discretionary plan assistance to suit the requirement of poorer States like Bihar. These schemes may be reduced drastically and the funds thus saved may be distributed to states through a modified formula as suggested earlier. In this regard, the pronouncement in the 1996-97 budget to transfer most of the Centrally Sponsored Schemes to States is in the right direction but the criterion envisaged by the Planning Commission for inter-state allocation on the basis of earlier years withdrawals is not satisfactory.

One may also raise a question whether Bihar can be included in the Special Category States which get 90 per cent of central plan assistance as grant against only 30 per cent for other states including Bihar. Moreover, the scale of funding is also more liberal since 30 per cent of the total formula-based central plan assistance to states is pre-empted for those states whose population is hardly 5 per cent (as per 1971 census figures which are used for allocation). During 1995-96, for example, the per capita gross allocation of central assistance to special category states was Rs. 1,612 which was about 10 times higher than the respective figure of Rs. 164 for the Non-special category states. Figures of earlier years depict the same picture. Bihar has a strong case for inclusion in this category if a reference is made to economic criteria. Bihar is more backward than most of the existing Special Category States. Besides, it has a very large population and the highest incidence of poverty. It is specially weak in terms of power and quality of roads—two basic factors of growth. It also has a huge tribal population which is poorer than that of the Special Category States. Besides, like many Special Category States, it has a long international border, i.e. with Nepal and Bangladesh. Moreover, control by Government of India over its basic resources of coal and minerals has deprived it of its natural advantages. Its taxable capacity, therefore, remains extremely poor. It is, therefore, suggested that Bihar may be brought under Special Category States at least for a period of 8 to 10 years.

B. TRANSFER THROUGH FINANCE COMMISSION

Finance Commissions have played a key role in transfer of resources to states arising out of the proceeds of income tax and union excise duties. As regards income tax, measures of poverty and backwardness have been given higher weightage since the 8th Finance Commission. Prior to this Bihar's share in the divisible pool of resources emanating from income tax was in the range of the 9-10 per cent However, this changed to 12 per cent since the backwardness weightage was introduced (8th and 9th Finance Commission).

As regards union excise duties, the share of Bihar has fluctuated over the years, specially in early years. With the changed index of backwardness, Bihar's share increased to about 13.81 per cent during the 5th Finance Commission as against the level of 10.03 per cent in earlier years. The share has so far remained at about 13 per cent.

The Tenth Finance Commission recommended for uniformity in allocation of proceeds of different taxes. The Central Government has already accepted it. However, even within the scope of uniform formula, there is a need to focus on poorer States, by allocating more resources for taking care of their glaring deficiencies in development of capital intensive infrastructure like power, transportation and communication. Faster the development in these sectors, faster would be the economic growth process leading to improved level of tax base and reduced level of central dependency. A beginning in this direction has already been made by including 'infrastructure' as a factor in the scheme of devolution recommended by the 10th Finance Commission with a weightage of 5 per cent. Two modifications are, however, suggested in this regard. Given the role of infrastructure in economic development, it is suggested that the weightage be raised to at least 50 per cent. Second, as already explained in an earlier para, the availability of power has come to occupy as the single most important factor in economic development. This factor is also amenable to easy measurement. Hence, per capita electricity consumption should be included as a separate factor in the scheme of devolution with a weightage of 50 per cent. A poorer State like Bihar can get justice only when this variable is taken into account with a sufficiently higher weightage. A simulation exercise carried out confirms this hypothesis. Bihar's share as per 10th Finance Commission's award is 12.861 percent. This increases to 15.099, 14.936 and 15.189 per cents respectively under Models I, II and III as explained earlier. (It may be noted that in the Finance Commission's case the percentages have been worked out after taking all states into account both special category and non-special category ones). In absolute terms, Bihar's share goes up by Rs. 3,698, Rs. 3,428 and Rs. 3,847 crores for the five year period 1995-2000 or an average of about Rs. 700 to 750 crores per year.

Over and above the transfer of resources under devolution of taxes and duties, the successive Finance Commissions have been using the mechanism of grants-in-aid as prescribed under Article 275 of the Constitution. For grants-in-aid, the Finance Commissions have been taking the difference of gap that remains after setting off the devolution amounts against the projected deficits of the States. Any balance that remains is met by grants-in-aid. This has been described as 'gap filling approach' by fiscal experts. This approach has fallen short of the objective of reducing inter-state disparities and removing fiscal disadvantages of the poorer States. Bihar has not derived much benefit from this clause. The Seventh Finance Commission placed Bihar in the category of post-devolution surplus States. As per the Xth Finance Commission, Bihar did not qualify for any grants-in-aid even though less poorer States like Rajasthan and Orissa became the beneficiaries.

Thus, the purpose for which grants were to be made use of has not been adhered to. The Finance Commissions have relied mainly on devolution of taxes and duties for meeting the gaps between State's revenues and expenditures. The attempt of the successive Finance Commissions to increase the share of States in the divisible pool of taxes and duties has been prompted by this consideration. But in this process the advanced States receive much larger share. Consequently, the inter-state disparity has widened rather than narrowed. This is a serious lapse on the part of Financc Commission. According to the 10th Finance Commission, the per capita surplus ranged from Rs. 0.82 for Orissa, Rs. 214.17 for Bihar, Rs. 3,057 for Karnataka and Rs. 3,657 for Haryana. It is obvious that judicious principles were not applied. It may be noted that grants are State specific as against devolution which is general and applied universally. Grants-in-aid, therefore, are more suitable for reducing inter-state disparities in financial resources. Inter-state equity would be promoted if grants are made with reference to provision of basic minimum services to people. This can be made by following the distance formula as already adopted for devolution of taxes. If the share of vertical distribution from taxes is reduced, the amounts flowing to advanced States with big surpluses would be reduced. The saved resources could then be allocated as grants-in-aid to the more needy States. This has the dual advantage of (i) serving as a buffer against erosion of revenues to them because of estimation-related errors of the Finance Commission, and (ii) the provision of funds would meet the requirement to secure basic national minimum standards to these people.

To illustrate, at present, on the recommendations of the Tenth Finance Commission, resources made available to states under tax shares and grants-in-aid for 1995-2000 are shown in Table 2.

Figures in Table 2 indicate that grant is an insignificant component of the resource transfer. Assuming income tax share at the level of 50 per cent (Rs. 40,994 crores) and the basic union excise duties at 30 per cent (Rs. 76,834 crores), the total resources available from these two taxes would be Rs. 1,17,828 crores. This would result in a saving of Rs. 66,629 crores. This sum could be distributed among the deficit States on the basis of their relative status in the SDP income measured from the national average. This would tend to inject equity and would account for larger resource availability to states which are poor as indicated by the per capita SDP. This method would not involve any larger transfer of resources from the Central exchequer than what has been estimated by the Commission. Before concluding this discussion, it is worth-mentioning that tax shares ensure share in buoyancy while grant is a fixed sum. Some modification of the grant system would be needed to take care of this aspect.

TABLE 2

Resource Transfer to States Under TFC

(Rs. crores)

	Taxes and Duties		
(i)	Income Tax	62,765	(77.5% of divisible)
(ii)	Basic Excise Duties	1,21,692	(47.5% of divisible)
(iii)	Additional Excise Duties	19,986	(Tax-rental)
(iv)	Grant-in-lieu of tax on Railway passenger fares	1,900	(Compensatory Grant)
	Sub-Total	2,06,343	(96.45%)
	Non-Plan Rev. Deficit grants	7,583	(3.55%)
	Total	2,13,926	(100%)

The methodology followed by the Finance Commissions to assess State's revenues and expenditures has been unsatisfactory. Usually, revenues are overestimated and expenditures are underestimated to reach an artificial equilibrium. The non-materialization of Finance Commission's forecasts has been particularly disadvantageous to states like Bihar which are deficit States before devolution and not so much to the advanced States which are surplus before devolution. As a consequence of revenue shortage, a poor state like Bihar has found it difficult to even maintain available level of development services as well as infrastructures, which are already inadequate. There is another problem. The Finance Commission's estimates are based on state specific rates of growth of expenditure (as also of revenue) rather than on norms of expenditure needed to maintain reasonable standards of services as per the national yardsticks. In the absence of a normative approach, it is the backward States like Bihar which have suffered as a result of resource crunch because their expenditure levels in the past were much below the national norms. A better alternative is to make assessment of expenditure on a normative basis, i.e. expenditure needed to maintain reasonable standards of services as per national norms. Further, the surplus and deficit of states should be computed on per capita basis. This will help highlight the difference between the actual and the minimum agreed level of services. In fact the estimates of revenue receipts and expenditures should be worked out on per capita basis.

Other Sources of Resource Transfer

There are several other sources of resource transfer to states. However, a relatively smaller quantum of funds is made available through such sources. These include the following:

(i) Externally Aided Schemes: A formula devised in December 1991 for allocation of plan funds gave the highest priority to such projects.
(ii) Special Central Assistance for Hill Areas, Tribal Sub-Plan and Border Areas and North-Eastern Council. This receives the second highest priority in allocation of resources to states.
(iii) Budgetary Support to Rural Electrification (Assistance through REC for Minimum Needs Programme).
(iv) Calamity Relief Fund.
(v) Loans Under Small Savings Collection.
(vi) Loans to Cover Gaps in Resources.
(vii) Helping the States to Raise Loans from the Market. This includes financial institutions like LIC, GIC, IDBI, HUDCO, UTI, etc. Government of India gives assistance to all States in raising loans from markets and from financial institutions.

Ironically, Bihar has received much below the national average from all these sources. For example, Bihar has got a negligible amount under externally aided schemes. During 1992-95, Bihar received 130.90 crores out of Rs. 11,15,158 crores allocated for all the states, i.e. 1.12 per cent only. Other States like Andhra Pradesh, Maharashtra, Uttar Pradesh, Tamil Nadu and Karnataka received substantial sums, i.e. Rs. 2,089.33 crores (18.74%), Rs. 1,800.48 crores (16.16%), Rs. 1,594.42 crores (14.29%), Rs. 1,463.09 crores (13.12%), and Rs. 1,021.15 crores (9.15%) respectively. Take another example. Bihar's share in total market borrowings for the country worked out to around 4 per cent during the Sixth Plan and to less than 5 per cent during the Seventh Plan (Bihar's Annual Plan, 1993-94, Vol. I, page V).

Other sources of funds are various subsidies on items like fertilizers, foodgrains, crop insurance, family welfare programmes, etc. Bihar, however, has received least allocation from all these sources too. The State has continuously been the worst suffer from natural calamities, particularly flooding. It has, however, continuously failed to receive adequate funds for relief and rehabilitation of affected people. The latest 10th Finance Commission also could not provide needed funds for overcoming this deficiency. This Commission took into consideration actual expenditures of States on natural calamities during recent periods and recommended fund allocation for meeting natural calamity relief expenditure between 1995 and 2000. Centre provided 75% of this fund as grant and on this basis Bihar would received Rs. 205.14 crores, whereas States like Andhra Pradesh, Gujarat, and Rajasthan would receive Rs. 490.33 crores, Rs. 551.17 crores and Rs. 706.89 crores, respectively. This again shows the discrimination against Bihar with respect to its requirements. Lower level of expenditures in earlier years by the States on natural calamities should not be the logical basis for allocation. The criterion needs to be changed. It should be with respect to likely incidence of damage as estimated from available data.

Another available source has been receipts from investment of national savings. Government of India releases 75% as loan to States under soft repayment basis. However, the policy decision taken by Government of India not to invest provident funds accuring from collieries and Government of India's public undertakings into national savings has very adversely affected Bihar's resource situation. Bihar has to persue its efforts to bring changes in it in order to derive additional resources of about Rs. 200 crores per annum which has been denied to the State.

Government of India releases funds to States on the basis of hill areas development. This accounts for 90% as grant and the remaining 10% as loans to the States. This assistance is determined by geographical consideration (an inclination of 30 degrees) as well as the tribal nature of its population. Bihar has a vast tract of hill area and big size tribal population. Unfortunately, Bihar has so far not received financial assistance for hill areas apparently because its hills do not have 30 degrees inclination. Again, it is surprising that Bihar has failed to take an initiative. Besides, special assistance provided to border areas also has not been available to Bihar even though it has a vast border with Nepal and Bangladesh. Bihar has a genuine case for seeking assistance from such a source.

Royalty from coal and minerals is an important source of Bihar's revenue. Bihar, however, received a raw deal from the 10th Finance Commission with respect to royalty from mines and minerals. The Commission had recommended that in case the actual realisation of the concerned State from royalty was higher than that assumed in their estimate, then it would be open to the Central Government to make suitable adjustments in the grants - in-aid under article 275 recommended by them for seeking their non-plan revenue deficits. Such a recommendation harms the interest of Bihar which will suffer in case higher revision in rate of royalty or any method to increase its receipt from mines and minerals causes enhancement in receipt from the forecast figure during 1995-2000. This needs to be reviewed.

Bihar's position becomes even worse if account is taken of resource flows through other sources like royalty on coal and credit from institutional sources. The royalty rates on coal are specific and not *ad valorem* as in the case of petroleum. This prevents the state government from getting the benefit of rise in prices. The CD ratio of commercial banks in Bihar has been extremely low. The amount of credit received from other financial institutions like IDBI, IFC, LIC, UTI has been quite meagre. It is, therefore, recommended that the royalty rates on coal be made *ad valorem* with rates fixed at appropriate levels so as to yield revenue equivalent to that under the earlier system when cess was being levied. This measure is estimated to provide an additional revenue of at least Rs. 700 crores per annum for the State government. All efforts should be made to increase the flow of institutional credit. This would require strengthening of the institutional base and staff capability of financial institutions. District level functional committees with both bankers and entrepreneurs along with project preparation cells be also constituted.

It may, however, be mentioned that bringing about a change in norms of horizontal distribution of central funds favouring

Bihar and other backward states would not be an easy task. It would require a change in national mindset which would be greatly facilitated if Bihar and also other backward states launch a campaign for the same through the media as well as though professional seminars, conferences and other opinion generating fora. Above all, Bihar, as well as other backward states have to take steps first to set their own house in order and to raise quantum of domestic resources. A concerted programme of action is needed for this purpose.

Growth and Structure of Exports of Industrial Goods from Punjab

INDERPAL KAUR

Punjab is a border state situated in the north-western corner of Indian Union. The state has an area of 50.38 lakh hectares which is about 1.6% of the total area of country. There will be hardly any exaggeration to say that Punjab is one of the most prosperous states of the Indian Union. The per capita income of the state is the third highest among all states of the India. PCI of Punjab is Rs. 14188 at current prices and Rs. 4167 at constant prices (1994-95). The economy is characterised by a strong agriculture sector, active small-scale industrial and tertiary sectors. Agriculture occupies a place of predominance in the net output of state. Share of primary, secondary and tertiary sectors in income at current price was 47.90, 20.47 and 31.63 percent respectively in the year 1994-95. Per hectare yield of principal crops is highest in the country. An important feature of the state's agriculture is its plural role, firstly to cater to the basic food requirement of the state and also aim at an export surplus and secondly to provide a strong base of industrial raw materials for growth of industry. Pattern of industries in Punjab has been influenced by the existence of skilled labour and enterprise. As a result, agriculture-based and non-resource-based industries dominate the industrial scene. There is no denying the fact that agriculture plays a dominant role in the State and that the share of industries in its total GDP is comparatively small. But the economy can no longer be sustained by agriculture alone which has touched almost a saturation point. For future development of the State further industrialisation is essential. The least share of secondary or industrial sector is a clear pointer to the lack of proper industrial development in the state.

Exports assume a strategic importance in the development process of a developing economy. Accelerating the rate of growth of export earnings is not the only way and the ultimate solution to the persistent problem of foreign exchange reserves, but it is also a possible way towards the achievement of self-sustained growth. The present study is an attempt to study the growth, pattern and structure of exports of industrial goods from Punjab. Moreover, the study of growth and structure of exports will truly reflect the nature and extent of industrialisation in the state. The study is entirely based on the secondary data. The time series data of exports of different industrial goods was mainly obtained from the various issues of the 'Statistical Abstract of Punjab. The study covers the period 1980-81 to 1994-95. For analytical purposes, the simple statistical tools such as percentages and average annual growth rates have been used. To avoid inconvenience and repetition, various symbols for different industries are being used in the study. The list of these symbols is being given at the end of the paper. Whole of the analysis has been carried out at current prices.

GROWTH AND STRUCTURE OF EXPORTS

To see the trend of exports industrial goods from Punjab, the analysis has been done for the period as a whole (i.e. 1980-81 to 1994-95) and also for the sub-periods, i.e. 1980-81 to 1984-85, 1985-86 to 1989-90 and lastly 1990-91 to 1994-95. The total value of the exports of industrial goods in Punjab increased from Rs. 16,213 lakhs in 1980-81 to Rs. 2,08,299 lakhs in 1994-95 thus showing the average annual growth rate of 20 per cent. Regarding the composition of exports, it was found that in absolute terms during this period the highest value of exports was achieved by Hosiery and Ready Made Garments, HRG i.e. (Rs. 2,41,842 lakhs) and was followed by Bicycles and Parts, BP (Rs. 1,84,828 lakhs) and Machine Tools/hand Tools, MTHT (Rs. 67,045 lakhs). On the other hand, the lowest value was recorded by Sewing Machine and Parts (Rs. 8648 lakhs) followed by Art silk (Rs. 8031 lakhs). Further, for the period as a whole the maximum growth rate (75 per cent) was achieved by HRG, which was followed by SRE with (33 per cent) and SMP, EGEA and OI with (27 per cent). Then came CT and RP (24 per cent), TCLG, MTHT (23 per cent), AP (20 per cent), SG (9 per cent), WT (8 per cent) and C (6 per cent), but PC and AS recorded negative growth rates.

Regarding the percentage share, as is visible from Table 1, that the percentage share was found to be highest (28 per cent), for HRG, followed by BP (15 per cent), SG (13 per cent), OI (10 per cent) and CMTHT (8 per cent) in 1980-81. The percentages share of WT was 5 per cent, followed by TCLG, RP, AP with (2 per cent) as a percentage share in the total value of exports of industrial goods from Punjab in the same year, i.e. 1980-81. Further, CT, SMP, PC and AS just had (1 percent) share in 1980-81. At the end of the study period, i.e. 1994-95 the trend was found to be somewhat different as discussed above by OI achieving the maximum percentage share (24 per cent) followed by BP (19 per cent) and HRG (17 per cent). A significant improvement was observed in the percentage share of OI (from 10 per cent to 24 per cent), RP (from 2 per cent to 9 per cent) and BP (from 15 per cent in 1980-81 to 19 per cent in 1994-95). The CT industry improved from 1 per cent in 1980-81 to 3 per cent in 1994-95. The industries like TCLG, SMP, SRE, MTHT and AS increased their share marginally during the study period. On the other hand, the maximum decline in the percentage share was noticed in HRG (from 28 percent to 17 percent) followed by SG (13 percent to 5 per cent) and C (from 8 percent to 3 percent) for the same period.

The growth and structure of exports of principle products from industrial sector during 1980-81 to 1984-85 are being shown in Table 2. As is evident from the table that the highest growth rate (38 percent) was achieved by CT, followed by TCLG (19 percent), HRG (10 percent), AP (9 percent) and OI (8 percent). The industry WT showed a growth rate of 5 percent per annum for the same period. Rest of the other industries namely RP, SMP, EGEA, PC, BP, SG, C, SRE, MTHT and AS experienced negative

TABLE 1

Growth of Exports of Principal Items from Industrial Sector in Punjab (1980-81 to 1994-95)

(Values in Rs. Lakh)

Product → *Year ↓*	*WT*	*CT*	*HRG*	*TCLG*	*RP*	*SMP*	*EGEA*	*PC*
1	2	3	4	5	6	7	8	9
1980-81	771.24 (4.75)	196.67 (1.21)	4518.54 (27.87)	322.92 (1.99)	295.41 (1.822)	153.13 (0.94)	205.90 (1.27)	236.81 (1.46)
1981-82	976.22 (4.34)	312.43 (1.39)	7867.69 (35.00)	546.69 (2.43)	168.97 (0.752)	105.66 (0.47)	170.95 (0.76)	1263.88 (5.62)
1982-83	1108.43 (7.66)	453.52 (8.18)	8426.75 (7.86)	488.62 (1.63)	307.43 (4.162)	110.51 (0.49)	112.84 (0.48)	951.47 (1.34)
1983-84	1176.35 (5.96)	568.00 (2.88)	5912.93 (29.98)	513.99 (2.60)	118.07 (0.599)	48.96 (0.00)	128.96 (0.64)	255.18 (1.29)
1984-85	917.89 (4.50)	733.80 (3.60)	8205.51 (40.30)	798.13 (3.92)	147.09 (0.722)	77.83 (0.38)	196.90 (0.96)	379.73 (1.86)
1985-86	518.66 (2.11)	720.76 (2.93)	10531.35 (42.95)	739.37 (3.01)	511.10 (2.084)	82.85 (0.33)	117.17 (0.47)	590.84 (2.40)
1986-87	541.29 (1.96)	1433.50 (5.21)	9739.27 (35.43)	898.22 (3.26)	187.74 (0.683)	130.93 (0.47)	411.90 (1.49)	710.97 (2.58)
1987-88	758.14 (2.21)	1620.77 (6.70)	13055.72 (38.21)	400.85 (2.63)	912.19 (2.670)	116.67 (0.34)	251.36 (0.73)	718.88 (2.10)
1988-89	961.30 (2.06)	3435.62 (7.37)	15388.26 (33.02)	2011.18 (4.31)	131.60 (0.282)	205.02 (0.43)	2463.98 (5.28)	1106.81 (2.37)
1989-90	697.06 (1.07)	1919.33 (2.96)	15982.43 (24.67)	2226.89 (3.43)	851.64 (1.315)	455.68 (0.70)	9490.60 (14.65)	978.98 (1.51)
1990-91	1394.14 (0.55)	2939.41 (3.82)	29054.76 (37.77)	2997.09 (3.89)	821.11 (1.067)	618.98 (0.80)	2504.53 (3.25)	908.29 (1.25)
1991-92	470.86 (0.55)	1880.56 (2.08)	26847.54 (29.80)	2995.50 (3.32)	965.18 (1.071)	429.61 (0.47)	2462.00 (2.73)	830.79 (0.92)
1992-93	1228.11 (1.02)	1907.53 (1.59)	18538.20 (15.54)	4005.04 (3.35)	1589.64 (1.333)	1408.58 (1.18)	1541.33 (1.29)	349.93 (0.29)
1993-94	6282.26 (3.46)	3598.37 (1.98)	33004.53 (18.17)	4668.98 (2.57)	630.41 (0.347)	828.22 (0.45)	2844.94 (1.56)	436.61 (0.24)
1994-95	3152.89 (1.51)	7169.77 (3.44)	34768.73 (16.69)	5855.23 (2.81)	18202.98 (8.739)	3875.56 (136)	599.06 (0.28)	245.34 (0.11)
Total	20954.84	28890.04	241842.21	29968.70	25846.56	8648.19	23512.42	9964.51
Average Annual Growth Rate								
1980-81 to	7.51	23.36	74.51	22.88	23.54	26.79	27.24	-0.76
1994-95	[1.94]	[9.53]	[10.91]	[18.30]	[3.82]	[6.07]	[3.96]	[-0.21]

TABLE 1 (*Contd.*)

(*Values in Rs. Lakh*)

Product → *Year* ↓	*AP*	*BP*	*SG*	*C*	*SRE*	*MTHT*	*AS*	*OI*	*Total Exports*
1	*10*	*11*	*12*	*13*	*14*	*15*	*16*	*17*	*18*
1980-81	391.43 (2.41)	2364.43 (14.58)	2033.84 (12.54)	1228.32 (7.57)	373.01 (230)	1259.59 (7.76)	16037 (0.98)	1701.02 (10.49)	16212.63
1981-82	453.03 (2.01)	3050.56 (13.57)	181437 (8.07)	1292.53 (5.75)	533.11 (2.37)	1079.95 (4.80)	. 76.44 (034)	2824.03 (12.56)	22476.56
1982-83	373.27 (2.13)	1798.37 (36.86)	1870.15 (1.98)	7753.12 (4.84)	427.53 (1.87)	1231.40 (5.38)	357.98 (1.56),	3110.85 (13.60)	22861.24
1983-84	802.15 (4.06)	1967.92 (9.98)	1932.91 (9.80)	1432.24 (7.26)	221.46 (1.12)	929.16 (4.71)	49.40 (0.25)	3656.61 (18.53)	19719.35
1984-85	446.51 (2.19)	2246.25 (11.03)	1714.25 (8.42)	1000.65 (4.91)	46.00 (0.22)	181.82 (5.80)	38.38 (0.18)	2225.03 (10.93)	20356.82
1985-86	499.17 (2.03)	2935.95 (11.97)	1668.53 (6.80)	927.00 (3.78)	—	1399.70 (5.70)	137.24 (0.56)	3092.03 (12.60)	24519.72
1986-87	543.27 (1.971	3874.66 (14.09)	1521.30 (5.53)	533.13 (1.93)	97.77 (035)	1363.20 (4.95)	244.96 (0.89)	5784.27 (21.04)	27488.25
1987-88	792.63 (232)	3947.63 (11.55)	1513.62 (4.40)	46.42 (0.13)	74.24 (0.21)	2164.62 (633)	169.19 (0.49)	7123.91 (20.85)	34166.29
1988-89	849.78 (1.82)	6276.68 (13.46)	1896.42 (4.06)	230.54 (0.49)	4037 (0.08)	2776.96 (5.95)	414.71 (0.89)	8410.29 (18.04)	46599.63
1989-90	1395.39 (2.15)	9632.22 (14.87)	2410.68 (3.72)	751.55 (1.16)	630.71 (9.75)	3360.19 (5.18)	1238.51 (1.91)	12743.53 (19.67)	64765.43
1990-91	1120.57 (1.45)	6587.93 (8.56)	2595.28 (3.37)	943.18 (1.22)	736.26 (0.95)	3186.97 (4.14)	879.14 (1.14)	19572.60 (25.44)	76920.24
1991-92	2663.05 (2.95)	17130.76 (19.01)	339935 (3.73)	183.03 (0.20)	1485.33 (1.64)	4703.08 (5.22)	1771.34 (1.96)	21863.00 (24.27)	90080.98
1992-93	2988.26 (2.50)	29607.85 (24.82)	4000.87 (3.35)	5221.67 (4.37)	3944.09 (3.30)	8605.00 (7.21)	249338 (2.04)	31893.95 (26.69)	119273.43
1993-94	4529.25 (2.49)	53270.01 (29.34)	3245.85 (1.78)	4615.15 (2.54)	4676.92 (2.57)	16688.05 (9.19)	—	42233.78 (23.26)	181547.33
1991-95	4418.58 (2.12)	40131.58 (19.26)	10018.96 (4.81)	6238.96 (2.99)	5593.91 (2.68)	18115.3 (8.69)	—	49843.05 (23.92)	208299.63
Total	22266.34	18482.80	41636.38	26397.49	18880.71	67044.99	8031.04	216076.04	975287.53
Average Annual Growth Rate									
1980-81 to	2008	26.46	8.52	5.45	33.18	22.96	-25.67	27.66	20.06
1994-95	[9.00]	[8.70]	[3.92]	[0.66]	[1.57]	[8.69]	[-1.33]	[14.79]	[12.63]

Note: Figures in parenthesis ( ) are percentages and Figures in [ ] are T-Values. Full form of the symbols is given in Chapter 3.
Source: Statistical Abstracts of Punjab.

TABLE 2

Growth of Exports of Principal Items from Industrial Sector in Punjab (1980-81 to 1984-85)

(*Values in Rs. Lakh*)

Product → *Year ↓*	*WT*	*CT*	*HRG*	*TCLG*	*RP*	*SMP*	*EGEA*	*PC*
1	*2*	*3*	*4*	*5*	*6*	*7*	*8*	*9*
1980-81	771.24 (4.75)	196.67 (1.21)	4518.54 (27.87)	322.92 (1.92)	295.41 (1.82)	153.13 (0.94)	205.90 (1.27)	236.81 (1.46)
1981-82	976.22 (4.34)	312.43 (1.39)	7867.69 (35.00)	546.69 (2.43)	168.97 (0.75)	105.66 (0.47)	170.95 (0,76)	1263.88 (5.62)
1982-83	1108.43 (7.66)	453.52 (8.18)	8426.75 (7.86)	488.62 (1.63)	307.43 (4.16)	110.51 (0.49)	112.84 (0.48)	951.47 (1.34)
1983-84	1176.35 (5.96)	568.00 (2.88)	5912.93 (29.98)	513.99 (2.60)	118.07 (0.59)	48.96 (0.00)	128.96 (0.64)	255.18 (1.29)
1984-85	917.89 (4.50)	733.80 (3.60)	8205.51 (40.30)	798.13 (3.92)	147.09 (0.72)	77.83 (0.38)	196.90 (0.96)	379.73 (1.86)
Average Annual Growth Rate								
1980-81 to	5.41	38.14	9.51	19.10	-16.08	-19.12	-3.71	-6.34
1984-85	[1.02]	[11.24]	[1.09]	[2.88]	[-1.47]	[-2.16]	[-0.40]	[-0.23]

(*Contd.*)

TABLE 2 (*Contd.*)

(Values in Rs. Lakh)

Product → *Year ↓*	*AP*	*BP*	*SG*	*C*	*SRE*	*MTHT*	*AS*	*CI*	*Total Exports*
1	*10*	*11*	*12*	*13*	*14*	*15*	*16*	*17*	*18*
1980-81	391.43 (2.41)	2364.43 (14.58)	2033.84 (12.54)	1228.32 (7.57)	373.01 (230)	1259.59 (7.76)	160.37 (0.98)	1701.02 (10.49)	16212.63
1981-82	453.03 (2.01)	3050.56 (13.57)	1814.37 (8.07)	1292.53 (5.75)	533.11 (2.37)	1079.95 (4.80)	76.44 (0.34)	2824:03 (12.56)	22476.56
1982-83	373.27 (2.13)	1798.37 (36.S6)	1870.15 (1.98)	7753.12 (4.84)	427.53 (1.87)	1231.40 (5.38)	357.98 (1.56)	3110.35 (13.60)	22861.24
1983-84	802.15 (4.06)	1967.92 (9.98)	1932.91 (9.80)	1432.24 (7.26)	221.46 (1.12)	929.16 (4.71)	49.40 (0.25)	3656.61 (18.53)	19719.35
1984-85	446.51 (2.19)	2246.25 (11.03)	1714.25 (8.42)	1000.65 (4.91)	46.00 (0.22)	181.82 (5.80)	38.38 (0.18)	2225.08 (10.93)	20356.82
Average Annual Growth Rate									
1980-81 to	8.704	-5.625	-2.747	-3.026	-39.73	-2.74	-28.08	8.27	3.29
1984-85	[0.825]	[-0.809]	[-1.621]	[-0.429]	[-2.40]	[-0.65]	[-1.20]	[0.80]	[0.69]

Note: Figures in parenthesis ( ) are percentages and Figures in [ ] are T-Values.
Full form of the symbols is given in Chapter 3.
Source: Stahstical Abstracts of Punjab,

growth rate. For the sub period (1980-81 to 1984-85) as a whole, the total value of exports increased from Rs. 16,213 lakhs to Rs. 20,357 lakhs showing the average annual growth rate of 3 percent only. Regarding the percentage share of the different industries in the total value of exports it was found that HRG improved its share significantly by increasing from 28 percent in 1980-81 to 40 percent in 1984-85. The percentage share of CT, TCLG, PC and OI also increased for the same period, but it declined for the industries namely ST, RP, SMP, EGEA, AP, BP, SG, C, SRE, MTHT and AS industries. The decline was found to be more in BP, SG and C industries. Therefore, it can be said that the disturbed conditions in the state, (i.e. the state of the economy before and immediate after the operation Blue Star) affected the performance of different industries (leaving a few) adversely.

For the sub-period 1985-86 to 1989-90, the situation was found to be very impressive by most of the industries achieving remarkable rate of growth. As is evident from the Table 3 that EGEA recorded a growth rate of (188 percent, because its initial base was very low), AS (64 percent), SMP (47 percent), OI (38 percent), TCLG (35 percent), CT and BP (33 percent), AP, MTHT (28 percent), PC (15 percent), HRG (14 percent), WT (12 percent) and SG (10 percent). Similarly, the industry SRE also recorded a significant increase in its growth rate because its initial base being very meagre. Only one product that is, C recorded a negative growth rate during the same period. The total value of exports increased from Rs. 24,519 lakhs in 1985-86 to Rs. 64,765 lakhs in 1989-90 exhibiting a growth rate of 28 percent. As per the percentage share of different component industries, it can be visualised from the Table 3 that HRG industry (which was major component in the previous sub-period) declined its share from (43 percent to 25 percent). But the percentage shares increased remarkably for EGEA (0.47 percent to 15 percent) and SRE (0.35 percent to 10 percent). The increase was also very much evident for the industries like BP and OI industries. The industries like TCLG, SMP, AP and AS also showed a moderate increase in their percentage share. On the other hand, the industries like WT, RP, PC, SG, C, MTHT showed a decline in their respective shares for the same period.

Now coming to the last sub-period of the analysis, i.e. 1990-91 to 1994-95, it was observed from the Table 4 that the highest

TABLE 3

Growth of Exports of Principal Items from Industrial Sector in Punjab (1985-86 to 1989-90)

(Values in Rs. Lakh)

Product → *Year ↓*	*WT*	*CT*	*HRG*	*TCLG*	*RP*	*SMP*	*EGEA*	*PC*
1	*2*	*3*	*4*	*5*	*6*	*7*	*8*	*9*
1985-86	518.66 (2.11)	720.76 (2.93)	10531.35 (42.95)	739.37 (3.01)	511.10 (2.08)	82.85 (0.33)	117.17 (0.47)	590.84 (2.40)
1986-87	541.29 (1.96)	1433.50 (5.21)	9739.27 (35.43)	898.22 (3.26)	187.74 (0.68)	130.93 (0.47)	411.90 (1.49)	710.97 (2.58)
1987-88	758.14 (2.21)	1620.77 (6.70)	13055.72 (38.21)	400.85 (2.63)	912.19 (2.67)	116.67 (0.34)	251.36 (0.73)	718.88 (2.10)
1988-89	961.30 (2.06)	3435.62 (7.37)	15388.26 (33.02)	2011.18 (4.31)	131.60 (0.28)	205.02 (0.43)	2463.98 (5.28)	1106.81 (2.37)
1989-90	697.06 (1.07)	1919.33 (2.96)	15982.43 (24.67)	2226.89 (3.43)	851.64 (1.31)	455.68 (0.70)	9490.60 (14.65)	978.98 (1.51)
Average Annual Growth Rate								
1985-86 to	12.36	32.75	13.78	35.13	6.88	47.07	187.99	15.63
1989-90	[1.83]	[2.28]	[4.14]	[4.38]	[0.20]	[4.32]	[4.49]	[3.47]

TABLE 3 (*Contd.*)

(*Values in Rs. Lakh*)

Product → *Year ↓*	*AP*	*BP*	*SG*	*C*	*SRE*	*MTHT*	*AS*	*OI*	*Total Exports*
1	*10*	*11*	*12*	*13*	*14*	*15*	*16*	*17*	*18*
1985-86	499.17 (2,03)	2935.95 (11.97)	1668.53 (6.80)	927.00 (3.78)	—	1399.70 (5.70)	137.24 (0.56)	3092.03 (12.60)	24519.72
1986-87	543.27 (1.97)	3874.66 (14.09)	1521.30 (5.53)	533.13 (1.93)	97.77 (0.35)	1363.20 (4.95)	244.96 (0.89)	5784.27 (21.04)	27488.25
1987-88	792.63 (2.32)	3947.63 (11.55)	1513.62 (4.40)	46.42 (0.13)	74.24 (0.21)	2164.62 (6.33)	169.19 (0.49)	7123.91 (20.85)	34166.29
1988-89	849.78 (1.82)	6276.68 (13.46)	1896.42 (4.06)	230-54 (0.49)	40.37 (0.08)	2776.96 (5.95)	414.71 (0.89)	8410.29 (18.04)	46599.63
1989-90	1395.39 (2.15)	9632.22 (14.87)	2410.68 (3.72)	751.55 (1.16)	630.71 (9.75)	3360.19 (5.18)	1238.51 (1.91)	12743.53 (19.67)	64765.45
Average Annual Growth Rate									
1985-86 to 1989-90	28.44 [6.38]	33.09 [6.14]	10.03 [2.14]	-11.82 [-0.28]	73..74 [2.14]	27.92 [6.43]	63.66 [3.31]	37.82 [7.16]	28.02 [9.50]

Note: Figures in parenthesis ( ) are percentages and Figures in [ ] are T-Values.
Full form of the symbols is given in Chapter 3.
Source: Statistical Abstracts of Punjab.

TABLE 4

Growth of Exports of Principal Items from Industrial Sector in Punjab (1990-91 to 1994-95)

(Values in Rs. Lakh)

Product → *Year ↓*	*WT*	*CT*	*HRG*	*TCLG*	*RP*	*SMP*	*EGEA*	*PC*
1	*2*	*3*	*4*	*5*	*6*	*7*	*8*	*9*
1990-91	1394.14 (0.55)	2939.41 (3.82)	29054.76 (37.77)	2997.09 (3.89)	821.11 (1.06)	618.98 (0.80)	2504.53 (3.25)	908.29 (1.25)
1991-92	470.86 (0.55)	1880.56 (2.08)	26847.54 (29.80)	2995.50 (3.32)	965.18 (1.07)	429.61 (0.47)	2462.00 (2.73)	830.79 (0.92)
1992-93	1228.11 (1.02)	1907.53 (1.59)	18538.20 (15.54)	4005.04 (3.35)	1589.64 (1.33)	1408.58 (1.18)	1541.33 (1.29)	349.93 (0.29)
1993-94	6282.26 (3.46)	3598.37 (1.98)	33004.53 (18.17)	4668.98 (2.57)	630.41 (0.34)	828.22 (0.45)	2844.94 (1.56)	436.61 (0.24)
1994-95	3152.89 (1.51)	7169.77 (3.44)	34768.73 (16.69)	5855.23 (2.81)	18202.98 (8.73)	3875.56 (1.86)	599.06 (0.28)	245.34 (0.11)
Average Annual Growth Rate								
1990-91 to	52.54	27.53	5.81	19.52	78.09	54.11	-23.78	-28.74
1994-95	[1.59]	[1.69]	[0.66]	[7.33]	[1.55]	[2.30]	[-1.56]	[-4.16]

(Contd.)

TABLE 4 (*Contd.*)

(*Values in Rs. Lakh*)

Product → *Year ↓*	*AP*	*BP*	*SG*	*C*	*SRE*	*MTHT*	*AS*	*OI*	*Total Exporter*
1	*10*	*11*	*12*	*13*	*14*	*15*	*16*	*17*	*18*
1990-91	1120.57 (1.45)	6587.93 (8.56)	2595.28 (3.37)	943.18 (1.22)	736.26 (0.95)	3186.97 (4.14)	879.14 (1.14)	19572.60 (25.44)	76920.2
1991-92	2663.05 (2.95)	17130.76 (19.01)	3399.35 (3.73)	183.03 (0.20)	1485.33 (1.64)	4703.08 (5.22)	1771.34 (1.96)	21863.00 (24.27)	900S0.9
1992-93	2988.26 (2.50)	29607.85 (24.S2)	4000.87 (3.35)	5221.67 (4.37)	3944.09 (3.30)	8605.00 (7.21)	2493.38 (2.04)	31893.95 (26.69)	119273
1993.94	4529.25 (2.49)	53270.01 (29.34)	3245.85 (1.78)	4615.15 (2.54)	4676.92 (2.57)	16688.05 (9.19)	—	42233.78 (23.26)	181547
1994-95	4418.58 (2.12)	40131.58 (19.26)	10018.96 (4.81)	6238.96 (2.99)	5593.91 (2.68)	18115.3 (8.69)	—	49843.05 (23.92)	203299
Avereage Annual Growth Rate									
1990-91 to	38.75	60.77	30.41	5.45	33.18	22.96	-25.67	27.66	30.90
1994-95	[3.89]	[3.78]	[2.32]	[0.66]	[1.57]	[8.69]	[-1.33]	[14.79]	[10.46]

Note: Figures in parenthesis ( ) are percentages and Figures in [ ] are T-Values.
Full form of the symbols is given in Chapter 3.
Source: Statistical Abstracts of Punjab.

growth rate was recorded by RP (78 per cent) followed by BP (61 per cent), SMP (54 per cent), WT (53 per cent), AP (39 per cent), SRE (33 per cent) and SG (30 per cent). Similarly, the industries OI and CT achieved a growth rate of 28 per cent, MTHT (23 per cent), TCLG (20 per cent), HRG (6 per cent) and industry C (5 per cent). The two industries namely EGEA and AS showed a negative rate of growth. The total value of exports increased from Rs. 76,920 lakhs in 1990-91 to Rs. 2,08,300 lakhs in 1994-95, showing a growth rate of 31 per cent. Regarding the percentage share of the different industries it is evident from Table 4 that the percentage share of HRG industry (which seems to be the most important industry in view of its absolute value and percentage share in the total value of exports) showed a declining trend (from 38 per cent in 1990-91 to 17 per cent in 1994-95). Similarly, the percentage share of BP industry increased from 9 per cent to 19 per cent, of RP from 1 per cent to 9 per cent, of MTHT from 4 per cent to 9 per cent. In case of the industries like WT, SMP, AP, SG, C and SRE the percentage share increased at a moderate rate. On the other hand, the industries like CT, TCLG, EGEA, PC and OI industries showed a decline in their respective percentage share.

It may be concluded from the above discussion that the export sector in the Punjab state has grown tremendously during the study period. For the period as a whole in absolute value terms the Hosiery and Ready-made garments, Bicycles and Parts and Machine Tools/Hand Tools emerged as the most prominent industries. Besides these, growth wise SRE Solvent Oil/Rice Bran Extraction, Sewing Machine and Parts, SME, Electrical Switch Gears and Electrical Accessories, EGEA, Cotton Textiles CT, Rubber Products RP, Tanned and Chrome Leather Goods CLG, Machine Tools/Hand Tools, MTHT Auto-parts AP, Other Items OI were amongst the leading industries, i.e. (growth rate ranging between 23 per cent to 33 per cent). The other industries like Sports goods SG, Woollen Textiles/Carpets WT and Coffee C, etc. also performed well (growth rate ranging between 5 per cent to 10 per cent).

Regarding the structure of the exports of industrial goods from Punjab, it is very much evident from the analysis that in the initial year of the study, i.e. 1980-81, the HRG Hosiery and Ready-made Garments, Bicycle and parts BP and Sports Goods SG were taking the first, second and the third places respectively. But at the end of the study period the Bicycles and parts BP took the leading position in terms of percentage share and was followed by Hosiery and Ready-made Garments. A significant increase was also observed in case of Rubber Products.

Sub-period-wise, it was found that during the period 1980-81 to 1984-85 the industrial production suffered a set-back due to apparent reasons, when most of the industries registered a negative rate of growth and only six industries namely WT, CT, HRG, TCLG, AP and OI showed a positive rate of growth. During the sub-period 1985-86 to 1989-90, the exports registered a very high growth rate (28%) as compared to the period 1980-81 to 1984-85 (3%). It was observed that only one product namely Coffee showed a negative growth rate and rest of the other products experienced a positive rate of growth. Exports of EGEA, SRE and Art Silk AS, increased at a rapid rate.

During 1990-91 to 1994-95 exports grew at an average annual growth rate of 31 per cent. Exports from the products like RP, BP, SMP and WT increased at a rapid rate whereas the EGEA, PVC Cables and Art Silk showed a negative growth rate. Rest of the other products showed a positive rate of growth.

Therefore, it may be concluded that the export sector in Punjab has undergone significant structural changes during the study period. The change has obviously been in favour of non-traditional products like Electrical Gears and Electrical Appliances EGEA, Bicycles Parts BP, Rubber Products RP, Sewing Machine and Parts SMP and Auto Parts AP, etc., but this change in the growth and structure of exports has not been stable and consistent, it was rather fluctuating in nature. Moreover, the liberal trade policy has significantly improved the performance of exports sector after mid-80's but the process has not been continuous and persistent. Such policies will help in long-run if the indigenous industrial sector becomes more efficient and strong. The development of domestic sector with more and more emphasis on quality and competitiveness is essential for long-run development of this sector. The export sector is also facing some problems like raw material, finance, supply problems like packaging and quality transportation to mention a few. Moreover, the infrastructural facilities have to be strengthened and in order to maintain quality and standardisation government should launch a campaign to create quality consciousness. Further, the procedure for granting loans should be simplified and timely supply at low rates should be provided. For modernisation of exportable products, imports of required machinery be allowed liberally and on duty free basis. Encouragement should also be given for upgrading the technology to turn out quality products. Although in terms of the 'total value of exports' at the 'All India' level the relative share of 'Punjab Economy's' industrial goods exports may appear to be very small. Yet, they are very essential for self-sustained process of economic development of the stake. Moreover, at the various levels the efforts are to be made to promote only high technology, electronic and information technology, consultancy services and importantly the export-oriented industries for future expansion and existence.

List of Symbols

1.	Woollen Textiles/Carpets	WT
2.	Cotton Textiles	CT
3.	Hosiery and Ready-made Garments	HRG
4.	Tanned and Chrome Leather and Leather Goods	TCLG
5.	Rubber Products	RP
6.	Sewing Machine and Parts	SMP
7.	Electrical Switch Gears and Electrical Accessories	EGEA
8.	PVC Cables	PC
9.	Auto parts	AP
10.	Bicycle and Parts	BP
11.	Sports Goods	SG
12.	Coffee	C
13.	Solvent Oil/Rice Bran Extraction	SRE
14.	Machine Tools/Hand Tools	MTHT
15.	Art Silk	AS
16.	Other Items	OI

References

Dass, Swadip, K. and Pant, Manoj, "*Economic Liberalisation; Industrial Structure and Growth in. India*," Oxford University Press, 1990, pp. 107-21.

Nayyer, Deepak, "India's Export Performance: Factors and Constraints," *Economic and Political Weekly*, Vol. 28, Nos. 10, 20 and 21, Annual No. (May 1987), pp. 73-90.

Singh, Pritam, "*Punjab Economy—The Emerging Pattern*", Enkay Publishers, New Delhi, 1995.

Eighth Five Year Plan, Government of India, Planning Commission, New Delhi.

The Need for Transforming Natural Resources for Sustainable and Balanced Development

S.K. Sharma

Every nation—developed or developing—is striving for development. Several models and approaches of development have been evolved since after second world war (Sharma, 1996). Ultimate goal of these approaches has been to increase production. The resultant scenario of resource exploitation and socio-economic development presents atleast three problems simultaneously in depressed regions. At the outset, people are viewed separated from resource endowment of the area. As such, exploitation of natural resources, most useful aspects of the biophysical environment, increased phenomenally in consonance with the increasing production in the economic sector. But motives behind this exploitation have been the maximization of output and revenue returns rather than the optimisation of net social benefits and regional development (Misra and Sharma, 1982, 6). Limited perspectives led to excessive and ruthless exploitation of natural resources; which in turn is not only creating multi-dimensional environmental problems and natural hazards but has degraded the environment in general. Development ultimately suffers with the degradation of environment (Kayastha, 1993, 56). Thus, resources are developed without caring for environment and society. The way in which natural resources have been developed in the past has made the potential adversities and dangers to natural resource system and to the human welfare the focal theme of current discussions. This problem is accentuated by the fact that all transportable resources of lagging regions and areas, instead of being utilized for the development of the region of their occurrence, are syphoned to dominant regions leaving degenerated ecosystem and dependent economy in their share. Third glaring problem is the dichotomy of the 'existence of poverty in plenty'. It means, most often than not, resource-rich regions are lagging far behind in level of development if they are not dominant. On their hand, developed regions and countries are capable of importing resources from outside.

Such problems of developing countries and of marginal areas have attracted attention of international institutions and a series of International Conferences have been conveyed in 1970s and early 1980s to emphasize the intricate and close linkages between development, population, resources and environment (U.N., 1984, 64-65). Resources have to be developed to enhance the economic development. At the same time, environmental equilibrium has to be maintained. Therefore, there is urgent need to synchronise both the resource development and the environmental management in the wider perspective of regional and national development on sustainable basis. With these views, the need of adopting transformational approach for the development of Madhya Pradesh has been discussed in the light of the problems of resource development in the following pages.

CONCEPT OF SUSTAINABILITY AND SUSTAINABLE DEVELOPMENT

The contemporary meaning of development is the continuous upliftment of the entire society and social system to betted conditions or towards more human conditions. In words of Drewnowski, 'development is the process of qualitative change and quantitative growth of the social and economic reality which we call either society or economy' (Drewnowski, 1974, 94-95). Fulfilment of the basic needs, participation, self-esteem, life sustenance and freedom from servitude are some of the characteristics of development. But the concept of sustainability has added more qualification to develòpment. The concept of sustainable development was propogated in early 1970s. By 1980 the International Union of Conservation of Nature emphasized the need for conservation of living resources to achieve sustainable development (IUCN, 1960). Later the same IUCN defines conservation as the management of human use of the biosphere so that it may yield the greatest sustainable benefit to current generations while maintaining the potential to meet the needs and aspirations of future generation (IUCN, 1987). Since then several attempts have been made to define sustainability and sustainable development (Pezzey, 1989). Lele (1989) has presented a critical review of the concept. Despite certain shortcomings, the concept has received wide recognision. Nevertheless, it carries different meanings to different people. Sustainable development, as defined by the World Commission on Environment and Development, 'is development that meets the needs of the present without compromising thc ability of future generations to meet their own needs', (WCED, 1987). The emphasis in this definition is on the satisfaction of basic human needs and maintenance of environmental equilibrium.

The tenet of this concept is the utilization of the environmental resources according to their capacity of replenishing so that their perpetual supply can be ensured. It is evident from David Pearce's view that sustainability refers to 'leaving the same or an improved resource endowment as a bequest to the future... (that is) the total stock of all forms of wealth (including environmental wealth) must not be depleted', (Pearce, 1989, 17-20). Many forms of development erode the environmental resources upon which they are based; which in turn, undermine present economic development and reduces future possibilities drastically. Therefore, sustainable development should keep in view the stability of the ecosystem. With this view, the International Union of Conservation of Nature defines sustainable development as 'improving the quality of human life while living within the carrying capacity of supporting ecosystem', (ICUN, 1987 and Naik, 1993, 11-13). Thus the question is not simply of sustenance of life but of good quality of life. Quality of life means different things to different strata of society. Usually it is equated with material self-sufficiency. In regional policies it is 'adequately perceived conditions of life'. Now it is accepted as a process, a relationship, a sense of belonging, and a sense of wholeness. For increasing material production people intervene in the environment and use inputs. Biophysical potentiality and inputs together determine the carrying capacity. But the bio-physical system has a limit to assimilate inputs, therefore the intervension should be limited.

Further, as Kayastha has pointed out, 'sustainability can also be understood in social sense, meaning a thriving economy and social order with productive structures and relationships, which ensure a fair distribution of incomes, power and opportunities, thus providing the basis for social peace (Kayastha, 1993, 63). Finally, sustainability is used in the sense of long-term carrying capacity of regions, where there is no negative impact on environment (Kuhnen, 1992). Thus essential elements of sustainability cover all aspects ranging from ethics, aesthetics, self-reliance, basic needs to stability of human population (Chattopadhyaya and Carpenter, 1991, 1). In fact, it is people-oriented and nature-oriented development concept, in which social justice, welfare, quality of life, and environmental protection are kept at par the economic growth. At the same time, local population, resources, needs, aspirations and capabilities are given due attention in the development planning. It is because, as Tolba has seen in case of Africa (1987), people had used local resources prudently for generations as the people observed religious, cultural and other practices finely honed to their environment. These traditions can be used to make resources sustainable.

RESOURCE STATUS: EXPLOITATION AND UTILIZATION

Madhya Pradesh presents a very good example of the dichotomy of 'poverty in plenty'. It is universal fact that the distribution of resources is localized, which is true in the case of Madhya Pradesh also. As far as bounty of resources are concerned, the eastern part is the richest in the state, but in economic development western part is far ahead, which has thin resource base. In the east, there are few developed enclaves associated with inland parts for export of natural resources. It is paradox enough that this part possesses most of the forest, mineral and power resources of the state and their production has also increased by leaps and bounds, raising the revenue many folds. But most of the resources are exported for processing to other parts of the state and even other parts of the country, leaving these areas lagging far behind in development. Distribution of natural resources has been analysed with the perspective of the comprehension of their role in enhansing economic development in this state. Only major resources have been looked upon.

LAND RESOURCES

Land is the basic resource and determines the economy of the State to a great extent. It assumes special significance because it is non-transportable resource and yields benefits to the local people. But the state is endowed with limited good agricultural land. Most of the area presents typical characteristics of a plateau. The Malwa plateau, Madhya Bharat Pathar, Bundelkhand upland, Vindhyan scarpment, Vindhyachal range, Satpura range, Baghelkhand plateau, Bastar plateau, Chhattisgarh basin and the Narmada valley of the north-central Peninsular India are the major physiographic units within the boundary of the State. Most of these plateau are highly dissected and present high local relief which reduce their agricultural suitability. Land of the following regions is usually not suitable for agricultural purposes: (i) Bastar plateau, (ii) Baghelkhand plateau, (iii) Satpura range, (iv) Vindhyachal range, and (v) Madhya Bharat Pathar. However, there are some pockets of level land between hills and dissected areas. Most of these areas are under forests. Contrary to it, land classed as suitable for cultivation are confined in (i) the Chhattisgarh basin, (ii) Narmada valley, (iii) Rewa plateau, (iv) Malwa plateau, and (v) on part of the Bundelkhand upland. Land of the Chhattisgarh basin covered with red and yellow soils is rated as very good and good in the capability classification, while of the Rewa plateau and the Narmada valley, with deep and medium black soils, are good land. Old alluvium and mixed red and black soils on level land of the Sindh-Pahuj plain of the Bundelkhand upland make it agriculturally productive area, gently.sloping land of the Malwa plateau, covered with medium black soils, is moderately good.

The quality of land has manifested itself through the net sown area. It is because in the country like India where agriculture, by experimentation over centuries, has well adjusted itself to the natural conditions. All cultivable area is under cultivation. All the above regions with good agricultural lands are widely cultivated. Conversely, dissected areas, with thin poor and unworkable soils have low and very low proportion of net sown area. It is extremely low in the Baghelkhand plateau, Bastar plateau, Maikal plateau and major parts of the Madhya Bharat Pathar and Bundelkhand uplands. These areas are deprived of such basic resources which provides stable footing to the economy and people.

WATER RESOURCES

Useability of land is further limited with the availability of moisture. Rainfall is the primary source of moisture supply. There is wide regional and seasonal distribution of rainfall. Normally south-eastern half of the state receives higher rainfall than 120 cm. In the north-west, it gradually drops to 72 cm in Jhabua and 68 cm in Morena. More than 90% of the rain comes during the south-west monsoon season, i.e. June to September. Vagaries of rainfall is so serious that eleven districts out of 45 have been identified as drought-prone districts. Eight of them are in the south-western part, while Datia is in the north and Sidhi and Shahdol in the east.

Nevertheless, the State has vast volume of surface water. Total volume of water drained by the rivers of this state is estimated at 183.3 billion cubic metres. Rivers radiate from high lands of this state and are tammed as they reach in the bordering states. Potential of under-ground water is also vast, and estimated at 83.8 lakh (5.8 million) hectares. There is marked variation in distribution of these potentials, depending upon climatic and structural characteristics. Usually, level lands are also endowed with rich water resources. Ultimate potential of water resources of this state can irrigate 102 lakh hectares. Only 59.3 lakh hectares (1995-96) are net irrigated at present which is about 58% of the ultimate potential. Most of the irrigated area is confined in the Chhattisgarh—the rice bowl of the state, Chambal region and Bundelkhand uplands. Conversely, the eastern part of the state but Chhattisgarh and Vidisha plateau and Jhabua fail even to employ such basic input as irrigation (Sharma and Jain, 1974).

FOREST RESOURCES

Forests are more abundant and valuable resources of this state. They constitute nearly one-third (32.8%) of the total geographic area of the state. It is estimated that nearly one-fifth (19.9%) of the total forested area and 14.3 of the growing stock of the country are confined within this state. There are five major belts of forest concentration. These are: (1) Satpura-Maikal-Baghelkhand plateau, (2) the Vindhyachal range, (3) the Panna-Vindhyachal range, (4) the Morena-Shivpuri plateau, and (5) the Bastar plateau. It is remarkable that there is close relationship between the distribution of forests and dissected topography. Generally, dissected and rugged parts are widely covered with dense forests due to their unsuitability for cultivation. Thus, most of the forests are confined in the south and south-eastern parts of state and forests and minerals are only resources available for development of these regions.

Forests have been exploited since time immemorial, but with the advancement of science and technology rate of exploitation increased tremendously. It can be guessed from the increasing trend of revenue accrueing from them. Gross revenue from forests was only Rs. 61.4 million in 1956-57, just before the reorganisation of the state, which reached to Rs. 3992.7 million in 1992-93. Thus forest revenue increased by more than sixty-five times during last three and a half decades from 1956.

Forests of this state produce a variety of products (Table 1). Timber is at the top as far as revenue is concerned. It is followed by tendu leaves, bamboo and sal seeds. Besides them Khair, Kulu and other gums, harra, leaves of mahul, lakh, aomla, bai birang, different types of grasses such as babor, sabai, rosa, bagai, etc., fruits of wild plants (i.e. bahera, chiraunji, bhilwa, mahua, imli), barks and leaves of several other trees, bones and horns are worth-mentioning.

These forest produces of the south and eastern parts of the state are capable of supporting several industries on all scales, particularly on medium and small scale. But these potentialities could not be harnessed within the state and most of the products are exported in raw form or in semi-finished form. Only few forest-based industries could be developed. Most of the forest produces are exported to surrounding states and as far as upto Punjab and Haryana.

TABLE 1

Madhya Pradesh: Output of Forest Produces, 1990-91

Produce	*Unit in thousand*	*Production*	*Revenue (Rs. Million)*	*% of total Revenue*
Timber	M^3	690	2227.7	59.7
Fuelwood	M^3	890		
Tendu leave	St. bags	6115	752.4	20.17
Bamboo	Notional tonnes	290	323.3	8.67
Sal seeds	Quintal	457	1.9	0.05
Harra	"	151	—	—
Gums	"	15	2.5	0.06
Khair	"	—	22.1	0.59
Gross Revenue	—	—	3730.8	100.00

MINERAL AND POWER RESOURCES

Madhya Pradesh has rich and extensive deposits of industrially important minerals and occupies first position in the mining economy of the country, contributing more than 24.0 per cent to the total value of mineral output (excluding petroleum and gas) in 1995-96. It is richly endowed with bauxite, coal, copper, diamond, dolomite, iron-ore, limestone and manganese ore. Besides them, and alusite, barytes, clays, corundum, flourspar, rock phosphate, ochre, sillimanite and steatite are also found. Estimated reserves of major minerals are presented in Table 2 below.

Besides these major minerals several other minerals of less significance are produced in the state. Among them, asbestos, barytes, calcite, corundum, diaspore, felspar, fireclay, kaolin, moulding sand, ochre, pyrophylite, quartz, silica sand, sillimaite, slate, steatite and tin concentrate are worth-mentioning.

Distribution of these minerals is very localised. Major tracts of their occurrences are the Baghelkhand plateau, Chhattisgarh basin, Bastar plateau, eastern Satpura and the Rewa plateau in the eastern part. Jhabua and lower Chambal valley are outside of these tracts (S.K. Sharma, 1988, 86).

TABLE 2

Madhya Pradesh: Reserves and Production of Important Minerals

Mineral	*Reserves million tonnes 1990*	*% of the country*	*Production (1995-96)*		*Rank in India*
			Qty 000 tonnes	*Value Rs. (Lakh)*	
Bauxite	140.8	5.6	518	1720	II
Coal	38115.39	19.3	79968	320202	I
Copper ore	95.89	29.5	2027	5463	I
Diamond*	1001.2	100.0	29.9	1309	I
Dolomite	1666.8	38.6	914	1665	II
Iron ore	2186.22	22.8	17426	34564	I
Limestone	9449.99	12.4	27451	19707	I
Manganese	16.54	9.4	359	4149	III
Rock Phosphate	15.66	13.8	85	657	III
Tine ore	28.89	99.9	NA	NA	I

* Reserve and production of diamond are in thousand carats.

Production of minerals increased many folds in last four and half decades. Total value of minerals was only Rs. 82.3 million in 1951 in this state which rose to Rs. 39899.7 million in 1995-96 recording an increase of nearly 500 times. It is estimated that more than two-thirds of the total value of minerals produced in the state are contributed by four districts, viz. Bilaspur, Shahdol, Surguja and Sidhi. These districts could reach to this level because of coal. Among other mineral producing districts mention be made of Chhindwara, Betul, Durg, Bastar, Balaghat, Satna and Jabalpur. Most of these districts are backward.

UTILIZATION OF MINERAL RESOURCES

This mineral rich state, increasing mineral production phenomenally, is still waiting for industrialization based on them on large scale. Instead of putting them on industrial uses within the region of their occurrences, most of them are exported to other parts of the country or to other countries usually unprocessed. It is fact that the natural resources are the property of the entire nation and not only to the region of their occurrences, but at the same time, it can also not be disowned that development of such poor regions, which lack all other factors of production than natural resources like minerals and forests, cannot be initiated without the efficient use of local natural resources. Simply collection of revenue from export of these resources will hardly create congenial structure for development. Despite this, prime motive behind the mineral exploitation in this state is export. As per act of mines and minerals all the major minerals are in the specified list and are virtually under direct control of the Central Government, and only minor minerals are in state control. Under such circumstances, location of mineral-based industries is not possible unless sanction is accorded by the central government. In some status, a few major minerals have also been excluded from the central list. For instance, Singreni coalfield of Andhra Pradesh is not in this list, consequently, the state government could establish two large fertilizer plants. But Madhya Pradesh could not get such concessions. Thus situation is like sailing in the sea where 'water is everywhere but not a drop to drink'. There is dire need of rethinking of mineral policies which deprive their utilization in the region of their occurrences.

Scanning of utilization of mineral resources in this perspective is pertinent. Let us start from iron ore. Out of total production of ore (12,536 thousand tonnes) only two-fifths (5390 thousand tonnes in 1989-90) is used in manufacturing iron and steel at Bhilai, and nearly three-thirds is sent out of state. The Bailadila project has been developed only for exporting rich iron ore to Japan and the Bailadila-Vishakhapattanam railway line has been constructed to facilitate the haulage of this confinement. In return, Bastar gets Rs. 6 to 7 per tonne of ore. Similarly, dolomite from this state is most often utilized in industries located in adjacent states, so and so the ferro-manganese plants, glass and refractory industries of Maharashtra and Gujarat also get dolomite from here, but such industries could not be established in this state. Bauxite is another example. State has vast reserves of coal in close proximity of bauxite deposits to meet the requirement of power of alumina plants. But this possibility could not be explored and three-fourths of produced bauxite is used for manufacture of alumina within this state and another one-fourth is used to meet the requirement of industries located outside. Limestone is the only mineral put to industrial uses extensively. Nearly 25 per cent (10,761 thousand tonnes in 1989-90) of total cement production in the country was manufactured within this state. This gives an insight as well as an example of industrial development. If this example is followed in case of other minerals this state can march far ahead in industrial development.

It was postulated that Madhya Pradesh would be constant source of power to the nation. It became true but at the cost of herself. She provides coal for power generation to Gujarat, Maharashtra, Rajasthan, Uttar Pradesh, Haryana and Delhi, but her three joint projects of super thermal power stations, viz. Bandhav (Sidhi), Mand (Raigarh) and Bisrampur (Surguja) could not get sanction, nor coal-based fertilizer plant could be brought up at Korba or Singrauli as has been done in Singreni coalfield. Story of other minerals is not different. Copper ore produced at Malanjkhand, Balaghat is sent to Khetri in Rajasthan for melting. Similarly, more than half of manganese ore is exported. Thus the entire structure of mineral exploitation is based on and is oriented to export. It functions as siphone for draining minerals out from this state. It can be said that minerals have not initiated industrial development in the region of their occurrences, excepting in the core of the Chhattisgarh. Bastar, producing 7.0 million tonnes of iron ore, Balaghat, producing 3 million tonnes of manganese, Surguja, Shahdol and Sidhi, each producing more than 7 million tonnes of coal each year, are still waiting for industrialization based on minerals.

RESOURCES AND REGIONAL DEVELOPMENT

The overall growth of different sectors of the state economy has been rapid and satisfactory during different plans. But still this state lags far behind the other states of the country in development in general and in socio-economic development in particular. The characteristics associated with backward regions, such as less than average income, lower employment, lower industrial and agricultural production, fewer social services and lesser commerce, etc. are present here. Even in this backward state there is marked regional inequality in the level of development. It is evident from the development block level analysis of the relative level of development (Sharma, 1994). Eleven variable have been used for the purpose. These variables are: (i) proportion of net sown area, (ii) intensity of cropping, (iii) percentage of irrigated area, (iv) proportion of cereal cropped area under HYV, (v) density of tractors per 1000 ha of cropped land, (vi) density of pumping sets per 1000 ha of cropped area, (vii) proportion of electrified villages, (viii) density of metalled roads per 100 sq km of area, (ix) proportion of literates to total population, (x) percentage of household workers to total main workers, and (xi) proportion of other workers. The data of each of above eleven variables for each block has been converted as percentage of the state average of respective variable. The eleven scores thus obtained for each block are summed to get composite score of level of development for each and all blocks.

The composite index of development thus obtained ranges from only 39 in Orchha block and 139 in Bhairamgarh block (both in Bastar district) to 2959 in Bhitarwar (Gwalior) and 2491 in Indore block. The composite index for the state would be 1100. Taking this median value into consideration 459 blocks of the state can be grouped into six classes.

Only 42.0 per cent (193) of blocks could cross the state average while 58.0 per cent (266) of them are below it. Again, 15.3 per cent of them are least developed with composite score below 50.0 per cent of the state, and more than one-fifth (21.8%) have composite scores between 50 and 75 per cent of the state average. Coincidently, these blocks, most often, happen to be tribal dominated.

Distribution of blocks above state average reveals several interesting facts. Most of these blocks are concentrated in Chambal, Sagar, Jabalpur, Ujjain and Indore divisions. Proportion of blocks belonging to developed classes in different divisions is presented in the Table 3.

It is evident from Table 3 that Hoshangabad division has highest proportion (90.0%) of the developed blocks followed by Chambal division (87.5%). It is more than three-fourths (76.3%) in Sagar, more than half in Gwalior and between 42 to 50 per cent in Bhopal, Indore and Jabalpur divisions. Contrary to it, Bastar division is at bottom with none of such blocks followed by Bilaspur (13.6%), Rewa (29.7%) and Raipur (35.4%).

On district level, there are seven districts viz. Bastar, Raigarh, Surguja, Shahdol, Guna, Seoni and Jhabua, where not a single block belongs to the developed class. Besides them, five districts, viz. Rajnandgaon, Mandla, Sidhi, Panna and Rajgarh have only one developed block each. There are nine districts where even the block of the district headquarters could not develop.

TABLE 3

Madhya Pradesh: Division-wise Distribution of Developed and Developing Blocks

Revenue Divisions	*Total No. of Blocks*	*Developed Blocks*	*Under-developed Blocks*	*Percentage of*	
				Developed Blocks	*Under-developed Blocks*
Indore	54	23	31	42.6	57.4
Ujjain	34	25	09	73.5	26.5
Gwalior	23	12	11	52.2	47.8
Chambal	16	14	02	87.5	12.5
Rewa	37	11	26	29.7	70.3
Sagar	38	29	09	76.3	23.7
Bhopal	37	17	20	45.9	54.1
Hoshangabad	10	09	01	90.0	10.0
Jabalpur	64	27	37	42.2	57.8
Bilaspur	66	09	57	13.6	86.4
Raipur	48	17	31	35.4	64.6
Bastar	32	00	32	00.0	100.0
Total	459	193	266	42.0	58.0

Thus, north-western part of the state is comparatively more developed. Significantly deprived areas in this part are the Jhabua-Dhar hilly tract, the Umatwara and Khilchiwara plateaus on north-eastern Malwa plateau and the Shivpuri plateau covering southern Madhya Bharat plateau. Contrary to it, deprived areas are long and wide in the south and east; and developed blocks are like drops in sea. These regions are the Satpura region including the Maikal plateau, the Baghelkhand plateau, three-fourths of the Chhattisgarh basin and the Bastar plateau.

The correlation of the distribution of resources other than the land and the level of development reveals that most of the districts poor in development have rich endowments of mineral, power and forest resources. For example, important minerals producing districts are Sidhi, Shahdol, Surguja, Bilaspur, Chhindwara, Betul, Durg, Balaghat and Bastar. Among them, only Bilaspur, Durg and Balaghat could figure in the list of highly and moderately developed districts, but not because of mining but because of industrialization and agricultural development. Similarly, districts with high productivity of forests are still far behind. Thus, scarcity of resources cannot be the cause of backwardness.

Infact, those socio-economic conditions which favour 'internal colonialism', determine the super structure of development. Among these characteristics, consciousness of the people and their cultural configuration lay down the corner stone of the development. Because of this fact, in most of the tribal development blocks rays of development could not reach and most of them are still in the darkness of under-development. Same is true for other poverty-risen areas. Thus, there is urgent need to create inner urge of developing themselves among such persons.

THE DILEMMA OF RESOURCE DEVELOPMENT AND ENVIRONMENTAL CRISES

It is evident from the preceding analysis that exploitation of resources increased tremendously but they have not contributed towards the economic growth of areas of their occurrences. Since resources have to be developed to enhance the development, it is bound to affect the environment adversely. It is accentuated by the narrow and wrong perspectives, faulty process of the planning and management and lack of proper institutions. In other words, resource development and environmental degradation are two faces of the same coin and go side by side. Some of the adverse consequences of the excessive resource exploitation are pointed out below.

Land Resources

Agriculture is the major contributor to the net domestic product and principal means of livelihood of the people. More than 75.3% (18.8 million in 1991) of main workers are engaged in cultivation. This excessive dependency on agriculture led to the excessive exploitation of agricultural resources, particularly of land. There is keen competition for grabbing land among people, rich and poor alike and virtually all cultivable lands, fallow lands and village common lands have already been brought under plough. Further, large extent of forests have also been cleared for the purpose. Extensive forest blanks can be seen on map prepared from satellite imageries. Total cropped area increased from 15.3 million ha in 1950-51 to 25.2 million hectares in 1995-96. Out of this, 5.9 million hectares were added during this period. Expansion of cultivation on physically unsuitable hilly and dissected areas make them vulnerable to erosion and presents threat in the sustenance of already distressed animals by reducing the grazing lands. Most of the animals depend on natural grazing lands for their feeding which are shrinking very rapidly and causing further deterioration in their efficiency. This situation directly through the supply of draught power, milk and other animal products worsens the living conditions of rural people.

Forest Resource

Most serious damage is caused to forests; and area under them is shrinking rapidly; and the entire forest eco-system, incorporating multistoried vegetative cover, wild life and supporting a large section of the society, stands disrupted and degenerated. Forests have been attacked not only for agricultural purposes but also for extracting forest products, for maximization of revenue but at the cost of almost disappearance of real forests. Phenomenal increase in revenue from forests presents only the partial story. Illegal and ruthless exploitation is only recorded on the face of forests. Bare stony land is left behind. Removal of forest cover on large scale has accelerated the process of soil erosion and flood. As a result, fertile soil is being washed away and reservoirs constructed down; streams are facing serious threat of silting (Sharma, 1987, 242). Thus thoughtless and ruthless exploitation of one resource, i.e. forest has become the real cause of the genesis of multi-dimensional problems never thought of. This expresses the real meaning of the interdependent relationship among natural resources.

Water Resource

Water is another 'common resources' which is still subject to *ad hoc* decisions. Though the central government had frame (comprehensive law regarding the use of water resource, little attention could be paid till now. Example can be cited of river water. Rivers, originating in this state, are treated as 'life sustaining' in boardering states but are neglected within this state. Recently they are being used as sources of domestic and industrial water supply and as means of disposal of residuals and wastes of urban centres and industrial units. Water channels of considerable large dimensions, carrying polluted water, characterise all big cities, viz. Indore, Bhopal, Jabalpur, Ujjain, Raipur, Sagar of the state. Because of location of industries with large quantity of waste materials for disposal, water of the Son, Tapti, Chambal, Kshipra, Shankhini, Kharun, Hasdo and Mahanadi suffers from pollution to a great extent. Thus, industrial development, while increasing industrial output, is adversely affecting the rural life—their health and economy by poisoning water which they have to use. Such pollutions always accompany industrialization and industrial development, no doubt, has become a must for the economic upheaval of the country. Only way left is that all possible means of treatment of wastes must be employed before their disposal in rivers.

Irrigation is the pertinent need of water. Individual farmers go for wells and tube wells because of economic reasons and use pumping sets for lifting water from them as well as from other water bodies. They use these sources for the best of their knowledge to get maximum individual benefits. Environmental degradation by them are of miniature scale, though high density of tube wells and excessive drafting of water can lead to dire scarcity of drinking water as is the case in the western Malwa.

Potential of irrigation by governmental sources has reached to 30.84 lakh hectares in 1991-92 from only 4.64 lakh hectares in pre-plan period. Nearly two-thirds of the potential is created by the major and medium projects. Planning for utilization of wasting precious water resource is auspicious omen but emphasizing particularly on large projects without paying due consideration on environmental and physio-cultural characteristics of these projects would be disasterous. At the same time, most of these projects are incapable of yielding benefits stipulated in the plans due to physical limitation or have created problems not thought of previously, such as salinity, alkalinity and water-logging. The Tawa, Chambal, Barna and Harshi projects have posed severe problems of water logging in their command areas. It is estimated that more than one-third of irrigated area suffers from this problem in the Tawa command area. It could have been avoided by selecting suitable site of dam, considering the lithological characteristics.

As far as irrigation is concerned, minor and small projects prove more efficient along with much smaller losses. It is found that 88 and 61 per cent of potential created by medium and minor projects were utilized while proportion was only 58% for major projects in 1986-87 in the state. More than 9.3 lakh ha. of potentials of these projects remained unutilized. Even of the Tawa project more than 37% of the potential could not be used. Thus simply creation of potentials has no meaning unless it is utilized. Otherwise vast amount of invested capital is wasted. Not only in terms of useability but also in terms of area submerged, the water-grid system, consisting of small, minor and check dams, barrage and weirs, can be most useful in context of settled valleys as in this country. This approach would be more profitable on several counts. The cost of construction would be much lower with least environmental disruption. It can be created within short period. At the same time, loss of forested and cultivated area would be small, and instead of displacement from their centuries old environment, people of the valley area will get opportunity to improve their lots. Small dams can be inundated even in little rains. Under these circumstances large reservoirs will neither be required nor water will be wasted.

Reality is quite different. Probably, not in any case, alternative methods and approaches of use of water resources have been evaluated in this state. Most often, it is presumed that amount of benefits accrueing from projects is directly related with the size of the reservoirs; and therefore, there is craze to plan for high and high dams. It is always thought similar to the large scale industries. Consequently, such projects are accompanied by large scale destruction of physical and socio-economic environment. At the time of planning of such projects only tangible costs payable in form of such losses are hardly paid due attention. Because of such partial accounting, large projects seem to yield much higher benefits than the costs incurred. The same story is being repeated in the case of the Narmada Sagar dam being constructed on the river Narmada, just above the Nimar plain (Sharma, 1987, 245-249). If instead of construction of Indira Sagar and Sardar Sarovar, attention had been paid to the construction of minor and micro-irrigation works it would have been more beneficial to local people.

Mineral Resources

As discussed earlier, this state has rich and extensive deposits of mineral resources and their production increased multifolds. But what are the consequences of export-oriented exploitation of mineral resources of this state can be sensed from the example of the Singrauli coalfield.

Singrauli is one of twenty-one coalfields of this state and has more than half (9000 million tonnes) of the estimated reserves of Madhya Pradesh. It is located in the south-eastern corner of Sidhi district (M.P.) and partially in Mirzapur district of U.P. This coalfield was opened in sixties which multiplied the hopes of development of this district through industrialization. Production increased by 528 times, from only 14 thousand tonnes in 1966-67 to 7.39 million tonnes in 1985. Coal produced here are utilized in industries located out of this state. Thermal power stations are chief consumers, receiving 93% of total despatch. Among them, Obra, Shaktinagar, Renusagar and Anpara stations in U.P., only a few kilometres from M.P. border, Gandhinagar in Gujarat, Kota in Rajasthan and power stations at Bhatinda, Badarpur, Faridabad, Tugalkabad and Ukai are worth-mentioning. Only Vindhyachal super thermal power station is erected in M.P. Thus, not a single industry based on coal could be initiated in Singrauli area of this state; while industrial complex has developed in adjoining Uttar Pradesh. Mining is entirely open cast employing Heavy Earth Moving machines which did not encourage even ancillary industries. These machines require highly skilled manpower, and therefore, there are bleak chances of employment of most illiterate ruralites. Normally they work as casual daily workers.

On the other hand, these machines have deformed the environment of this area. They have brought devastation over good quality rice land and dense forested area. Over burden has been dumped as hillocks on level land. People living in plain area have been displaced atleast thrice. For the first time Rihand dam made them homeless; later, opening of collieries again snatched their lands and recently Super Thermal Plant and Special Area Development Authority have made them almost helpless. Now, they have become victims of constant grabbing of land. They are desperate refugees on their own lands; and have lost their shelter, livelihood and social security and are exposed to very fastly moving alien economy. All social corruptions have reached there. Whatever land is available for farming it is subject to all disadvantages of pollution generated from coal mining and power houses. Devastating effects of mining on forests is not less deplorable. Not only forests are cleared ruthlessly, but tribal people living there and making livelihood from forests are displaced. They have not the ownership of land, and hence they are not entitled for compensation. At the cost of such environmental, economic, social and psychological losses due to the development of coal mining, this state gets royalty. In 1985-86, revenue realized from coal was Rs. 89 million, while value of coal produced in this area was Rs. 1414 million. How the economics of cost-benefit analysis fits here is hard to understand. In fact, as mentioned earlier, all intangible costs being paid in form of natural, economic, social and psychological environmental disruptions have not been included in the total costs of project development which results in higher benefits on lower costs for the region.

POSSIBLE REMEDY: RESOURCE TRANSFORMATION FOR DEVELOPMENT

The crux of the Problem lies on the policies of development. Planning for social well-being should incorporate both local needs and resources as well as national interests at a time. To meet such objectives, resources are to be managed rather than developed. It means their development is planned in such a manner that their sustained supply can be maintained, for longer time to larger section of the society with least deterioration in ecosystem. For this purpose, two general approaches to the implementation of development strategies have emerged in recent years: transferential and transformational. The former is based on the assumption that technologies and institutions already proven successful in industrialized countries could be transferred to the poorest developing country. But this approach has been failure. Transformational patterns of man-resource-environment exist because they have evolved over time as successful adaptive mechanism within given social, cultural and bio-physical conditions; and therefore must be used as the base for future development (Ruddle and Rondinelli, 1983, 25-26). It requires multi-level planning for implementing equitable growth policies. It accommodates local people, resources and institutions, adopts modern technologies to local conditions, resources and capacities without much deterioration in the environment. Thus, it is capable of synchronising both resource management and environmental protection. Transformational development seeks to increase incrementally the productivity of indigenous institution and practices and reinforcing and building on those appropriate to local conditions and needs and adaptive to changing circumstances and gradually displacing those that are not. Ruddle and Rondinelli have elaborated eight principles of transformational development and conclude that the success of the transformational approach depends on the organisation of technologies and institutions that are appropriate to the socio-cultural, economic, biological and physical environment of the particular areas to be developed (1983, 26). The eight principles are:

1. Building on existing culturally embedded resources, institutions and practices;
2. Involving local people who will be affected by the development planning and implementation;
3. Adapting modern technologies, services and facilities to local conditions, resources and capabilities;
4. Promoting specialization in production based on existing resource, human and spatial comparative advantages;
5. Using appropriate low-cost, culturally acceptable methods;
6. Planning for displacement of unproductive and unadaptable traditional methods, institutions and practices;
7. Establishing preconditions for change and transformation in social, technical, political and administrative structures and processes; and
8. Creating a planning process that is flexible, incremental and adaptive.

It is almost universally accepted that the development planning should be on the territorial basis (Friedman and Weaver 1979). Particularly in parts of marked diversity there is partinent need for territorial closure, atleast partially, to comprehend and alleviate poverty, to fulfil minimum needs, to check the drain of resources and even to plan counter measures to non-spatial causes of inequality. To make planning unit viable they should be based on local resource endowments as well as on functional complementarity. The approaches ranging from growth pole to agropolitan development do not incorporate both of these aspects simultaneously. While, the Russian approach of the economic regionalization while hinges upon the present position if resource development ignores inter-regional and intra-regional linkages. Appropriate territorial units can be identified incorporating both of these aspects. This can be carried out at two stages. First of all resource regions can be carved out based on the concept of least dissimilarity. At the second stage, functional regions can be demarcated on functional centrality principles. Demarcation of such resource-based development planning units has been illustrated else-where (Sharma, 1984, 1-7).

CONCLUSION

To sum-up, it may be accepted that there is marked regional inequality in distribution of resources in this state. Exploitation of resources increased tremendously. But they contributed least towards the economic growth of areas of their occurrence. Rather they have created several environmental crises and threat to sustained supply of natural resources. Still poverty coexists with resource exploitation on gigantic scale. Thus there is urgency of protecting local interests in perspective of national development as well as of protecting environmental equilibrium.

To accommodate different interests on varied spatial scale is really a tricklish problem. The proceeding discussion of resources intend to present the varied nature of problems. The poorest groups have had little or no alternatives but to continue exploiting fragile or marginal lands more intensively, which severely degraded the biological and physical environment. Unless a comprehensive plan incorporating local problems of population, unemployment and resource management, is seriously formulated and local people are involved in its implementation, it is hard to snatch even the degrading resource base from poor peasants. They can hardly cooperate in environmental management until they are sure of their livelihood and welfare. The root of the problem lies in viewing people separated from their resource endowments. Resources which could be utilized for their upheaval, have outward tendency and are exported.

In these perspectives, the need for regional analyses and planning is becoming more widely recognized not only because regional resource systems differ from each other but also because elements of resource system are intricately linked. New perspectives of the role of natural resources in meeting basic needs and increasing the productivity and income of poor emerged with new perceptions of socio-economic development. It became more apparent that closer attention must be paid to preserving and renewing biophysical systems and to transforming resources for human development,

REFERENCES

Chattopadhyay, S. and R.A. Carpenter (1991), Sustainable Development: Scientific Jargon or A Practical Management Alternative? *Annals, NAGI*, Vol. XI, No. 2, pp. 1-12.

Drewnowski, J. (1974), *On Measuring and Planning the Quality of Life*, Mouton: The Hague.

Friedmann, J. and J.C. Weaver (1979), *Territory and Function*, London: Edward Arnold.

IUCN (1980), *World Conservation Strategy: Living Resources Conservation for Sustainable Development*. IUCN-UNEPWWF in collaboration with FAO and UNESCO, Switzerland.

IUCN (1987), *Population and Sustainable Development*. Report of the IUCN Task Force on Population and Conservation for Sustainable Development. Gland, Switzerland. The World Conservation Centre.

Kayastha, S.L. (1993), Environment, Development and Quality of Life, *Annals, NAGI*, Vol. XIII, No. 2, pp. 54-75.

Kuhnen, F. (1992), Sustainability, Regional Development and Marginal Location, *Applied Geography and Development*, Vol. 39, 101-05, Tubingen.

Misra, V.C. and S.K. Sharma (1982), Social Dynamics of Resource Development, *Hill Geographer*, Vol. 1, No. 1, 1-7.

Naik, M.K. (1993), Sustainability and the Environment with Special reference to Food Production in the Semi-Arid Tropics, *Every Man's Science*, Feb.-March, pp. 11-13.

Pearce, David (1989), An Economic Perspective on Sustainable Development, in Development, Vol. 2/3, Special issue on New Perspectives on Development.

Pezzey, J. (1989), *Economic Analysis of Sustainable Growth and Sustainable Development*. S.P. No. 15, Environment Department, World Bank, Washington, D.C.

Ruddle, Kenneth and D.A. Rondinelli (1983), *Transforming Natural Resources for Human Development: A Resource Systems Framework for Development Policy*, Tokyo: The United Nations University.

Sharma, S.K. (1984), Resource-based Development Planning of Sagar Division, M.P., *Geog. Rev. Ind.*, Vol. 46, No. 4, pp. 1-7.

Sharma, S.K. (1987), Dilemma of Resource Development and Environmental Crises in M.P., pp. 236-54 in H.S. Sharma and M.L. Sharma, eds. *Environmental Design and Development*, Jodhpur: Scientific Publishers.

Sharma, S.K. (1988), Regional Resource-base and Pattern of Economic Development in M.P., pp. 123-44, in V. Vidyanath and Mohan Rao, eds. *Development of India's Resource-base*, New Delhi: Gyan Pub. Co.

Human Development in India: An Inter-State Comparison

Naseem A. Zaidi and Md. Abdus Salam

The experience of the fast developing East Asian countries has shown that it is human resources of a nation, not its capital and material resources, that ultimately determine the character and pace of its economic and social development. A World Bank study of 192 countries concluded that "only 16 per cent of the growth is explained by physical capital (machinery, building and physical infrastructure), while 20 per cent comes from natural capital. But no less than 64 per cent can be attributed to human and social capital."[1] A determined effort to expand human capabilities through improved education health and nutrition may help in accelerating the pace of economic growth even in low income and low human development regions. The central issue of quality of growth is whether it is genuinely serving human development in a country as a whole or in its political boundaries.

During 1960s and 1970s India remained in the group of 'weak link' countries characterised by slow progress of human development constrained by low level of economic growth. Without economic growth, resources to invest in human development are limited—and with poor standard of health, education and nutrition rapid economic growth becomes a distant dream. Since the decade of 1980s India has been suffering from the problem of lopsided development with rapid economic growth and slow human development. The problem of human development in India has been pointed out as follows:

> "Although there has been a significant improvement in social indicators, India still lags behind most Asian countries in these aspects. Poverty remains a serious problem; a large fraction of population has limited or no formal education and there are substantial disparities in social indicators across the states."[2]

THE HUMAN DEVELOPMENT INDEX

The HDI prepared by UNDP since 1990 has passed through a process of continuous modification. It is a composite index of achievements in basic human capabilities in three areas—a long and healthy life, knowledge and a decent standard of living. Life expectancy, educational attainment and income are the three variables which have been chosen to represent these three dimensions. The HDI value for each country indicates how far it has to go to attain certain defined long-term goals such as an average life span of 85 years, access to education to all and reasonably high per capita income for enjoying a decent standard of living. The index is used for inter-country comparison of human development and has been proved useful in boosting up the efforts of the governments of the countries deficient in human development.

A study on similar lines is necessary to examine interstate differences, as in a federal set-up like in India education and health services primarily come under the purview of the state governments. Some efforts have been made earlier in the direction but the studies are not comprehensive as these do not correlate the indices with the other parameters of the economies. A.K. Shiva Kumar[3] constructed HDI for 17 Indian states and ranked the states along with the countries for which the HDI for 1987 was computed by UNDP in Human Development Report, 1990. Recently Shiva Kumar[4] computed gender-related development index (GDI) on the lines proposed in UNDP's Human Development Report, 1995 for 16 Indian states for which data were available and ranked them along with 130 countries of the world. Kumar found that there were only 13 countries in the world that had low GDI value than Uttar Pradesh and Bihar. Twice as many people live in Uttar Pradesh and Bihar in such abysmal conditions of human deprivation than in the remaining 13 countries that had lower GDI values. He concluded, "such low levels of human development and gender inequalities for such a large Indian populations are indeed a sad reflection of the poor state of social progress in the country."[5] Kumar's findings may provide interesting academic readings but fail to provide policy guidelines as no effort has been made to correlate various indices with the other parameters of the state economies.

The objective of the present study is to enumerate and correlate various indices denoting to life expectancy, educational attainment and real GDP per capita to other parameters of the economies of 15 states for finding out the causes of varying values of these indicators in different states.

METHODOLOGY

UNDP adopts a method[6] for calculation of HDI which is based on three indicators: longevity, as measured by life expectancy at birth; educational attainment, as measured by a combination of adult literacy (two-third weight) and combined primary, secondary and tertiary enrolment ratios (one-third weight); and standard of living, as measured by real GDP per capita (PPP$).

For the construction of index, fixed minimum and maximum values have been established for each of these indicators.

(a) Life expectancy at birth: 25 years and 85 years.
(b) Adult literacy and combined enrolment ratios: 0% and 100% in both the cases.
(c) Real GDP per capita (PPP$): PPP$ 100 and PPP$ 40,000.

For any component of HDI individual index can be computed according to a general formula:

$$\text{Index} = \frac{\text{Actual } x_i \text{ value} - \text{minimum } x_1 \text{ value}}{\text{Maximum } x_i \text{ value} - \text{minimum } x_1 \text{ value}}$$

where x_i value is the value of any indicator.

HDI is a simple average of the life expectancy index, educational attainment index and the adjusted real GDP per capita (PPP$) index.

UNDP uses the formula for calculation of HDI with the objective of international comparison. For inter-state comparison, such as in the present study, while calculating life expectancy and educational attainment indices the same method with slight modification may be followed but for calculation of per capita income index the methodology is to be modified due to the following reasons:

(a) For international comparison, per capita real income expressed in home currency is converted in PPP$ as purchasing power of different currencies is different. For inter-state comparison within the country this exercise seems to be futile as majority of the consumption goods in different states are available at national prices. Some locally produced goods may be available at lower prices but this difference may be neutralised by higher prices in case of some other goods. Shiva Kumar[7] (1996) converted per capita SDP for 16 states in India into real GDP per capita in PPP$ by multiplying the ratio of state SDP per capita at constant prices for a particular states and national SDP per capita, with national per capita income expressed in PPP$. For international comparison such as in Kumar's study the method may be workable but for inter-state comparisons the state's real per capita SDP may be a sufficient indicator to reflect the level of living in the state.

(b) UNDP adopts minimum and maximum value of per capita income which are the most extreme values

> observed or expected over a long period say 60 years. The minimum are those observed historically going back about 30 years, and the maximum are the limits of what can be envisioned in the next 30 years. Recent economic growth rates indicate that the maximum income that the richest countries are likely to achieve by 2020 is $40,000 in 1990 PPP$. Such a high level of income is unrealistic under Indian conditions, therefore, a minimum of Rs. 100 and maximum of Rs. 10,000 at 1980-81 prices have been taken into account in the present study.

The HDI reduces all three basic indicators to a common measuring rod by measuring achievement in each indicator as the relative distance from the desirable goal. The maximum and minimum values for each variable, which are fixed, are reduced to a scale between 0 and 1 with each country (or state) at some point on the scale. In the present study due to non-availability of complete data for all the Indian states only 15 Indian states have been selected for constructing HDI and for inter-state comparison.

(A) Longevity

Table 1 shows life expectancy indices for 15 states on the basis of formula adopted by UNDP. Data of life expectancy relate to average over 1988-92 as estimated by Sample Registration System and Centered at 1990.

(B) Educational Attainment

Empirical studies suggest positive effects of schooling on GDP growth. It has been found that increasing the labour force's average education by one year raises GDP by 9%, but this holds only for the first three years of extra education. After that, the returns to each additional year diminish to around 4% of GDP.[9] The returns appear to be highest for basic schooling (primary, and later secondary), for which further expansion will mainly involve enrolling more children from poor families.[10] Considering the significance of education most of the developing countries have committed themselves to the goal of universal education in the shortest possible time.

Educational attainment was originally measured only

through the adult literacy defined as "the percentage of persons aged 15 and over who can, with understanding, both read and write a short simple statement on everyday life."[11] HDR-1991 broadened this measure to incorporate mean years of schooling. As reliable data on mean years of schooling were not available the variables for educational attainment now included adult literacy, with a two-third weight, and gross combined primary, secondary and tertiary enrolment with a one-third weight. In India upto now, the literacy rate data are available for population aged 7 years and above, therefore, the UNDP methodology has been slightly modified to include literacy rate in place of adult literacy.[12]

TABLE 1

Life Expectancy Indices for 15 States

States	*Life Expectancy at birth (years) 1988-92*	*Life Expectancy Index*	*Rank*
1. Andhra Pradesh	60.2	.586	08
2. Assam	54.1	.485	14
3. Bihar	57.5	.542	10
4. Gujarat	59.5	.575	09
5. Haryana	62.5	.625	04
6. Karnataka	62.2	.620	05
7. Kerala	71.3	.772	01
8. Madhya Pradesh	53.4	.473	15
9. Maharashtra	63.4	.640	03
10. Orissa	55.4	.507	12.5
11. Punjab	66.6	.693	02
12. Rajasthan	56.3	.522	11
13. Tamil Nadu	61.5	.608	06
14. Uttar Pradesh	55.4	.507	12.5
15. West Benoal	61.4	.607	07

Source: Economic Survey, 1995-96, p. 171.

COMBINED ENROLMENT RATIOS

UNDP in its Human Development Reports gives one-third weightage to combined primary, secondary and tertiary enrolment ratios for computation of educational attainment indices. The gross enrolment ratio has been defined as "the number of students enrolled in a level of education, whether or not they belong in the relevant age group for that level, as the percentage of the population in the relevant age group for that level". The relevant age group in different levels of education has not been specified in the Reports. Age-specific literacy rates data in India as per the 1991 census are not yet available. Whatever data are available[13] from the Ministry of Human Resource Development do not seem to be reliable particularly at primary level of education as enrolment ratio for Tamil Nadu at this level is shown as 148.4 per cent and in case of 6 out of 15 states gross enrolment ratio exceeds 100 per cent which is possible but does not seem to be realistic. For solving the problem of deficiency of desired data the following methodology has been adopted in the present study:

(a) State-wise data of population in various age groups are available upto 1981. Population data of different states in the desired age groups have been inflated considering the population growth in the decade 1981-91 in corresponding state with the assumption that growth of population was evenly distributed in the various age groups. The break up of age groups is as follows: primary level 5-9 years, middle and higher secondary level 10-19 years, higher education 20-29 years. Projected population data in different age groups in different states are given in Table 2.

UNDP considers combined first, second and third level gross enrolment ratio. In India state-wise break-up of enrolment data is available for primary, middle, higher secondary and higher education levels.[14] As data about combined population in the age group 5-29 years have been projected for 1991, enrolment data for 1991-92 may give more realistic results. Combined enrolment ratio may be calculated as percentage of enrolment with combined population in the relevant age group. Educational attainment indices may be calculated by assigning two-third weightage to literacy percentages in the various states and one-third to combined enrolment ratio. The results have been shown in Table 2.

TABLE 2

Educational Attainment Indices for 15 States

Sl. No.	States	Combined Population in the age group 5-29 years 1991 (lakhs)	Combined Enrolment primary to higher education 1991-92 (lakhs)	Combined Enrolment ratios (2) as % of (1)	Literacy Rate 1991 %	Educational attainment indices	Rank
1	2	3	4	5	6	7	8
1.	Andhra Pradesh	342.6	117.6	34.3	44.1	.408	11
2.	Assam	119.9	55.2	46.0	52.9	.506	06
3.	Bihar	447.6	125.2	27.9	38.5	.350	15
4.	Gujarat	224.9	92.7	41.2	61.3	.546	04
5.	Haryana	91.9	31.3	34.0	55.8	.485	8.5
6.	Karnataka	268.2	90.1	33.6	56.0	.485	8.5
7.	Kerala	158.8	61.6	38.8	89.8	.728	01
8.	Madhya Pradesh	346.9	117.7	33.9	44.2	.407	12
9.	Maharashtra	413.8	175.0	42.3	64.8	.573	03
10.	Orissa	168.1	57.6	34.2	49.1	.441	10
11.	Punjab	108.8	37.7	34.6	58.5	.505	07
12.	Rajasthan	169.6	71.3	42.0	38.5	.396	13
13.	Tamil Nadu	274.7	131.0	47.6	62.7	.576	02
14.	Uttar Pradesh	722.5	188.7	26.1	41.6	.364	14
15.	West Bengal	376.8	139.4	37.0	57.7	.508	05

Sources: 1. CMIE, India's Social Sector, Feb. 1996.
2. Govt. of India, *Economic Survey*, 1995-96, p. 171.

Looking into the break up of combined enrolment ratio and literacy percentage in different states some interesting conclusions are drawn:

1. Kerala has the highest educational attainment index but this does not reveal the whole of the story. Though literacy percentage was the highest in Kerala, the combined enrolment ratio in Kerala ranks 6th out of 15 states. This is due to poor enrolment percentage in higher education in which Kerala's rank is 11th out of 15 states. Due to two-third weightage given to

literacy percentage Kerala's already high literacy percentage pushes up the educational attainment index. While Kerala has the highest literacy percentage (89.8 per cent) far ahead of the next highest, i.e. Maharashtra (64.8 per cent), the enrolment ratio in Kerala at primary level stood at sixth place out of 15 states indicating the role of private missionaries in expanding non-formal education. Literacy is necessary but not sufficient condition for economic development of a region/state. Higher per capita income is a direct outcome of more weightage given to higher education in a state. The coefficient of rank correlation between per capita income and literacy percentage comes to 0.7322 while the same between per capita income and enrolment in higher education is 0.9238 indicating a high degree of association between income and education at higher level. In spite of the fact the state governments, motivated by political factors, spends more money for universalisation of education rather than allocating larger chunk of budgetary resources for higher education. The enrolment ratio in higher education (total enrolment in higher education as percentage of total population in the age group 20-29 years) for Maharashtra was the highest (5.94) followed by Gujarat (4.55)—the two states having high per capita income rank. From the above analysis the conclusion may be drawn that emphasis on higher education rather than universalisation of education is more conducive for human development in a state.

(C) Per Capita Real Income

Per capita income of different states for the year 1991-92 at 1980-81 prices is given in Table 3. Per capita income indices have been calculated by assuming a minimum value of Rs. 100 and of Rs. 10,000 which may be maximum expected per capita income during the next 25-30 years.

HUMAN DEVELOPMENT INDEX

HDI may be calculated by taking simple average of life expectancy, educational attainment and real per capita SDP indices of 15 states. The difference between real SDP per capita rank and HDI rank indicates that Kerala and Orissa are the two states in the country where HDI rank is higher as compared to SDP rank.

Bihar is on the bottom in both HDI and SDP per capita index. No state of the country comes near the level of high human development (HDI 0.8 or more), only Kerala, Punjab and Maharashtra come in the category of medium human development (HDI between 0.5 and less than 0.8) and all the other states have low level of human development. Even Kerala has lower level of HDI (0.558) as compared to HDI average of all the developing countries of the world (0.563).

TABLE 3

Per Capita Income Indices for 15 States

States		*Per capita SDP at 1980-81 Prices Rs. (1991-92)*	*Per capita Income Index*	*Rank*
1	*2*	*3*	*4*	*5*
1.	Andhra Pradesh	1788	0.171	10
2.	Assam	1887	0.181	08
3.	Bihar	1122	0.103	15
4.	Gujarat	2321	0.224	04
5.	Haryana	3455	0.339	02
6.	Karnataka	2255	0.218	06
7.	Kerala	1826	0.174	09
8.	Madhya Pradesh	1621	0.154	12
9.	Maharashtra	3381	0.331	03
10.	Orissa	1530	0.144	14
11.	Punjab	3869	0.381	01
12.	Rajasthan	1773	0.169	11
13.	Tamil Nadu	2309	0.223	05
14.	Uttar Pradesh	1589	0.150	13
15.	West Bengal	2015	0.193	07

Source: Government of India, Ministry of Finance, *Indian Public Finance Statistics*, 1995, p. 82.

HDI AND SOCIAL EXPENDITURE RATIOS

In India expenditure on health and education is much lower as compared to other developing countries. "The Republic of Korea invests $160 per person a year in health and education, Malaysia $150, India, by contrast, investing only $14, Pakistan $10

TABLE 4

Human Development Index of 15 States

Sl. No.	*States*	*Life Expectancy Index*	*Educational attainment Index*	*SDP Per capita Index*	*HDI*	*Rank in HDI*	*Rank in SDP*	*HDI & SDP Rank difference*
1	*2*	*3*	*4*	*5*	*6*	*7*	*8*	*9*
1.	Andhra Pradesh	0.586	0.408	0.171	0.388	10	10	0
2.	Assam	0.485	0.506	0.181	0.391	09	08	-1
3.	Bihar	0.542	0.350	0.103	0.332	15	15	0
4.	Gujarat	0.575	0.546	0.224	0.448	06	04	-2
5.	Haryana	0.625	0.485	0.339	0.483	04	02	-2
6.	Karnataka	0.620	0.485	0.218	0.441	07	06	-1
7.	Kerala	0.772	0.728	0.174	0.558	01	09	+8
8.	Madhya Pradesh	0.473	0.407	0.154	0.345	13	12	-1
9.	Maharashtra	0.640	0.573	0.331	0.515	03	03	0
10.	Orissa	0.507	0.441	0.144	0.364	1 1	11	+3
11.	Punjab	0.693	0.505	0.381	0.526	02	01.	-1
12.	Rajasthan	0.522	0.396	0.169	0.363	12	11	-1
13.	Tamil Nadu	0.608	0.576	0.223	0.469	05	05	0
14.	Uttar Pradesh	0.507	0.364	0.150	0.340	14	13	-1
15.	West Bengal	0.607	0.508	0.193	0.436	08	07	-1

Source: Tables 1, 2 and 3.

and Bangladesh $5." Broadly speaking the governments spend more funds on human development according to availability of resources, but apart from this factor much depends upon the priorities set by the governments. This aspect may be studied in terms of public expenditure, social allocation and social priority ratios as done by UNDP in Human Development Report, 1991. Public expenditure ratio is the percentage of national income that goes into public expenditure. In developing countries 20-30 per cent of GDP goes for public expenditure. In the present study these ratios are satisfactory as these ranged from 17.5 per cent in Maharashtra during 1993-94 to 30.5 per cent in Rajasthan. What is more important is Social allocation ratio which is the percentage of public expenditure earmarked for social sectors such as education, health and social security, water supply and sanitation. These items are considered to be positively correlated with progress in human development. The international norm for this ratio was taken as 20 per cent for 61 countries for which data were available.[16] But these norms are determined on the basis of expenditure on these items by central government, while in case of India the larger chunk of expenditure is incurred by the state governments. UNDP in its HDR-1991 defined social priority ratio as the percentage of social expenditure devoted to basic social services such as basic education, basic health care and nutrition, etc. In India the ratio cannot be calculated as state-wise break up of data about these items of expenditure is not available.

It was revealed in the present study that public expenditure has closer association with educational attainment than it has with the life expectancy as the latter is influenced by multiplicity of factors like heredity, racial climatic and environmental factors apart from public expenditure on health, nutrition and sanitation, etc. The coefficient of rank correlation between per capita expenditure on education (Table 5) and educational attainment (Table 2) came to 0.833 while for per capita expenditure on health (Table 5) and life expectancy (Table 1), the same was 0.611.

TABLE 5

Per Capita Expenditure on Education and Health in 15 States (1991-92)

States		*Per Capita Expenditure (Rs.)*		*Rank in*		*Expenditure as %age of SDP at current prices*	
		Education	*Health*	*Col. 1*	*Col. 2*	*Education*	*Health*
1	*2*	*3*	*4*	*5*	*6*	*7*	*8*
1.	Andhra Pradesh	174	52	12	12	3.09	1.01
2.	Assam	252	70	06	04	5.40	1.49
3.	Bihar	150	49	14	13.5	5.14	1.67
4.	Gujarat	261	69	05	5.5	4.30	1.14
5.	Haryana	229	63	07	08	2.50	0.71
6.	Karnataka	195	61	9.5	09	3.60	1.13
7.	Kerala	293	80	02	02	5.65	1.53

(Contd.)

1	2	3	4	5	6	7	8
8.	Madhya Pradesh	157	48	13	15	3.55	1.07
9.	Maharashtra	267	69	03	5.5	3.26	0.84
10.	Orissa	175	54	11	11	4.42	1.37
11.	Punjab	295	97	01	01	2.95	1.57
12.	Rajasthan	203	68	08	07	4.45	1.49
13.	Tamil Nadu	262	79	04	03	4.42	1.33
14.	Uttar Pradesh	148	49	15	13.5	3.67	1.22
15.	West Bengal	195	60	9.5	10	3.68	1.14

Source: 1. CMIE, *Public Finance*, June 1996, pp. 205-06.

TABLE 6

Per capita Expenditure and Revenue Structures of High and Low Human Development States during 1991-92

(in Rs.)

Sl No.	*States*	*HDI Rank*	*Expenditure*			*Revenue*		
			All Social Services	*Education*	*Health*	*Total Receipts**	*Tax Rev.*	*Tax Income ratio (%)*
1	2	3	4	5	6	7	8	9
A.	**High Human Development States**							
1.	Kerala	1	491	293	80	1360	773	14.9
2.	Punjab	2	528	295	97	2409	904	9.0
3.	Maharashtra	3	485	267	69	1652	909	11.1
4.	Haryana	4	462.5	229	63	1675	927	10.4
B.	**Low Human Development States**							
1.	Rajasthan	12	414	203	68	1378	556	12.3
2.	M.P.	13	337	157	48	975	515	11.5
3.	U.P.	14	263	148	49	1035	448	11.2
4.	Bihar	15	267	150	49	783	374	12.1

*Includes revenue, capital receipts and grant from the Centre.

Sources: 1. CMIE, *Public Finance*, June 1996.
2. CMIE, *India's Social Sector*, Feb. 1996.
3. Govt. of India, *Economic Survey*, 1995-96, pp. 5-11.

Expenditure structure, to a great extent, depends upon revenue structure of a state. The low human development states of the country are caught in a vicious circle of low revenue base and low expenditure on education and health. The vicious circle is discernible from the pattern of expenditure and revenue of high and low human development states given in Table 6. Apart from revenue constraint much depends upon priorities assigned to social sector. In Kerala, in spite of low per capita total revenue and tax revenue receipts per capita expenditure on social services including education and health is quite high and this results in first rank in HDI for Kerala but Haryana, in spite of high per capita total and tax revenue gets fourth place due to low weightage assigned to social sector including expenditure on education and health.

CONCLUSION

A higher per capita tax, non-tax revenue, a larger expenditure on social sector, specially on education and health and an efficient utilisation of funds so allocated are necessary to achieve higher standard of human development. Economic growth requires effective policy management if it is to enrich human development.

A high literacy percentage is necessary but not sufficient condition for economic growth. Though literacy percentage was the highest in Kerala in 1991, it stood 6th out of 15 states in combined enrolment ratio. This was due to poor percentage in higher education in which Kerala ranked 11 out of 15 states. The coefficient of rank correlation between per capita income and literacy percentage came to 0.7322 while the same between per capita income and enrolment in higher education was 0.9238 indicating a high degree of association between income and higher education. In spite of the significant role of higher education in economic growth, state governments, motivated by political reasons, spend more on universalisation of education.

NOTES AND REFERENCES

1. UNDP (1996), *Human Development Report*, 1996, Oxford University Press, New York, p. 7.
2. Asian Development Bank (1996), *Asian Development Outlook 1996 and 1997*, Oxford University Press, New York, p. 128.
3. Kumar Shiva, A.K. (1991), UNDP's Human Development Index—A Computation for Indian States, *Economic and Political Weekly*, Mumbai, October 21, 1991, pp. 2343-45.

4. Kumar Shiva, A.K. (1996), UNDP's Gender-Related Development Index—A Computation for Indian States, *Economic and Political Weekly*, Mumbai, April 6, 1996, pp. 887-95.
5. *Ibid.*, p. 893.
6. UNDP: *Human Development Report*, 1996, *op. cit.*, p. 106.
7. *Op. cit.*, Table 4 Column 14 and 15.
8. UNDF, *Human Development Report*, 1994, *op. cit.*, p. 92.
9. *Human Development Report*, 1996, *op. cit.*, p. 76.
10. *Ibid.*, p. 76.
11. *HDR*, 1990, pp. 182-83.
12. *HDR*, 1994, p. 219.
13. Government of India, *Economic Survey*, 1995-96, p. 173.
14. CMIE (1996), *India's Social Sector*, Economic Intelligence Service, Mumbai, pp. 182-87.
15. *HDR*, 1996, *op. cit.*, p. 8.
16. *Ibid.*, p. 71.

Fallacies and Constraints of Balanced Regional Development in India

M.L. Patel

THE CONCEPTUAL ISSUE

Different disciplines explain the concept of development in different terminologies. George Dalton holds—what economist, call development, political scientist call modernization[1] (economic) development, sociologist call its role differentiation[2] and anthropologist call it culture change.[3] Development of mental scale is the complete awareness of phenomenon pertaining to the advantages to self, others or the human kind at the global level. In contrast to the stagnation as a phenomenon is indicative of a situation which is fully devoid of change, therefore, it closes the scope for further widening of mental horizon in relation to a given phenomenon. Thus, rethinking analysis, of the obtaining and developing situation and exposure to alliwed activities of other's command are the process through which development or change can be realized as mental make-up and preparedness leading to acquiring of desired changes and transfers in physical activities.

Thus, awareness is a starting point, which is instrumental to onward transmission of self-inculcated or acquired knowledge from the others. Rejection of further designed change is stagnation which may even be proved more conducive to retardation and wholesale closure of the scope for any positive change.

Abrupt interruption may even devastate the total thinking process, which is a pre-condition for developing any awareness, which in turn is a pre-condition for any development or positive change. Thus, what Gunnar Myridal held in his theme of spread effect[4] is an implication of development for positive change, while the retardation is latent in the process of 'Back wash effect' in his own words. The whole action and reaction of a positive and negative changes in due course of time will lead a person, society or nation to achieve a targeted rate of growth. This will perhaps help in resurgence of the country in various fields viz. economic, scientific, cultural and even on super-natural programme to realize world human rights via global faternity and "Vasundhra Kutumbam". These all would ultimately lead to fallacies borne and perpetuated in Globalization process of acquiring World's total wealth via possessing world powers. Development, however is not confined to faithful imitation of the developed alone as held by J.K. Galbraith and propagated by him in his work.[5] His concept *prima facie* no doubt, be easy to understand that development is the faithful limitation of the developed in a market economy model. However, imitation is not all that matters, because it only manifests communication of awareness of development in a particular context of socio-economic sector and unfolds the process of adoption of new technology and strategy to achieve the fixed target. Awareness, thus is a pre-acceptance stage in adoption of the new idea and the technology, which may be self-inculcated, imitated or borrowed from others, without awareness of desirable change towards benefits no growth for development can be envisaged.[6] However, a recent rejoinder to this norm is on the sustainability.[7] In the overall sense of the word, Target groups benefit is no more a supreme objective in new world order because the development has to be adjudged from the point of view of environment and ecological balances and in fitness with their natural order and system both, whatever may be scientific achievement of chemical weapon or other nuclear advancement and space research. Ultimately, all these achievements have to be tested and found sustainable to the entire world order governed by the environmental balance to save the universe.[8]

DEVELOPMENT STRATEGY

Development of Human resources is different from the development of backward areas or for that matter, optimal utilization and exploitation of resources potentials obtaining in backward areas.

The basic difference in approach of development of human factor is that supply of the skill development, education, care of health through safe water, and balanced diet availability, etc. is sponsored by the community efforts or for that matter by joint efforts, but their demands are controlled by the individual beneficiaries, who first develop adequate degree of awareness of development of human capital, which can in future be more productive and conducive to yield more socio-economic gains to the individual, family, society and the nation all at various level at one or the different times. Thus, development of human resources is highly intricate and a phenomenon, which requires not only incentive, as a propelling factor, but also some times— the economic austerity and administrative manipulation to make the supply side of the development components, largely depending upon the political will and capacity to make their supply prompt by way of development of necessary infrastructure for durable and wider use and benefit of the community as a whole, which inhabits the society of a nation.

If the target society or ethnic group for such human resource development is full of traditional embargos, stigmas and taboos, social infrastructures developed at any large scale efforts remain under utilized and prove largely wasteful as larger society is experiencing about the Tribal Sub-Plan expenditures exclusive for ethnic groups, which are 461 in number in 1991 and make a total tribal population of over 6.77 crores at All India level. Since tribal population is generally concentrated in given patch of areas their development has been based on the area development as well as on community development programmes in addition to family-based programmes. Tribal Sub Plan Areas have been identified all over the country since 5th Five Year Plan. People's participation in terms of capital investment in this sector is negligible for want of adequate income and savings. Therefore, the Government policy to provide capital subsidy has been adopted. Measurement of cost and benefit of Tribal development is futile, because everything is being done on public cost of Central and State Government Funds in varying proportion. At the national level, therefore, when the cost and benefit returns are to be derived towards evaluation of such Tribal development projects, it hardly measures to the targeted outputs, which perhaps could be of more advantage at the National level, if their utilization otherwise could be made in wider interest of Indian society possessing higher level of technology and effective demand for such infrastructure and support services.

DEVELOPMENT OF BACKWARD REGION

It needs to be clearly defined on conceptual level first, as to what is Backward region? It is commonly believed that the areas, which are inhabited by backward people, are obviously backward regions. This contention however, does not suit to these, who held that human factor alone is not all that should be a deciding factor to distinguish a backward area from that of an advanced area.

In Indian context, the experience reveals that backward regions have large unexploited resource potentials as natural resources and offer big scope to industrial developments and mining works. For want of local initiative and awareness perhaps, the area could remain isolated and inaccessible for which, the attributing factors were absence of transport and communication, and lack of knowledge about the hidden reserve of the wealth of nation. Thus unsurveyed mineral potentials, or even forests resources together and separately remain out of the purview of the relevant agencies, which possess expertise to exploit them with effectants technical know-how and equipments. Thus, there is always a paradex obtaining in existing backward regions with high resource potentials.

In situations, when free market forces within the economic region do play important role in canceling out the uneconomic productive units and firms on grant of incurring higher marginal costs and the additive transport cost, etc. of a product to be transferred from one point to another within the economic region or even between the two or more economic regions, the marginal production unit fails to survive and stand against the market competition. Thus to ensure in Intra region or International balance a hevy economic burden of trade with duty free import - substitute will be unavoidable. Thus public income gets unnecessary reduced overtime. It is therefore on all such counts of economic gains latent in the rationale of Balanced sectoral development, the balanced regional development gets lost in political subjugation of backward regions. Intra and Inter-regional liquidity of resources input and output are therefore quite imperative.

FREE PLAY OF MARKET FORCES LEAD TO REGIONAL INEQUALITIES

The theory of Balanced regional development pre-supposes the political pressure point to be developed in backward regions, which would meet out for a public demand to install such public projects. Gunnar Myrdal has very rightly held the views that free play of market forces generally lead toward inequalities. The Economist's approach to the problem of Balanced Development is global one while socialistic approach is regional one.[9] Politicians want every region to develop equally by way with offering equal opportunity to each voter living in backward regions. This approach is highly perceptible by resource short people of this backward region who would always wish to raise inter-regional liquidity of capital, and productive resources disregarding the economic loss involved in such endeavors.

However, there is always a human in making a case for applying egalitarian theory of the equity and even distribution of income sources all over the region—so to make over all self-sufficiency as the foundation of raising higher relative advantage and profitability with minimum cost of new economic proposition. Rationale of Balanced Economic Development laysits foundation on the balanced sectoral development so as to minimize the dependence of one on other region or country to meet own basic requirements, for which every economic region may not be rich in resource potentials. Thus, uneven distribution of natural resources defeats the basic postulation to bring about economic equality in various economic fronts and economic regions. The barriers caused by existing and growing intra-regional liquidity of capital, labour and enterprise can be mitigated partly by resolving through amicable deals with heavy political cost and interference in their respective areas.

PRAGMATIC APPROACH TO MITIGATE REGIONAL IMBALANCES

Pragmatic planning for Balanced Regional Development has remained a far cry so far, because of 2 basic reasons that in a macro-level, the nations involved in second world war, had been ruined economically and called for judicious economic recovery programme further so that regions, which had met the devastation caused on their productive units and loss of resource potentials could avoid damage to their future too. Secondly, those poor countries, which were of colonial status and had been placed as fully parasitic on those economic fields also, for which their possessed sizeable potentials hither to remained unaware of their own productive potentials. The advanced regions also allowed them to remain unaware as their interests were bracketed. Thus, sectoral development problems and Regional Development problems co-existed side by side in interest of advanced countries/ regions, which highly lacked in marketing scope for their own products. The problems, thus remains on going to call for New Economic World order in which friendly countries could wave their regional barriers for international liquidity on the one hand and ensure optimal use of Global inventories of Natural resources on the other. Global Recovery of environmental degradation has added third angle to this problem, where third world countries have to pay heaviest costs. With the onset of 21st century, the world demand for available resources inventories obtaining on earth surface, underground and under water, will be inadequate, promoting the old Dilemma.

The Un-resolved Dilemma

"Dilemma of Balanced Regional Development in India", is unique, encompassing systematic thinking about balanced economic development, balanced regional development and fallacies thereof. Economic rationale under the system of free economy does not warrant any argument in favour of any of the above two, because both of them directly or indirectly violate the principle of comparative advantages. While attempting to remove regional inequalities in economic development and making every region self-contained, it is more probable that even uneconomic production units have to be installed in backward regions, despite their cheap substitute available in the neighbouring advance regions. Harry W. Richardson in the famous writing (Regional Growth Theory, 1973) has rightly held—"The doctrine of regional growth both within and between regions, does not make good economic sense, though it is easy enough to formulate abstract models that yield predictions of this kind."

Notes and References

1. Apter David, The Politics of Modernization, Chicago University, Chicago Press, 1965.
2. Neil, J. Simelser, Mechanisim of Change and Adjustment in Industrialization and Society, B.F. Hoselitz and W.E. Moore of the Hague UNESCO, Mounten, 1966.
3. (i) T.S. Epstein, Economic Development and Social Change in South India, Manchester University Press, 1967.
   (ii) Mary Douglas, The Lele Resistance to Change in Market in Africa, Paul Bohanan and George Dalton (eds.), National History Press, New York, 1965.
4. M.L. Patel, Dilemma of Balanced Regional Development, Progress Publishers, Bhopal, 1975, p. 24. To explain, how spread effects and back-wash effects travel from growth centre to growth potential areas and how re-bound effect can degenerate backwash effect continium can be measured with given assumptions; for details see ch. 4 on Regional Planning for Economic Development, *ibid*, pp. 24-44.
5. John Kenneth Galbraith, Economic Development, Harvard University, London, pp. 3-8, 1969.
6. Valueable mineral resource reserves in backward region or countries, have turned the power of bargaining in their favour, subject to availability of cheap import substitutes. This has necessitated the need for new World Trade Organization to come for rescue of the so-called advanced countries.
7. M.L. Patel, 'Awareness in Weaker Sections', 1997, (M.D. Publication), New Delhi, see chapter 4.
8. K. Gopal Iyer (Ed.), Sustainable Development, Vikas Publication, New Delhi, 1995.
9. The recent attempts of old member countries of GATT, WTO and other recent common currency pact to be effective from 1999 are well planned attempts to retaliate the fear generated due to rising bargaining power of the Third World Countries, which will not leave any chance to heavily discount the future and forward trading pacts between the resourceful and resource short but with high technological know-how countries.

An Alternative Approach into the Process of Regional Development

P.G. Marvania

INTRODUCTION

Now, no one disputes the wisdom of intervention to bring about speedy balanced regional development. The science of regional development has come to forefront in the post-war era. Efforts are being made to make this science more and more useful to regional, urban and development planners.

However, many of the crucial issues like, 'where', 'how' and 'when' to intervene, demand a new insight into the process of regional development. This has now been possible as new realities are coming up from the interventions which were undertaken in the past.

This paper concentrates on highlighting the role of, kind of spatial system formed by industrial and urban locations, in dispersal of industries. The phenomenon of axial or corridor type of development is probed in detail. This axial or corridor type of development is partially the outcome of interventionist policy. To relocate industrial locations, incentive packages are devised to lure entrepreneurs at the backward area locations. The state plays an active role in formulation and implementation of strategy for guiding fresh industrial investments and creating new industrial urban nodes in the lagging regions. Some good has undoubtedly come about, yet this strategy cannot be said to have been eminently successful. This paper focuses upon the fact that in some lagging regions this strategy bore fruits, whereas the same could not succeed in other such regions. This paper attempts to show that why did such a lopesided performance take place? This paper attempts to bring out the weaknesses of conceptualisation of the present strategy. That is, this strategy has failed to address adequately the issue of 'where' and 'when' to intervene, though its 'mode' of intervention is reasonably a good prescription.

This paper first presents divergent conceptual views about rationale of intervention. Secondly, the gaps in the conceptual base of the present strategy are outlined. Thirdly, paper presents an alternative approach called, the 'Multi-Nodal Urban Industrial' approach which provides a better insight into the process of regional development and imbalances therein. Lastly, an empirical evidence is presented to verify the efficacy of the main tenets of this approach.

CONCEPTUAL VIEWS

Spatial disparities of development have been a top priority of development theorists as well as planners world over for last four decades. Persistence of such inequality for a longer duration leads to uneven and lope-sided growth of the national economy, which may result into socio-political tensions and violence leading to retardation of prospects of long-term growth of the economy. In the initial phase of the post-war era, there were two divergent views regarding the nature of regional inequality of development. One such view held that the regional inequality was a function of 'stage' of development. Hence, policy intervention was unwarranted. Because, progress in the process of development would take care of these inequalities in the due course of time as economy moves from the stage of "take-off" to that of "drive to maturity". The secular trend of growth process in many industrialised countries showed this characteristic. Works of Kuznets (1955), Perloff *et. al.* (1960) and Williamson (1965) supported this automatic convergence hypothesis, as it was popularly known then. Whereas, another diagonally opposite view was held by Myrdal (1957) and Hirchman (1957). According to them, the process of regional development would occur in polarised fashion only. Therefore, for reducing regional inequality, intervention would be essential. They held view that without intervention, the process of development would push economy upon growth path by creating inequality of spatial development. And process of development would not cease such inequality in absence adequate intervention. The other researchers and writers like Schultz (1950), North (1955) and Friedmann (1966) who had examined empiral evidence of process of development in different countries arrived to conclusion that as economy moves from predominantly agrarian status to highly industrialised one, a 'core-periphery' type of spatial structure is created. Where 'core' is dominated by concentration of activity and the 'periphery' lacks in such activity concentration. It was also suggested that to break this dualistic structure intervention is essential for creating new 'core' regions within such peripheral regions.

Richardson (1973) found the evidence of performance of automatic conversion as mixed ones. The market forces have proved too weak for rapid convergence. Therefore, objective of dispersal of industrial activity away from large urban centres, ahead of polarisation reversal, needs a carefully designed policy intervention. It is believed, that the most potent way to reduce regional disparities of development is, dispersal of industries in the backward regions. To achieve this, 'growth pole' and 'growth centre' strategies in their variant forms were applied during 1960s and 1970s. Underlying assumption for application of these strategies was that impulses of growth created at these poles/ centres would be transmitted to the hinterland. Perroux (1955), Boudeville (1966), Nicholas (1969), McCrone (1969), Paar (1973) and Lausen (1974) were the fore-runners of advocacy of growth pole and growth centre strategies for achieving the balanced regional development. However, studies made by UNRISD (1971); UNCRD (1976) and Stohr (1975) indicated that this strategy though produced some results, could not bring about the desired reduction in the imbalance in development.

Partial success of this type of strategy could not be explained by the existing development literature then. It demanded a better insight into the process of regional development. This posed a typical question that why did the growth pole/centre type of strategy succeed in some backward areas and failed in others? What was wrong with its conceptualisation? What were those unique features of the spatial-system in which it fared relatively better? Why did the dispersal of industrial activity take a shape of axial development ? Were there any special features for which the spatial systems could differ from one another in case of success and failure of activating the growth impulse ? To what extent the intervention played important role in activating the growth impules in the backward regions where it succeeded? One needs to answer these questions in the light of some conceptual framework and empirical evidence.

GAPS IN THE PRESENT CONCEPTUAL UNDERSTANDING

Over the years, attempts have been made to develop analytical tools for getting better insight into the process of development in general and regional development in particular. Such efforts have no doubt, raised the level of sophistication and scope of analytical tools. Yet, these tools, classical, neo-classical and Marxian, could not explain fresh realities of spatially uneven development despite implementation of well-thought out interventionist strategy. Not only that but these approaches could not explain that why such a strategy could generate impulses of growth in some backward regions and failed in others.

The inadequacy of the present approaches are (Classical, Neo-classical, Marxian, Growth Pole, Development from Below or Above; Critical Minimum Efforts; Trade Dependency Theory, etc.) due to two conceptual omissions.

First, it is because of lack of incorporation of spatial context of the process of regional development in these approaches. The above stated approaches have not taken into account the influence exerted by the spatial system upon the magnitude and dispersal of the growth process. Though, process of growth is intimately related to 'space', none of these approaches has any explicit or implicit conotation to the relationship between 'space' and process of 'economic growth'.

Second is due to their lack of multi-dimensional view of the process of regional development. That is, these approaches have perceived the process of regional development as an uni-dimensional process. In fact, the process of regional development is a multidimensional process. It cuts across several disciplines like, 'urban economics', 'industrial economics', 'agrarian economics', etc. The process of regional development is quite closely related with sectoral development of particular region. Hence, the regional growth process has to be perceived as a multi-dimensional growth process.

LACK OF SPATIAL CONTEXT

The classical and neo-classical approaches of process of development are 'spaceless'. That is, these approaches of development have not taken into consideration the casual influence of 'spatial system' on the 'growth process'. The classical were more concerned with process of income generation and its distribution among the factors of production. The neo-classical concentration was on obtaining conditions for general equilibrium. Both these approaches overlooked the contribution of the spatial system in the growth process. The Leonfief types of growth models were more concerned with inter-sectoral consistency of physical inputs and outputs for development plans. The Keynesian and Post-Keynesians were more concerned about providing a smooth path for development process. Whereas the emphasis of development economists like Rosenstein-Rodan (1945), Prebisch (1950), Rostow (1952), Nurkse (1952), Myint (1957), and Hirschman (1958) mostly dealt with causes of under-development and mode of sectoral allocation of resources. They too did not take much of a cognizance of the causal relationship between the 'space' and 'development'.

A set of approaches (Myrdal's 'cumulative causation', Hirschman's 'Unbalanced Growth Strategy', and Friedmann's 'Core-periphery Model') which sought to explain the process of development, did lay emphasis upon the need for intervention for accelerating the process of convergence. But, these approaches did not examine in detail the spatial aspects of an efficient intervention, i.e. 'where', 'when', and 'how' to intervene in the space.

Both, activity as well as human habitats have a spatial dimension in the sense that both are related to specific locations in the space. Therefore, any policy manipulation for achieving desired distribution of activity and settlements have to take into account its spatial implications. Hence, any conceptualisation of intervention which is devoid of spatial context, cannot fully explain dynamics of regional growth and development.

LACK OF MULTI-DIMENSIONAL CONCEPTUALISATION

The process of regional development cuts across several processes like, urbanisation, industrialisation, agrarian development, etc. Hence, it is truly speaking a multi-dimensional process. While conceptualising about this process one has to take into account inter and intra-sectoral relationships. The uni-dimensional view does not explain fully this process. Usually, the policy intervention has been advocated for achieving the spatial equity of development ahead of the on set of polarisation reversal process. To achieve this goal, relocation of industrial investment and human settlement are undertaken by way of providing positive and negative incentives. The intentions are to shift both, activity and settlements from 'core' to 'periphery'. Following are the underlying assumptions of such a strategy. First, entrepreneurs are willing to move away from already developed, urban centres to the backward regions when they are offered incentives. Second, the incentive packages themselves are sufficient to make any location in the backward region and economically viable and self-sustaining centre of growth. Lastly, locations in different lagging regions are equally preferred by entrepreneurs.

Usually writers from different disciplines have laid emphasis upon their own discipline while explaining regional development. Urban theorists have laid emphasis upon city-size, hierarchical structure of cities, rank-size distribution, etc. in explaining the variations in the spatial development. The industrial economists have explained such variations in terms of cost and market considerations. However, for explaining partial success of dispersal of industrial activity and settlements in the backward regions, one needs a synthesised approach involving more than one discipline. Such a framework would explain the success of intervention in some backward regions and failures in others.

MULTI-DIMENSIONAL CONCEPTUAL FRAMEWORK

The multi-dimensional conceptual framework is evolved through synthesis of concepts from urban, industrial and development economics.

The urban theorists have perceived city as a generator of surplus and creator of wealth. It is also perceived as centre equipped with better living amenities. Moreover, the city has been identified as a centre of mixing discoveries and innovations and benefiting from scale and agglomeration externalities. The urban theories are chiefly concentrated around explaining the 'rank-size' distribution of cities, urban primacy and urban amenities management. (Zipf, 1949). Only three decades ago, a few geographers and urban planners started investigating link between urban primacy and the level of development (Berry, 1961; El Shakhs, 1972, 1980; Alonso, 1968).

Similarly, the industrial location theorists have laid emphasis upon cost and market consideration in growth of industrial locations. Weber (1909), Palander (1955) and Hoower (1937, 1948) indicated that 'cost of production' was the chief determinant of location of a plant. Whereas, Christaller (1933) and Losch (1940) showed that proximity of market was the chief determinant in location of a plant. Each of these approaches precluded the tenets of the other one. The least-cost locational approach emphasised search for the least-cost location in conditions where demand factor is held constant and the locational interdependence of firms and their externalities are assumed away.

But when demand was allowed to vary in space it was possible to move to a new location even with higher unit cost as the greater sales would have increased total profits. The Christaller-Losch type of approach had recognised locational interdependence of the firms. Yet, it suffered from assumption of identical costs and sales conditions.

The development theorists perceived backwardness as result of lack of adequate investment. Hence, to promote development of a region, fresh injection of investment was prescribed by them.

While evolving the synthesised framework for explaining dynamics of spatial development above three considerations have been taken into account. This framework emphasises that the spatial system plays an important role in dispersal of industrial activity in the backward regions with the help of incentives. This approach tries to explain that why only some of the lagging regions get industrialised through intervention whereas, others remain as non-starter.

Firstly here, urban spatial system is defined as the system of settlements constituted by urban nodes. Each urban node is characterized by several functions which it performs. Among these functions one is pre-dominant, i.e. centre of industrial activity, or trading, or administration, post or educational centre, service centre, etc. This particular aspect is known as 'nodal function'.

Moreover, each urban node is having functional linkages with other urban nodes in the space. Together, they all form a system of nodal functional 'roles' and 'relations'. The functional roles are characterised by node's own locational situation. In the spatial system. Whereas, 'functional relations' are characterised by node's locational situation *vis-a-vis* other locations in the spatial system. The functional roles are in form of node's own urban agglomeration economies, socio-cultural and economic infrastructure facilities, character of pre-dominant activity, people's perception of quality of life at this node, etc. While functional relations are in form of flow of factors, inputs, produces, services, information, facility of transport linkages and net-working, etc. These roles and relations are location specific. They are likely to differ with regard to their contents and characteristics from node to node in the spatial system.

The totality of functional roles and relations gives each urban-node a unique locational and functional characteristic which we shall term as urban nodal function. The urban nodal functions can be varied like service centre, manufacturing centre, trading centre, etc.

This urban nodal function generates two types of forces at and around the urban-node for which it has been specified. One is centripetal and another is centrifugal. Former attracts more and more concentration of activity and population at and around urban node. While the later, repels them away from the node. Their combine effects result into ringular shaped urban influence zone around the node. Following are some of the important factors which influence the size and shape of this zone:

(i) type of pre-dominant activity at node;

(ii) size of agglomeration economies of production;
(iii) quality of urban amenities and urban infrastructure services;
(iv) prices of land and housing rents; and
(v) socio-cultural dimension.

POLE-NODE AND URBAN-INDUSTRIAL INFLUENCE ZONE

An urban-node possing following characteristics is defined as the pole-node:

(i) An urban node having industrial manufacturing activity as its pre-dominant function; and
(ii) It should have a large concentration of population.

Thus the pole-node is characterised by concentration of industrial activity and population. The ringular shaped urban-influence zone created at and around the pole-node has distinct features of centripetal and centrifugal forces. To distinguish the urban influence zone of the pole-node let us term it as 'urban-industrial influence zone.'

Besides, when two pole-nodes are linked through a well developed transport network, a ribbon-shaped urban-industrial influence region is created between them. Following are some of the factors which decides the intensity and size of this influence region:

(i) Numbers of pole-nodes and other urban nodes along the transport corridor linking two pole nodes;
(ii) their spatial arrangement pattern, i.e. linear triangular etc.;
(iii) inter-nodal distances; and
(iv) size of population and manufacturing activity at pole nodes.

The intensity of ribbon-shaped urban-industrial influence is increased with increase in number of pole-nodes, their linear arrangement along transport corridor and short inter-nodal distances. Further, well developed infrastructure of transport and commutation increase intensity of urban-industrial influence.

So far we have conceptualised, urban spatial system; functional roles and relations of an urban node; urban nodal function, urban influence zone; pole node and urban industrial influence zone. With help of these concepts now we shall define, multi-nodal urban-industrial spatial system as follow. Any urban spatial system having following characteristics is defined as a 'multi-nodal urban-industrial' spatial system:

(i) it has two pole nodes;
(ii) the size of population and activity at each pole-node is quite large;
(iii) pole nodes are situated on the linear transport corridor which has well developed transport and commutation infrastructure; and
(iv) inter-urban nodal distances along the transport corridor are quite short.

The multi-nodal urban-industrial spatial system offers a host of locational advantages to entrepreneurs to set-up industry within its urban-industrial influence region. These advantages are as follow:

(i) an easy access to agglomeration benefits of production and marketing at pole-nodes;
(ii) an easy access to multiple markets of pole-nodes and other urban nodes within the system.
(iii) an easy access to urban amenities at pole-nodes and that of other urban nodes within the system;
(iv) an easy access to the pool of skilled workers and maintenance service facilities at pole-nodes;
(v) an easy access to transport and commuting facility within the urban-industrial zone; and
(vi) an easy access to business support facilities at pole-nodes.

Here, the functional roles and relations of the pole-nodes as well as that of other urban-nodes falling within the ring-ribbon type of urban industrial influence region of the pole nodes, create a spatial-system which offer above stated locational advantages to entrepreneurs.

The industrial theorists have identified following pre-requisites for locational consideration:

(i) access to large national and foreign markets for procurement of inputs and sales of output;
(ii) access to transport and communication facilities of national and international networks;
(iii) access to benefits of urban and industrial agglomeration externalities;
(iv) smooth supply of basic and key inputs like water, electricity, manpower, etc.;
(v) access to urban life amenities;
(vi) access to business and production support services like, maintenance of plants and machineries, accounting, advertising, marketing, etc.;
(vii) well developed locational infrastructure facilities like road, water, educational service, etc.;
(viii) access to cost reducing means; and
(ix) access to market enlarging means.

Without any sort of external intervention, all those locations which offer above mentioned locational advantages will flourish. Without on set of polarisation process, it would be difficult to prevent concentration of industries at these locations. When a deliberately designed intervention is undertaken, following incentives are offered to make locations in the lagging region more attractive and viable:

(i) supply of two critical inputs of industrialisation, namely, water and electricity are supplied at the concessional rate;
(ii) provisions of tax holiday like exemptions from Sales-tax and excise duty for a period of first five years of production;
(iii) cash subsidies to set-off loss of benefits of agglomeration externalities;
(iv) provision of well developed locational infrastructure; and
(v) institutional finance at the concessional rate of interest.

Also benefits of 'pioneering unit' status and 'export-oriented' units are also bestowed upon them.

So far we have outlined the characteristics of the multi-nodal urban-industrial spatial system and its locational advantages. Moreover, we have identified the type of considerations or factors which play a very crucial role in deciding locational priorities of entrepreneurs. We have also identified the benefits offered through incentive package to make backward area locations viable. Now let us explain the phenomenon of partial success of incentive packages in dispersing industries at the backward area locations.

If one compares the list of entrepreneurial pre-requisites for locational choice with that of benefits offered by the backward area industrialisation incentive packages, one finds that such benefits refers to only a few of entrepreneurial pre-requisites. But if, such a backward area location falls within the multi-nodal urban-industrial spatial system, then, it has added locational advantages offered by the spatial system. Now, such locational advantages are lacking at the backward area locations falling outside the multi-nodal urban industrial spatial system. Hence, in terms of industrial locational advantages the backward area locations within the multi-nodal urban industrial spatial system have more advantages than their counterparts falling outside the multi-nodal urban-industrial spatial system. Therefore, though incentive package offers uniform benefits at all backward area locations, the ones falling within the multi-nodal urban-industrial spatial system have more locational advantages. Hence, all these backward area locations falling within the multi-nodal urban-industrial spatial system are preferred when incentives of industrialisation of backward area are offered. Thus the type of spatial system plays an important role in success of incentives to attract entrepreneurs at backward area locations. As the multi-nodal urban industrial spatial system puts the backward area locations within itself on a higher preference scale *vis-a-vis* those outside such a spatial system. And this produces more efficient results of intervention at balanced area locations falling within this spatial system.

CASE STUDY

The efficacy of tenets of the above framework is examined by taking intervention experience of the State of Gujarat. It is hypothesised that the multi-nodal urban-industrial spatial system has important bearing on locational preferences of entrepreneurs. For this purpose two backward area locations with almost identical characteristics were selected. They are Ankleshwar in Bharuch district and Wadhwan in Surendranagar district. Both were centrally declared backward districts. They bore similarities of their developmental status, then, except their locational situation. The former fell within the multi-nodal urban industrial spatial system formed by pole nodes of Ahmedabad and Mumbai, whereas the later fell outside such a system (see Map 3). The intervention was successful at Ankleshwar whereas it failed at Wadhwan.

As shown in the Maps 2 and 3 a multi-nodal urban industrial spatial system is created due to pole-nodes of Ahmedabad add Bombay along the rail and road corridor linking both of them. This spatial system extends from Mahesana in the north to Vapi in the South. We can see in the, Map 3 that a stripe of approximate length of 385 km. and having a width of 08-12 kms. alongside the national highway No. 8 and double track-broad gauge rail line linking Ahmedabad and Mumbai forms a multi-nodal urban industrial spatial system which runs through district of Bharuch which is a backward district (see Map 1). The system has other urban nodes with substantial industrial activity. (see Maps 2 and 3).

A stratified random sample of 192 entrepreneurs was selected as outlined in Table 1. They were asked to reveal their locational preferences. As given in Table 2, fifteen locational factors were identified and each entrepreneur was suppose to rank the role of these factors in their locational choice (refer Table 2). The preferences were analysed using the PCA (Principle Component Analysis) with help of the SPSS software. The findings of the analysis presented in Tables 3 to 7.

The PCA extracted five factors. The factory and constituent variables were as follow:

F_1 : ROAD, RAIL, MARKET, POWER, WATER, SPECI;
F_2 : LAB, LAND;
F_3 : BIGIND, SSI;
F_4 : TOWN, INCE, ESTATE;
F_5 : GROWTH, EXPECT.
(Refer Table 2 for variable abbreviations)

TABLE 1

Size-Activity Distribution: Universe and Sample (Total)

Activity	*Universe*				*Sample*			
	L	*M*	*S*	*T*	*L*	*M*	*S*	*T*
Chemical	10	31	125	166	2	5	27	34
Dyes	1	11	111	123	0	2	23	25
Engineering	14	26	167	207	3	6	37	46
Textiles	7	18	138	163	1	4	28	33
Plastics	5	7	69	81	1	1	16	18
Pharmaceuticals	14	13	43	70	3	3	10	16
Packaging	3	4	20	27	1	1	04	06
Pesticides	7	0	01	08	2	—	—	02
Ceramic	0	0	20	20	0	0	06	06
Miscellaneous	0	1	26	27	0	0	06	06
Total	61	111	720	892	13	22	157	192

L = Large; M = Medium; S = Small; T = Total.

TABLE 2

Locational Variables

What was the significance of each of the following factors in your locational choice ?

1. Provision of backward area incentive benefit package (INCE)
2. Estate facilities (ESTATE)
3. Availability of cheap labour (LAB)
4. Availability of land at low cost (LAND)
5. Assured power supply (POWER)
6. Assured water supply (WATER)
7. Easily accessible well-developed road-transport network (ROAD)
8. Easily accessible well-developed rail-transport network (RAIL)
9. Easy access to major markets (MARKET)
10. Proximity of a town (TOWN)
11. Good prospects for growth of the unit (GROWTH)
12. Product specialisation (SPECI)
13. Existence of big industrial units at this place (BIGIND)
14. Presence of SSIs in substantial numbers (SSI)
15. Your expectation that this location would grow into an industrial nucleus (EXPECT)

(Contd.)

Significance Rating Scale:

	Level of Significance	*Rank Value*
(a)	Not significant at all	1
(b)	Desirable but not compulsory	2
(c)	Important	3
(d)	More important	4
(e)	Most important	5

These factors can be meaningfully interpreted as follow :

F_1 : "Infrastructure and Market Facilities";

F_2 : "Basic Inputs";

F_3 : "Industrial Agglomeration Economies";

F_4 : "Urban Proximity and Intervention Benefits"; and

F_5 : "Growth Expectation."

From the results presented in Tables 3 to 7, it is clearly indicated that entrepreneurial choices are more powerfully explained by F_1, F_2 and F_3 than F_4. Which implies that entrepreneurial locational preferences are more influenced by classical locational advantages rather than interventionist's control variables used for attracting entrepreneurs at the backward area locations.

This means, when entrepreneur has to make a choice among the backward area locations, he would prefer the. locations falling within the multi-nodal urban-industrial spatial system rather than those falling outside such a system. Here in this case Ankleshwar has grown rapidly whereas the Wadhwan has failed to attract industrial activity. As in Map 3, several estates falling within the multi-nodal urban industrial spatial system have also got industrialised, though, these estates fell into the backward areas. Thus, the type of spatial system is a crucial factor which planners should take into account while designing the industrial dispersal policies for the backward area development through industrialisation.

TABLE 3

Correlation Matrix

	INCE	*ESTATE*	*LAB*	*LAND*	*POWER*	*WATER*	*ROAD*
INCE	1.00000						
ESTATE	.29190*	1.00000					
LAB	.15428	.28343*	1.00000				
LAND	.24097*	.23869*	.65567*	1.00000			
POWER	-.12433	-.16430	-.24810*	-.20278	1.00000		
WATER	-.13622	-.10910	-.11364	-.15563	.51365*	1.00000	
ROAD	-.07591	-.01734	-.10048	-.07834	.40931*	.33681*	1.00000
RAIL	-.09164	.03034	-.05895	-.03176	.34807*	.28654*	.68320*
MARKET	-.05174	-.22798*	-.21465	-.15495	.54100*	.38376*	.54331*
TOWN	.22558*	.19164	.01758	.03897	-.17636	-.04440	-.06206
GROWTH	.00460	.15535	.05010	.07701	-.17634	-.25134*	-.13318
SPECI	-.12419	.12593	.09195	.01509	-.19932	-.11664	-.26893*
BIGIND	-.20619	-.01673	-.12691	-.15575	.10568	.03811	-.10409
SSI	-.12133	..07497	.05913	.07715	.12262	.04593	-.01510
EXPECT	-.03129	.09509	-.03054	.06009	.02293	.06357	-.04453

	RAIL	*MARKET*	*TOWN*	*GROWTH*	*SPECI*	*BIGIND*	*SSI*	*EXPECT*
RAIL	1.00000							
MARKET	.49310*	1.00000						
TOWN	-.08782	-.15660	1.00000					
GROWTH	-.08387	-.29415*	.05556	1.00000				
SPECI	-.34441*	-.38105*	.05624	.21670	1.00000			
BIGIND	-.20818	-.03352	-.02794	.11524	.13695	1.00000		
SSI	-.00967	.00913	-.00759	.12788	.04801	.65304*	1.00000	
EXPECT	.04584	-.04559	-.05320	.31262*	.01435	.17573	.13558	1.00000

Determinant of Correlation Matrix = .0141676
Kaiser-Meyer-Olkin Measure of Sampling Adequacy = 0.68074
Bertlett Test of Sphericity = 788.21660, Significance = 0.00000
* 1-tailed significance.

TABLE 4

Initial Statistics

Variable	*Communality*	*Factor*	*Eigen value*	*Pct of Var*	*Cum Pct*
INCE	1.00000	1	3.37461	22.5	22.5
ESTATE	1.00000	2	2.07942	13.9	36.4
LAB	1.00000	3	1.72805	11.5	47.9
LAND	1.00000	4	1.21516	8.1	56.0
POWER	1.00000	5	1.16281	7.8	63.7
WATER	1.00000	6	.96580	6.4	70.2
ROAD	1.00000	7	.88543	5.9	76.1
RAIL	1.00000	8	.74458	5.0	81.0
MARKET	1.00000	9	.64997	4.3	85.4
TOWN	1.00000	10	.51628	3.4	88.8
GROWTH	1.00000	11	.43248	2.9	91.7
SPECI	1.00000	12	.36829	2.5	94.2
B.IGIND	1.00000	13	.33079	2.2	96.4
SSI	1.00000	14	.30736	2.0	98.4
EXPECT	1.00000	15	.23897	1.6	100.0

PC Extracted 5 factors.

TABLE 5

Final Statistics

Variable	*Communality*	*Factor*	*Eigen value*	*Pet of Var*	*Cum Pet*
INCE	.55215	1	3.37461	22.5	22.5
ESTATE	.53984	2	2.07942	13.9	36.4
LAB	.80264	3	1.72805	11.5	47.9
LAND	.77957	4	1.21516	8.1	56.0
POWER	.58897	5	1.16281	7.8	63.7
WATER	.42453				
ROAD	.66668				
RAIL	.71905				
MARKET	.67053				
TOWN	.63051				
GROWTH	.67870				
SPECI	.31906				
BIGIND	.82012				
SSI	.79363				
EXPECT	.57406				

TABLE 6

Factor Matrix

	Factor 1	*Factor 2*	*Factor 3*	*Factor 4*	*Factor 5*
MARKET	.80104	.11152	.10080	-.05225	.05951
POWER	.72467	-.14458	.18105	-.04529	.08992
ROAD	.70828	.25311	.27373	.14889	.06208
RAIL	.66137	.31863	.31484	.20430	-.19815
WATER	.60545	-.06134	.16242	-.07725	.14783
SPECI	-.46251	-.31016	-.03564	-.02663	-.08341
BIGIND	-.04104	-.76160	.37502	-.13138	.28372
INCE	-.23845	.50521	.09926	.24004	.41543
SSI	-.01973	-.53536	.61984	-.21653	.27486
LAND	-.37579	.48589	.49964	-.36866	-.12930
ESTATE	-.33890	.28503	.46599	.28780	.20921
EXPECT	-.05933	-.25080	.42795	.42185	-.38279
GROWTH	-.38229	-.22112	.30040	.49440	-.38599
LAB	-.40848	.45197	.45613	-.45717	-.12026
TOWN	-.23816	.15887	.02246	.40974	.61657

TABLE 7

Rotated Factor Matrix

	Factor 1	*Factor 2*	*Factor 3*	*Factor 4*	*Factor 5*
ROAD	.80734	-.00148	-.08837	.00100	.08414
RAIL	.79836	.06999	-.18137	-.02131	.20838
MARKET	.77824	-.12666	.01728	-.12742	-.17972
POWER	.67289	-.19873	.24768	-.16506	-.09003
WATER	.57979	-.12296	.21182	-.08196	-.14719
SPECI	-.51137	-.00351	.16606	-.07911	.15398
LAB	-.13154	.88400	.00111	.05021	-.03689
LAND	-.07067	.87321	-.02500	.10189	.03277
BIGIND	-.10766	-.15655	.87728	-.07429	.09423
SSI	.04826	.14014	.87165.	.00523	.10886
TOWN	-.11341	-.15570	.04999	.76674	-.05488
INCE	-.01659	.19414	-.18641	.68683	-.08769
ESTATE	-.03580	.33914	.06647	.57985	.28792
GROWTH	-.26008	.00624	.02929	.05221	.77938
EXPECT	.05977	-.00355	.13928	-.05134	.74056

Map 1: Gujarat State: District-wise Development Status

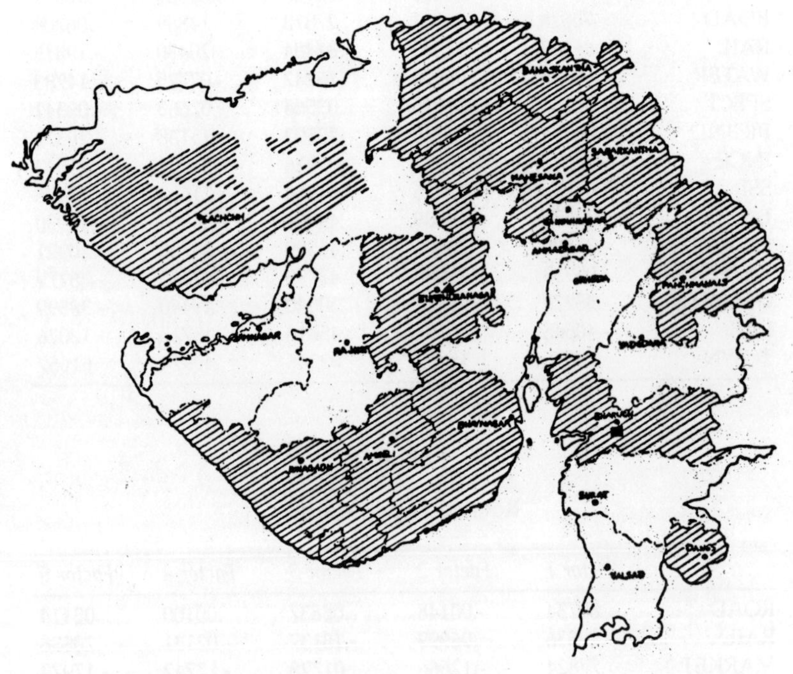

 INDUSTRIALLY BACKWARD DISTRICTS.

SAMPLED LOCATIONS

▲ WADHWAN G.I.D.C.

 ANKLESHWAR G.I.D.C.

Map 2: Gujarat State: Class-I Cities Major Road-Rail Routes and MNUI Spatial System

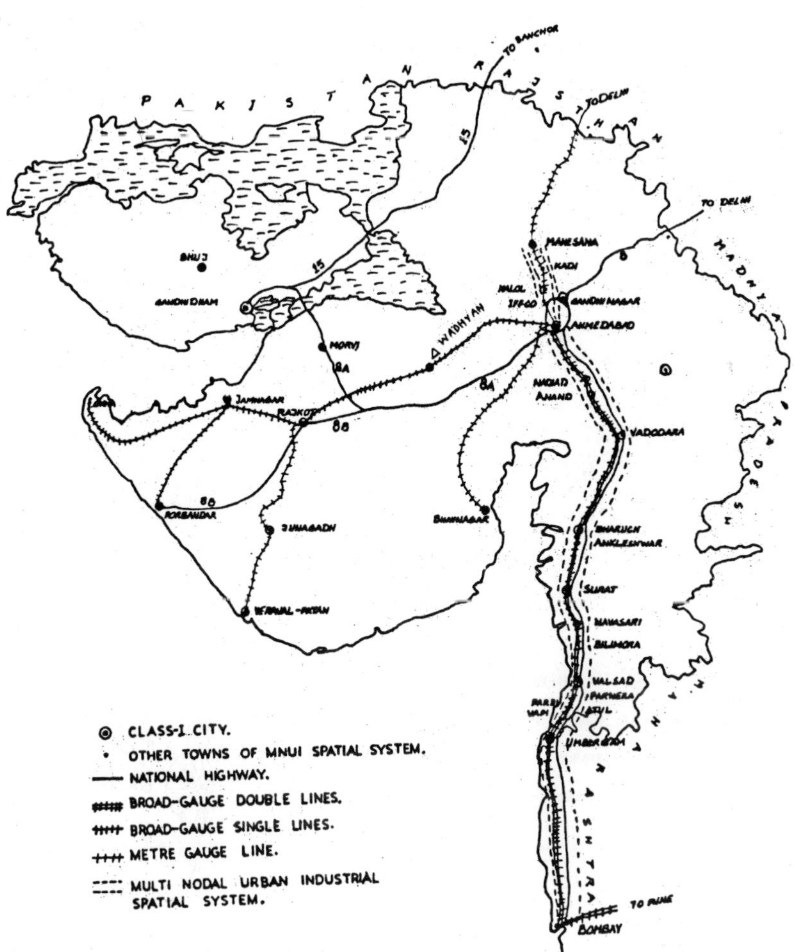

Map 3: Gujarat State: The Multi-Industrial Spatial System

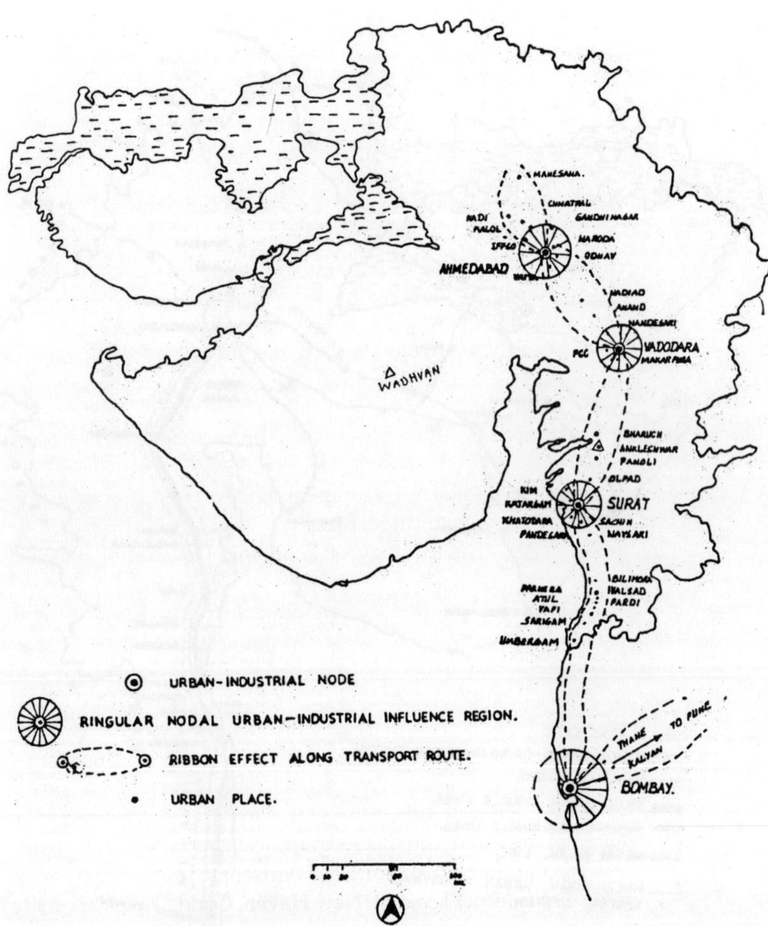

REFERENCES

Alonso, W. (1968), Industrial Location and Regional Policy in Economic Development, Berkeley, California, IURD, UCLA, Working Paper 74, 1968. Reprinted in, Friedmann, J. and Alonso, W. (eds.), Regional Policy: Readings in Theory and Applications, Cambridge, Mass, 1975.

Berry, B.J.L. (1961), "City Size Distribution and Development", *Economic Development and Cultural Change*, 9, 973-87.

Boudeville, J.R. (1966), Problems of Regional Economic Planning, Edinburgh University Press, Edinburgh.

Christaller W. (1933), Die Zentralen Orte in Suddeutchland Tr. by Baskin, C.W. (1966) as Central Places in Southern Germany, Printice-Hall, Englewood Cliff, New Jersey.

El-Shakhs, S. (1972), 'City Systems, Primacy and Development, *Journal of Developing Areas*, 7, 1972, 11-36.

—— (1980), 'National and Regional Issues and Policies Facing the Challenges of the Urban Future', In UNFPA, Proceedings of Conference on Population and Urban Future, Rome, Sept. 1980.

Friedmann, J. (1966), Regional Development Policy : A Case Study of Venezuela, MIT Press, Cambridge, Mass.

Hirschman, A.O. (1958), 'The Strategy of Economic Development', New Haven.

Hoower, E.M. (1948), 'The Location of Economic Activity', McGraw Hill, New York.

—— (1937), 'Location Theory and the Shoe and Leather Industries', Harvard University Press, Cambridge Mass.

Kuznets, S. (1955), 'Economic Growth and Income Inequality', *American Economic Review*, 45 (1), March 1955, 20-21.

Lasuen, J.R. (1974), 'A generalisation of Growth Pole Notion', In Thomas, R.S. (ed.), Proceedings of the Commission on Regional Aspects of Development of the International Geographical Union, Vol. 1, Canada.

Losch, A. (1940), Die Raumliche Ordnung der Wirtschaft Translated by W.H. Woglom, *The Economics of Location*, New Haven, Conn., Yale University Press.

McCrone (1969), 'Regional Policy in Britain', George Allen and Unwin, London.

Myint, H. (1957), 'An interpretation of Economic Backwardness', Oxford University Papers, 6 (2), June 1954, 132-63.

Myrdal G. (1957), 'Economic Theory and Underdeveloped Regions', Duckworth, London.

Nichols, V. (1969), 'Growth Poles: An Evaluation of the Propulsive Effects', *Environment and Planning*, 1, 193-208.

North, D. (1955), 'Location Theory and Regional Economic Growth', *Journal of Political Economy*, 63 (3), 243-58.

Nurkse, R. (1952), "Some International Aspects of the Problem of Economic Development', *American Economic Review*, 42, 571-83.

Paar, J.B. (1973), 'Growth Pole, Regional Development and Central Place Theory', Papers of Regional Science Association, 31, 172-212.

Palander, T. (1935), 'Beitrage Zur Standorts theorie', Ref. in Smith D., *Industrial Location*, John Wiley, New York, 1981, pp. 75-93.

Perloff, H.S. *et al.* (1960), 'Regions, Resources and Economic Growth', John Hopkins Press, Baltimore.

Perroux, F. (1950), 'Economic Space: Theory and Application', In Friedmann J. and Alonso, W. (eds.) 1964.

Prebisch, R. (1950), 'The Economic Development of Latin America and its Principal Problems: The UN Department of Economic Affairs', New York.

Richardson, H.W. (1973), Regional Growth Theory; Macmillan, London.

Rosenstein-Rodan, P.N. (1943), 'Problems of Industrialisation of Eastern and South Eastern Europe', *Economic Journal*, 53, (June-Sept. 1943), 205-11.

Rostow, W.W. (1952), 'The Process of Economic Growth; Norton, New York.

Schultz, T.W. (1950), 'Reflections of Poverty within Agriculture', *Journal of Political Economy*, 53, 1-16.

Stohr, W. (1975), 'Regional Development: Experience and Prospects in Latin America', Mounton, The Hague.

UNCRD (1976), 'Growth Pole Strategy and Regional Development in Asia', UNCRD, Nagoya, Japan.

UNRISD (1971), 'Regional Development Experience and Prospects', Vol. 1; South and South-East Asia; UN Research Institute of Social Development, Mounton.

Weber, A. (1909), Uber den Standort der Industrien; tr. by Friedrich, C.J.; Alfred Weber's Theory of Location of Industries; University of Chicago Press, Chicago, 1929.

Williamson, J.G. (1965), 'Regional Inequality and the Process of National Development: A Description of Patterns', *Economic Development and Cultural Change*, 13, 1965, 3-43.

Zipf, G.K. (1949), Human Behaviour and Principle of Least Effort; Cambridge Mass : Addison-Wesley.

POLICY MEASURES FOR BALANCED AND SUSTAINABLE AGRICULTURAL DEVELOPMENT

KANCHAN CHOPRA

I
THE CONCEPT AND ITS POLICY SIGNIFICANCE

Sustainability of agriculture has been interpreted in a number of ways in the recent literature. It is however, not a new concept. Organic methods of farming or 'permanent agriculture' which respected the integrity of the soil and related ecological systems have been referred to as 'sustainable'.[1] Among recent writers on the subject, Conway (1985) maintains that an agricultural system that can overcome a stress, defined as a discontinuity in the situation to which it is subject, can be referred to as sustainable. The FAO (1989), on the other hand, defines sustainable agriculture as the successful management of resources for agriculture to satisfy changing human needs while maintaining or enhancing the

This paper was earlier published in *Indian Journal of Agricultural Economics,* Vol. 48, No. 3. It is published with kind permission of the editor and author.

quality of environment and conserving natural resources. Parikh and Ghosh (1991) consider soil in particular to be an important resource base and think it should be treated as the reference point for defining sustainability. Jodha (1991) treats sustainability as a characteristic of the agricultural system: "It is the ability of the system to maintain a certain well defined level of performance over time, and if required to enhance the same through linkages with other systems without damaging the ecological integrity of the system."

The notion that seems to underlie most of the above ways of viewing the concept is that growth must be achieved without impairing the resource base. In other words, the land/soil and its intrinsic qualities should be maintained unimpaired in the process of growth. And this should hold true over a relatively long-run. A period of high growth rates should not be followed by a period in which a so-called plateau in productivity is reached. Sustainability is, in other words, the desired ideal of achieving growth while maintaining natural capital intact.

This concept of sustainable growth has existed in economic thought in one form or the other. Classical political economy was concerned with the notion of sustainable growth, in particular in relation to land. Malthus considered resources to impose a limit to growth and the focal point of Ricardo's analysis was relative growth on non-homogeneous plot of land. Mill's notion of a stationary state in which outputs and inputs grew at the same rate provides the closest approximation to the present approach to the notion of sustainability. Marx too stressed that "work is not the source of all wealth, nature is just as much the source of use value as work, which is itself only an expression of a natural force, human labour power."

Later day extensions of these ideas have resulted in alternative approaches to the problems. In neo-classical economics the attempt to take account of this area has seen the emergence of resource management models. These models view the maintenance of environmental standards as another constraint to maximising/minimising discounted streams of utility/disutility either over finite or infinite time horizons. Alternatively, the new institutional economics stresses property rights. It states that a well spelt out system of property rights, be it private, public or common, would solve many of the problems encountered due to ecological constraints. The new science of bio-economics traces the origin of scarcity and consequently the limits to growth to the operation of the laws of thermodynamics. Simultaneously, a dis-satisfaction with the monolithic concept of land and an appreciation of the interdependence between different natural processes have become a part of mainstream economics. As Daly (1990) puts if, "The production process functions within the ecosystem and its links with the ecosystem should determine the optimal level at which it should function."

At the present juncture in Indian agriculture, the concept of sustainability in agriculture has attained a certain policy significance. The reasons for this have to be viewed in the context of the evolution of agricultural policy in India which has been preoccupied primarily with the issue of increasing productivity. This was natural and correct in a country where foodgrain shortage was endemic. The sixties saw the emergence of the high-yielding variety (HYV) technology and the thrust of policy was towards increased production in selected areas—the so-called intensive development areas. In a sense, the last thirty years have seen the culmination of the success of this policy approach manifested in the spread to oilier areas of the country. Even in the late seventies, however, the need for a new policy thrust in agriculture was already beginning to emerge.[2] It had become obvious that an extension of the same irrigation-fertiliser-based technology to a large number of new regions was not possible and/or viable. An examination of productivities across regions indicated that the ecological parameters were significant in determining both correct policy options and levels of productivity to be aimed at. By the late eighties, the two important policy questions had become: (1) a high level of productivity with a plateau was being reached in some high productivity regions; (2) large parts of the country seemed to continue to have low levels of productivity: an appropriate strategy for them was required. In both cases, it seemed as if the ecological factors and the limits to productivity imposed by them were emerging as significant. It is this emergence of ecological constraints within the context of an economic view of productivity potential that brought sustainability issues to the fore. The empirical question that arose was: Would Indian agriculture be sustainable over the next decade or more?

Before examining sustainability issues in the Indian context, some significant inter-relationships between the process of technological change and the presence or otherwise of sustainability in the ensuing agricultural growth are examined.[3] Technological change increases productivity as a consequence of introduction of new inputs or through new methods of combining old inputs. When this technological change operates as an exogenous factor, the high levels of productivity that follow do not necessarily address the issue of the maintenance of natural capital over time. Further, required change in institutions is assume to take place. The outcome is that if these institutional factors happen to be favourable and if the correct configuration of ecological factor is available, the change becomes a success in terms of both productivity and sustainability. Preservation of the natural resource-base not central to such a process of technological change. It may be an outcome given a favourable combination of the new technology and emerging institutional and location-specific ecological factors.

Alternatively, if requisite technological change begins with location-specific natural resources and asks the question: what kind of increases in productivity can be obtained by improving on the management and use of these factors within the institutional constraints of the region, the emerging technology considers both productivity and sustainability as equally significant characteristics. Such a view of technology as specific to regional ecological and institutional factors implies that productivity of the ensuing agricultural process is left unspecified in the first instance. It is an output variable in the simultaneous system.

Such an analysis of the links between productivity and sustainability, on the one hand, and technological change, institutions and ecology, on the other, emphasises that sustainability is a characteristic of the process of economic growth. It is a characteristic that shall have to be contended with either *ex post* as in the situation of exogenous technological change or at the outset as when planning for growth with appropriate natural resource management. Growth is in the final analysis "the consequence of positive feedbacks between the socio-system and the eco-system whereby these systems can evolve in a manner favourable to man."[4] It also implies value judgements with respect to the model of development being looked for. Such a model should include planning and adaptation of the farming system to the environment of the region and focus on a harmonious use of the various biological resources within the agro-system.

II
SUSTAINABILITY OF EXOGENOUS, PRODUCTIVITY-ORIENTED TECHNOLOGICAL CHANGE

The bio-chemical technology introduced in the mid-sixties has been the major exogenous technological change witnessed by Indian agriculture. This irrigation-fertiliser-based HYV technology has spread to roughly one-third of the 140 million hectares of net sown area in this country. What is the track record of this technology with respect to the issue of leaving natural capital intact? In this case, the erosion of natural capital could have taken two major forms: land degradation and/or over-use of water. One of the key issues then is: has irrigation-based agriculture resulted into waterlogging, salinity or other forms of land abuse either in the catchment or the command area that will undermine its future productivity.

Estimates of waterlogging and salinity in the country are subject to wide variation. Definitions of the phenomenon, time of measurement and method of measurement have all affected the magnitudes arrived at.[5] An estimate based on Central Water Commission (CWC) data places waterlogging as a percentage of irrigation potential created at between 0.22 per cent and 14 per cent for different states in India. Further, it is not related solely to the level of development in the state.

In Punjab, which epitomises the success story of Indian agriculture, waterlogging is limited to about 5 per cent of irrigation potential created. It must be noted also that this is a state where groundwater potential has been almost fully utilised, and there exists a network of canals. It is the conjunctive use of surface and ground water, the appropriate soil and drainage conditions and the suitable institutional support which have made the new technology sustainable at the level of productivity that it reached in the late eighties.

TABLE 1

Waterlogging and Salinity

Sl. No.	*State*	*Waterlogged area as a percentage of irrigation potential created (upto 1990)*
1.	Andhra Pradesh	8.65
2.	Bihar	13.19
3.	Gujarat	7.07
4.	Haryana	11.11
5.	Karnataka	1.83
6.	Kerala	2.40
7.	Madhya Pradesh	0.22
8.	Maharashtra	0.31
9.	Orissa	13.80
10.	Punjab	5.17
11.	Rajasthan	9.25
12.	Uttar Pradesh	0.94
13.	Tamil Nadu	1.14
14.	Jammu and Kashmir	0.97
	Total	5.90

Source: CWC unpublished data from Office of Member, Water Planning, Government of India, New Delhi, 1989.

It does not follow from this that an expansion of the same technology to other areas will have similar impact. Reports from the command area of the Indira Gandhi Canal in nearby Rajasthan confirm this (for detailed information, see Urmul Trust, 1992). The hard pan layer underlying the desert soils creates a hydrological barrier which, by preventing seepage, results in rise in water tables at a rate of 1 to 8 metres per year. Whereas large areas are already facing the problem of waterlogging, the threat of probable degradation of 38.09 per cent of the Stage 1 command area remains. Further, studies carried out in Stage 2 reveal that in 33.8 per cent of the area a hard pan existed within five metres of the surface. This seems typical as similar situations have arisen with regard to irrigation projects elsewhere.[6] Such situations are clear instances of an ecological barrier to the unquestioning replication of a top-down irrigation-fertiliser-based technology. Under some sets of circumstances, the process of agricultural development that it results in is bound to be unsustainable.

Expansion of irrigation-fertiliser-based technology often implies the construction of large reservoir-based projects at appropriate sites. These mega projects alter natural systems by affecting patterns of land-use in their catchment areas as well. The total impact on the system must induce this change, which at times takes the form of forest degradation as well. Two questions can be asked in this context. Firstly, what is the incremental cost of the alteration in natural systems in the catchment in addition to that in the command? Alternatively, in view of the irreversible nature of some kinds of changes in natural eco-systems, is it permissible at all? Some estimates which have a bearing on both these questions[7] are now presented.

It is postulated that the increased cost of creating a hectare of irrigation potential depends on the relative location of the catchment and the command areas of the project being considered. This seemingly apparent statement is the consequence of the variety in the forest types found in India and the variation in the magnitudes of waterlogging and salinity in different canal commands. Data from about 105 projects are put together to determine the catchment/command area ratio and further, the ratio of forest area in the command. Further, on the basis of alternative estimates of the value of a hectare of forest land lost,[8] the incremental cost of creating irrigation potential (equal to one hectare in the command) is obtained. The results, presented in Table 2, give an estimate of this increase for projects affecting different kinds of forests and having command area lying in different states. If only use value of forests is taken into account, this increase lies in the range of 21 to 26 per cent. Such an increase is likely to affect economic viability, and more important, sustainability even if it is assumed that the loss can be made up for.

Availability of groundwater has been the basis for the expansion and entrenchment of the irrigation-fertiliser-based biochemical technology in some regions. Notable cases are Gujarat and Western Uttar Pradesh. The use of this common property resource has had diverse impacts. While at the macro-level, only some 18 million hectare-metres of the 47.5 million hectare-metres of available groundwater is currently used, the picture with respect to level of exploitation varies from region to region. From the viewpoint of sustainability of the process of agricultural development, it is important to see that tendencies towards over-exploitation are kept in check.[9] In view of the fact that over 95 per cent of the area served by groundwater in India is commanded by privately owned wells, the possibility of over-exploitation is a very real one unless it is limited either by legal restrictions or by organisational structures. Further, in a regime of private ownership, water markets have emerged in many parts of the country. Though these markets are claimed to have ensured equitable distribution, studies have pointed out towards the danger of over-exploitation being encouraged by them. One method of avoiding this could be increasing the private cost of water exploitation in these areas by imposing a pro-rata tariff on electricity.

TABLE 2

Environmental Cost of Creating an Additional Hectare of Irrigational Potential

(as percentage of capital cost)

Location of command area	*Forest type in catchment area*		
	Tropical dry deciduous	*Tropical moist deciduous*	*Tropical thorn*
Andhra Pradesh	24.37	23.11	22.07
Gujarat	23.66	22.40	21.36
Orissa	26.71	25.46	24.42

Note: Only 'use value' of forests has been considered.

Another of these problems is concerned with long-run productivity deficiency, which reduces the marginal productivity of highly productive crop lands. Larger application of fertilisers is no substitute for poor agronomic management. The Indian Council of Agricultural Research (ICAR) has reported that micronutrient deficiencies have become a major constraint on crop production in India's present agricultural programmes. Two surveys done by ICAR in 1982-83 and 1988-89 indicate some broad trends. There has been increased incidence of zinc, copper and manganese deficiency in soils, as well as boron and molybdenum in some case, with samples showing growing deficiencies in micronutrients concentrations as reported in Table 3.

TABLE 3

Micronutrient Deficiency in Selected States

State	Percentage of samples with zinc deficiency		Percentage of samples with copper deficiency		Percentage of samples with iron deficiency		Percentage of samples with manganese deficiency	
	1982-83	1988-89	1982-83	1988-89	1982-83	1988-89	1982-83	1988-89
Andhra Pradesh	37	72.6	0	0	0	10	0	6.2
Bihar	58	48.2	29	2	3	4	2	0.6
Gujarat	26	N.A.	0	N.A.	17	N.A.	0	N.A.
Haryana	80	18.3	0	0	72	62	1	0
Madhya Pradesh	86	67.1	0	0	3	7	3	0
Pondicherry	10	—	0	N.A.	0	N.A.	2	N.A.
Punjab	25	12.5	0	2.5	110	4		
Tamil Nadu	31	81.2	5	23	44	31	3	9
Uttar Pradesh	94	69.0	3	48	30	29	1	40
All States	47	67.0	2	15	24	23	1	7.2

Source: All India Coordinated Scheme of Micro and Secondary-Nutrients and Pollutant Elements in Soils and Plants, 22nd Annual Report, 1988-89, Indian Institute of Soil Science, Bhopal, 1991; All India Coordinated Scheme of Micronutrients in Soils and Plants, 16th Annual Report, 1982-83, Indian Council of Agricultural Research, New Delhi.

On balance, most productivity-oriented environments seem to come up against constraints, when viewed from the sustainabilily angle. A close watch needs to be kept on their ecological costs. Simultaneously, a good mix of market and non-market instruments to keep these costs within acceptable ranges has to be evolved. Even so, it is clear that new technologies with a focus on sustainability also need to be developed.

III
SUSTAINABILITY INVESTMENTS AS AN ALTERNATIVE STRATEGY

Another equally significant issue concerns the form that agricultural development in rainfed areas of the country takes. A large part of non-forest wasteland, estimated to be about 95 million hectares, lies in this zone. And for wasteland where the potential productivity is higher than actual productivity, the challenge of formulating sustainable (or for that matter any) agricultural development strategies remains, by and large, untackled. More than 60 per cent of this land lies in the Central Plateau region where terrain is undulating and exploitable water is lower than the national average. This resource endowment coexists with a variety of property rights in land. The two together make the area unsuited for the adoption of a state-run canal system or a privately operated tubewell system. Simultaneously, however, the percentage of the population below the poverty line is in the range of 40 to 49 per cent as compared to 38 per cent for the country as a whole so that income and productivity are crucial.[10]

The strategy that is beginning to emerge in this context is the outcome of a variety of experiments conducted at local level.[11] The common element underlying these experiments, diverse though they are, is "the preservation of land and water resources, *in situ* for intensive use and management through a holistic perspective of agricultural systems". Simultaneously an in-depth understanding of local resources and institutions is the other starting point of most of such initiatives, be it the Pani Panchayat of Salunkhe, Annasaheb's experiment in Ralegaon Sidhi or the Sukhomajri experiment. The technology adopted varies from region to region. In regions with annual rainfall above 700 to 800 mm, and with appropriate sites, rain water harvesting has been tried successfully. In regions with lesser rainfall, other measures for soil and water conservation have been attempted. In some situations, the focus has been on agro-forestry; in others on groundwater recharge for rangeland protection and in still others on rain water harvesting for irrigation.

From the viewpoint of agricultural development, gains from such experiments may be limited. Cropping intensity increases by 5 to 15 per cent and incremental yields by 0.5 to 1.0 per tonne hectare. However, the consequent increases of 60 to 100 per cent in the productivity of large tracts of arid and semi-arid land will make a significant difference to the nation's foodgrain budget. More importantly, this increase shall be compatible with the protection of soil and forest resources. In other words, natural capital is kept intact in this approach which aims to increase productivity by starting from the local level.

The increasing number of such local level experiments

emerging in different parts of India validate the viewpoint that this approach constitutes an alternative. Note, however, that its success is ensured only under a specific set of circumstances. In regions where degradation has crossed a certain critical level, it may need to be supplemented by direct government intervention to constitute an effective poverty alleviation strategy.[12] Further, the socio-legal system must evolve in a complementary fashion. The major requirements of such evolution are a decentralised system of decision-making and a degree of participatory resource management with a set of communal norms that govern such management. In other words, the process of technological change rooted in the preservation of local level resources reveals the complementarities as well as the incompatibilities between ensuring sustainability and achieving productivity increases in the context of existing institutional structures.[13] Similar problems are steam-rollered by top-down technologies in initial stages. Later, they result in inconsistencies between productivity, sustainability and equity goals. Grass-root-based technological change, on the other hand, tackles these issues head on. It requires, however, a large input of local level leadership, a resource which may be in short supply in most developing country situations.

IV
DIRECTIONS FOR FUTURE POLICY

Two types of agricultural investments have been focused in this paper: those that increase productivity but may not necessarily sustain agricultural productivity in the long-run and those that ensure conservation and to a limited extent raise productivity.[14] In the next phase of its development, Indian agriculture shall have to consider both types for adoption. It shall, however, have to be kept in mind that when the primary goal is one or the other, negative repercussions for the other are kept within limits.

Another significant policy conclusion is that the two types of investments seem to indicate different kinds of approaches to government intervention in the agricultural sector. A top-down approach to such intervention shall have to rely on easily replicable, capital intensive solutions. Approaches that start from the grass-roots are not, in general, as capital intensive. The major input they require is human resources to act as catalysis in the process. The corresponding benefit in the latter kind of approaches is that social acceptability of the technological change has to be reckoned within the initial stages. Large scale centrally engineered technological change seems to assume that both ecology and social institutions shall mould themselves in its wake. At times such assumptions are realised. When they are not, both the ecological and social sustainability of the change may be threatened. In the climate of decentralised decision-making, it shall become important to examine seriously the potential of technological change which begins at the other end of the spectrum.

Notes and References

1. An early writing in this area is the article by King (1911) (as quoted by Tibaldi, 1991) who referred to the centuries old agriculture of East Asia as sustainable. See also Tibaldi (1992).
2. See Swaminathan (1977) for an expression of such a view.
3. For further analysis of these interlinkages, see Chopra and Rao (1992).
4. See Norgaard (1981) for an exposition of this view.
5. See Sinha (1986) for a discussion of these issues.
6. See Holling (1992) for details of a case study for a semi-arid part of Spain. Large areas in the U.S. are known to face similar problem.
7. See Chopra *el al.* (1993), in particular Section 9 for the detailed estimates.
8. In one approximation, only the use value is taken whereas in another use, option and existence value is taken. The latter accounts in some way for the irreversible nature of the loss of forest land.
9. For an analysis of groundwater and related problems, see Shah (1991).
10. One could argue alternatively that these regions be supplied by the state subsidised net works of food distribution. However, the track record of public distribution systems in India is one of increasing cost and poor targeting efficiency with respect to the poor. See, among others, Tyagi (1990) and Dev and Suryanarayana (1991).
11. For a description of such experiments, see Alagh (1990), Rajagopalan (1991) and Chopra and Kadekodi (1993).
12. See Chopra and Kadekodi (1993). Note, however, that under some circumstances, a natural-capital-based strategy shall be the only one that results in self-sustaining growth.
13. A study of attempts at such change, for instance, the Chakriya Vikas Pranali in Bihar brings out these issue succinctly.
14. To recapitulate, examples of the first are intensive use of irrigation and

the second category includes tie-ridging that prevents run-off and conserves the soil, integrated pest management or biotechnology.

REFERENCES

Alagh, Y.K. (1990), "Agro-Climatic Planning and Regional Development", *Indian Journal of Agricultural Economics*, Vol. 45, No. 3, July-September.

Chopra, Kanchan and Gopal, K. Kadekodi (1993), "Watershed Development: A Contrast with NREP/JRY", *Economic and Political Weekly*, Vol. 28, No. 26, June 26, pp. A61-A66.

Chopra, Kanchan and C.H. Hanumantha Rao (1992), "The Links Between Sustainable Growth and Poverty", *Quarterly Journal of International Agriculture*, Vol. 31, No. 4, pp. 364-79.

Chopra, Kanchan; G.K. Kadekodi, and Nandita Mongia (1993), *Environmental Impacts of Projects: Planning and Policy Issues*, Working Paper, Institute of Economic Growth, Delhi.

Conway, G. (1985), "Agro-Ecosystem Analysis", *Agricultural Administration*, Vol. 20, No. 1, pp. 31-35.

Daly, H.E. (1990), "Towards Some Operational Principles of Sustainable Development", *Ecological Economics*, Vol. 2, pp. 1-6.

Dev, S. Mahendra and M.H. Suryanarayana (1991), "Is PDS Urban Biased and Pro-Rich: An Evaluation", *Economic and Political Weekly*, Vol. 26, No. 41, October 12, pp. 2357-66.

Food and Agriculture Organization of the United Nations (FAO) (1989), *Sustainable Agricultural Production: Implications for International Agricultural Research*, Rome.

•Holling, C.S. (1992), "New Investments, New Science for the New Class of Problem", Paper presented at the Second Meeting of the International Society for Ecological Economics, Stockholm.

10. Jodha, N.S. (1991), "Sustainable Agriculture in Fragile Resource Zones: Technological Imperatives", *Economic and Political Weekly*, Vol. 26, No. 13, March 30, pp. A-15-A-26.

King, Franklin (1911), *Farmers of Forty Centuries: Permanent Agriculture in China, Korea and Japan*.

National Wastelands Development Board (1987), *Cultivating India's Wastelands*, Ministry of Environment and Forests, Government of India, New Delhi.

Norgaard, R.B. (1981), "Socio-System and Eco-System: Coevolution in the Amazon", *Journal of Environmental Economics and Management*, Vol. 8, pp. 238-54.

Parikh, K. and U. Ghosh (1991), "Natural Resource Accounting for Soils: Towards an Empirical Estimate of Costs of Soil Degradation for India", DP-48, Indira Gandhi Institute of Development Research, Bombay.

Rajagopalan, V. (1991), "Integrated Watershed Development in India: Some

Problems and Perspectives", *Indian Journal of Agricultural Economics*, Vol. 46, No. 3, July-September, pp. 241-50.

Shah, Tushaar, (1991), "Water Markets and Irrigation Development in India", *Indian Journal of Agricultural Economics*, Vol. 46, No. 3, July-September, pp. 335-47.

Sinha, B.P.C. (1986), "Waterlogging and Drainage Problems in India: An Overview", in Central Ground Water Board (1986), *Seminar on Conjunctive Use of Surface and Groundwater Resources*, New Delhi (Pre-Seminar Volume Papers).

Swaminathan, M.S. (1977), "Indian Agriculture at the Cross-roads", *Indian Journal of Agricultural Economics*, Vol. 32, No. 4, October-December, pp. 1-34.

Tibaldi, E. (1992), "Organic Agriculture for Sustainable Development", *Journal of Society for International Development*, Vol. 3, pp. 77-80.

Tyagi, D.S. (1990), *Managing India's Food Economy: Problems and Alternatives*, Sage Publications, New Delhi.

Urmul Trust (1992), *The Nahar Yatra: A Report on the Indira Gandhi Canal*, Mid-Day Publications, Bombay.

PART B

Decentralised Planning: Issues and Training Implications: An Analytical Framework

Amitava Mukherjee and B.N. Yugandhar

I. RECENT DEVELOPMENTS IN DECENTRALISATION

Against the background of rising expectations and belied promises, governments in all developing countries have been turning their attention once more to decentralisation of planning. Decentralised planning was viewed more as a policy option rather than a theoretical scheme because the factors promoting the change of direction are the leaders 'concern about the deteriorating quality of life, particularly in rural areas; the increasing disenchantment with contemporary development theory; the belief that shifts in policy, if not in ideological positions, were warranted, and the determination to overcome the bottlenecks emanating from over-centralisation in every sphere of economic activity.

*This paper was published in *IASSI Quarterly* (Vol. 10, No. 2). It is published with kind permission of the editor of the journal.

Governments in several developing countries had taken on too many responsibilities in the first place because they felt that in a period of transition, centralised leadership was necessary to instil planning discipline and ensure rapid socio-economic development. As it turned out, in many developing countries, central direction reached an extreme limit, and the *ex post* consequences were different from the *ex ante* ones: instead of rapid economic development, several developing countries sank into the depth of economic poverty and the dream of economic and technological advancement turned into a nightmare, tormented by the scarcity of food, energy problems, balance of payments and external debt crisis, as well as the crisis of economic management. India has been no exception to this general rule.

The inhabitants of our rural areas have particularly been exposed to unbelievably harsh conditions. The damage done to their home and hearth, and to food and cash crops by floods, droughts and desert encroachment has been phenomenal, and for years, the rural communities have borne their pains and sufferings in silence. They provided back-breaking labour which produced crops for export and for domestic consumption, but their direct incomes remained very low and the real incomes which urban dwellers enjoyed, in terms of access to amenities and conveniences such as electricity and water supply subsidized energy, specialist and general medical treatment, basic technical and vocational education, etc. were denied to the majority of rural inhabitants. Poverty, illiteracy, disease, malnutrition, shorter life-expectancy and high rates of infant mortality are major maladies afficting all poor communities, but they are particularly malignant in rural India. Bringing the benefits of science and technology to the threshold of the common people to relieve them of their distress is one of the greatest challenges facing our society.[1]

In line with the general disenchantment with the living conditions in rural areas, some countries have come to the conclusion that contemporary development theory needed to be re-examined. In several African countries, for instance, the government began to take a broad view of development as early as from the late 60s and the early 70s that "development" was viewed as being more than economic growth alone, and it was believed that the concept of growth ought to encompass socio-cultural and political development.[2] In particular, there has been a growing recognition that the extent to which a community participated in decisions affecting its welfare and destiny was a mark of development, which is deemed by many as a direct onslaught on the "modernization" theory which for years lent credence to the centralised structure of government planning and the paternalistic orientation of bureaucrats and public officials. There can be no debate that if cultural pluralism is not antithetical to the goal of development, then decentralisation in planning and governance cannot be an illegitimate strategy of nation-building and national integration.

Moreover, despite the absence of any system of governance and planning that is completely centralised, the systems which most countries adopted at Independence were characterised by a higher centralised bias, but the prevailing political imperatives in most countries (which include ideological stances and, in some cases, competing social/group interests), coupled with administrative imperatives, (emanating out of administering far flung territories with under-developed social and economic infrastructure, large and unevenly distributed rural populations, and diverse and complex local conditions) have driven an increasing number of countries to go in for more decentralised systems of governance, planning and administration. Decentralisation of planning, therefore, is viewed, as a political strategy directed towards, *inter alia*, the promotion of increasing people's participation in the initiation, planning and implementation of development programmes, equity in resource allocation, and greater accountability of bureaucracy and public administrators to elected bodies. It is increasingly being recognised as a more effective system for developing local level economy, and for managing public affairs. It can be argued that decentralisation in planning is likely to increase: one, the flexibility in planning operations both with regard to plan formulation and implementation, as the decision-making process is brought nearer to the scene of action and, therefore, increases the speed of response and cuts down administrative costs; two, mobilisation of local resources towards solving immediate problems; and three, more effective coordination of development activities at the levels to which powers have been handed down.[3]

II. MAIN FORMS OF DECENTRALISATION

The two most commonly recognised forms of decentralisation are devolution and decentralisation, though admittedly all decentralised planning system may not fit clearly into either of the two prototypes.[4] The distinction between the two is based on: (a) the types of powers to plan or planning functions that have been transferred from the higher to the lower tiers, (b) the way in which powers and functions of planning have been handed downs, and (c) the persons or agencies to which these have been handed down.

	Devolution	*Decentralisation*
(a) Powers of functions transferred.	Decision/policy-making powers	powers to execute central or State Government policies.
(b) Mode of transfer	Constitutional or ordinary legislation.	Administrative measures.
(c) Person/agencies to which power has been handed down.	(Quasi) autonomous regional/local bodies Special statutory bodies.	Local representatives of central government. Field units of some department or level of government.

The nature or form that decentralisation in planning takes and the extent of delegation that occurs are determined primarily by:

(i) Political considerations, particularly so, the motivation or demand for decentralisation (whether it is in response to pressure from below or to values or ideas articulated by political leadership), and

(ii) Political and administrative expediencies, which terms include the economics of polities.

III. PRE-REQUISITIES FOR SUCCESSFUL DECENTRALISATION OF PLANNING TO LOCAL LEVEL

This brings us to the issues of pre-requisites for successful decentralisation to local level. The most important pre-requisites for effective decentralisation of planning and administration are:

(a) Political will and confidence of the higher levels of political leadership to genuinely hand down powers and required resources to lower levels: whereas political will to resort to decentralised planning is born out of the conviction of the desirability of decentralising planning and commitment to take positive action to decentralise planning, the confidence to decentralise planning is generated by the trust that the political executive at higher levels has in the motives and capabilities of the lower tiers of governance and planning to exercise powers to plan and administer the powers, handed down to them in a positive and effective manner.

(b) Institutional arrangements adequate for effecting decentralisation in planning coupled with a clear definition and division of responsibilities between different tiers of administration and planning.

(c) Capability (in terms of technical competence and availability of resources) to tackle effectively planning at the local level itself.

(d) Linkage and coordination between local and higher levels of governance and planning.[5]

IV. DECENTRALISATION: FUTURE PRIORITIES

There is little doubt that substantial progress has been achieved in implementing decentralisation of planning in our country, nevertheless the battle against "non-decentralisation" in planning (we deliberately avoid using the word over-centralisation) is far from being won. A scheme pointing towards meaningful decentralisation in planning must resort to policies which *inter alia*, have the features of:[6]

(a) empowerment of the people,

(b) self-reformation,
(c) unity of direction,
(d) institutional flexibility and adaptability,
(e) rural transformation, and
(f) training for decentralisation.

It would be worth our while pondering over these for a short while.

(a) Empowerment of the People

The principle underlying the decentralisation of powers to plan at the local level, is that of articulating the will of the people, but many of us merely pay lip service to the idea of popular participation without being committed to it. Even when "local governments" are established, their planning operation seemingly proceeds as directed by some form of central authority or State authority. (For instance in Karnataka though local level planning through Zilla Parishads and other Panchayati Raj Institutions have had been established in 1986, plans for local level development were drawn up till 1987-88 at the State headquarters). The "field units" of planning departments of the government do not fare better, for their staffing, accounting and financial processes are decided upon at the State headquarters rather than out there in the field. For the objectives of decentralisation in planning to be successful in the true sense of the term, the powers that be, should seriously consider alternatives to their paternalistic, top-down and, most frequently, condescending attitudes to local level planning machinery and plan implementation machinery. The people or functionaries who man the local level planning and plan implementation machinery should be credited with some intelligence, and should be encouraged to take decisions affecting their areas of concern and jurisdiction notwithstanding the mistakes that will be committed during the initial phases.

(b) Self-reformation

Closely related to empowerment of the people is self-reformation. While the Central Government or the State Governments have a vital role to play in setting broad development targets and defining the code of conduct for local leaders, the decision appertaining to particular local functionaries being retained in office or otherwise should be left to the discretion of each community. Yea, the local communities require the services of persons who are public spirited, dedicated, with managerial capability, and who have foresight, probity, and sensitivity to environmental needs. Nevertheless, the best performance appraisal of local leaderships on the touchstone of the above attributes is done by the local people, and not by administrative fiat by State or Central political directive. Accountability should be to the people served and not to an authority operating far away from the scene of action at the Central Government or State capital.

(c) Unity of Direction

Any future attempt at decentralisation in the process of planning, should be informed by the fact that, the development of a structure capable of ensuring that all the institutions operating at a local level towards the same direction, with service to the community as their aim, is imperative. These institutions (like, local "field" offices of development agencies and departments, local offices of Central and State parastatal organisations, farmers' unions, non-governmental organisations, and community development associations) should be part of an integrated Local Development Authority under the general and managerial control of a Local Government Chairman, like the Adakshya, or the Sabhadipati, howsoever diversely designated they may be in various states. If the hopes and aspirations of the local people are not to be belied the discordant tunes produced by the "solo players" must be replaced with the beautiful symphony of an orchestra under an able conductor.

(d) Institutional Flexibility and Adaptability

Institutional flexibility (the design and operation of a local level planning machinery and plan implementation machinery which responds to the specifine needs of the various communities) is the fourth problem which should be of major concern for policy-makers both at the Central and at the State levels. Bias towards a "uniform" local arrangement for plan formulation and plan implementation needs to be critically re-examined bearing in mind that the problems facing the different local level areas are as diverse as the areas themselves: some are densely populated, others have their populations scattered over vast territories: some are located in riverine areas, others are somewhere in the middle of a desert, some are industrialised, others are agricultural or fishing communities and so on.

(e) Rural Transformation

Granted that the bulk of the people in India reside in the villages and in the rural areas, decentralisation in planning should be used as a strategy for transforming the rural communities into islands of development and for correcting the urban-rural imbalance. We shall have occasion to discuss this in detail later, and therefore suffice it to say for the present that rural communities must feel the impact of governments' development efforts having a bearing on their lives.

(f) Training for Decentralisation

It is clear from the preceding sections that training has an important role to play in promoting the objectives of decentralisation of planning upto the local level. The training question can be better looked into if we are clear in our minds about the key issues and challenges of decentralised planning, to which we shall presently turn.

V. DECENTRALISATION: KEY ISSUES AND CHALLENGES[7]

The most fundamental issue relates to the concern and limitations of Central and State Governments as instruments of development; governments whether Central or State, ought not to assume total responsibility for economic development because:

> Firstly, government efforts to do so are inevitably circumscribed by the need to accord priority to the interest of the individuals and groups who constitute 'the government' and because 'development' is only meaningful for people if it is initiated and controlled by them. The development forces to be long-lasting and all-pervasive must be based fundamentally in the developing community. The role of Central and State governments should, therefore, be that of a facilitator to the people to develop themselves and not to direct or determine the direction and magnitude of such development.

Secondly, decentralisation in planning is inextricably linked with popular participation, in making, implementing and evaluating the impact of decisions pertaining to local level development. Furthermore, popular participation in the planning system appears to be a necessary condition in bringing about adequate decentralisation of administrative powers and resources to the local level to ensure that decisions pertaining to local level development are taken and acted upon by people themselves according to their felt needs and aspirations.

Thirdly, the issues appertaining to decentralization of planning are those that evoke the idea akin to that of a conflict of 'power struggle' between the centre and the periphery and, therefore, it is often viewed with suspicion by central or higher level authorities, which is, to some extent, inevitable because decentralisation of planning carries with it the implication of handling down of control over resources and power from the higher levels to the lower tiers. The circumstances under which and the extent to which the State or the Central Governments are ready and willing to introduce genuine decentralisation in planning and tolerate the establishment of effective participatory institutions and organisations at the local level leading to further redistribution of power and command over resources to the particularly disadvantaged groups and communities in society throw up extremely sensitive issues. A large part of the "conflict" partaking the nature of a fight between the "Centre" and a "Periphery" would perhaps be resolved if the body of notions of planning which treats the people as the "periphery" *vis-a-vis* the Central or State Government as the "Centre" is reprobated.

Fourthly, as has been stated above, decentralisation of planning is often aspired to, as a means of achieving several different political and administrative ends, but given both the historical background of our planning system and the political reality now obtaining, many of these ends are not only difficult to achieve but also, are, at least in a few cases, in conflict with each other. There are, for example, some who maintain that an inherent conflict exists between the ends of efficiency in planning and in resource allocation and use on the one hand, and those of peoples' participation in planning and plan implementation on the other. The manner in which the major prerequisites for achieving the principal aims of decentralisation in planning are achieved and the manner in which the requirements for decentralised planning and administration, warranting the decentralisation of effective power and authority over resources, reconciled with the apparent requirement of some central authority to implement and coordinate important activities, need to be looked into at length.

Fifthly, the administrative viability, in terms of availability of manpower and financial resources of the right variety, at the level to which powers to plan and implement plans are decentralised, as well as the scope and degree of people's participation within that level, largely influence the effectiveness of decentralised planning. What then is the optimal size of the areas or units to which planning powers should be decentralised: the region/province, district, sub-district or village? These and related issues have generated considerable debate but the issues are as yet far from conclusively resolved.

Sixthly, decentralisation of planning essentially concerns the distribution of powers within a political system, and administrative organisation at various levels of government is closely related to the division of powers. The question then is: which individuals or organs should exercise what powers or responsibilities (including powers appertaining to policy-making, raising resources and controlling expenditure in each subject area) at each level of governance and planning. Should the entities exercising these powers be political or elected representative bodies (such as Panchayati Raj Institutions) or should they be appointees of State or Central Government. And, most difficult of all, is the question relating to the steps that are to be taken to ensure that the distribution of power that is agreed upon, is actually implemented in action and does not remain confined to the statute book.

Finally, the role that training can play in improving

individual and organisational performance, particularly so within a newly-instituted decentralised system of planning organisation and administration has to be addressed, which raises the additional question of what should be meant by 'training', in the context of decentralization of planning to the local level. Our concern should be with how those involved in decentralised planning can acquire a body of knowledge, skills, attitudes and values essential for operating effectively a decentralised system of governance and planning. Appropriate knowledge, skills, attitudes and values can be acquired through several avenues, and through exchanges between many different types of actors, including the people themselves and not necessarily only through conventional training activities. In other words, the concern is with 'learning' rather than 'training' in the conventional sense, and learning in its broadest sense. The word 'training' here is, therefore, used in its broader connotation, and with reference to the fifth issue listed above.

VI. ISSUES IN TRAINING FOR DECENTRALISED PLANNING

Flowing from the last issue read with the fifth issue in the preceding section, the insufficient number of technical as well as administrative personnel within the various levels of decentralised government structures and the changing roles of the different actors within the system, are areas of major concern for us. Granted that any decentralised system of planning requires, in order to be both efficient and effective, a comprehensive and dynamic approach to training, the main issues pertaining to training, therefore, are basically eleven:

1. How can training be linked to the individual and organizational needs of the different actors (or target groups) within a decentralised system of planning and governance at the different levels of operation to increase the effectiveness of decision-making appertaining to planning, execution and coordination of development efforts?
2. What should be the mode of assessing training needs for

Decentralised Planning in our present multi-level planning structure?

3. In view of the "scarcity of resources", who should constitute the main target groups for training, and in what order: the central political and national leaders, the elected representatives particularly those at the local levels to which powers and authority to plan have been decentralised, the functionaries of central and state governments (including officials of central government in the field and local self-government managers/ administrators), the field level technical/functional workers, or local/village level leaders and the general public?

   The mechanisms for identifying training needs of the various categories of actors in the area of decentralised planning can be regrouped into two types: one, the new entrants into the system and two, those already working in the system. While for the former, their training needs will be determined by their educational background and work experience, for the latter group, training needs will be a function of their educational background, their performance appraisal, their job description as also the goals of the government with regard to their succession planning. In either case, how should the individual training needs be matched with the institutional requirements and expectations of the functions to be discharged by the various actors?

4. What should constitute the main content or elements of training for each of the different target groups: appropriate technical and administrative skills; an understanding of the socio-political imperatives of the decentralised planning environment in which the various actors would operate, or re-orientation of the main actors of a decentralised planning set-up? These aspects have to be considered in relation to the changing roles of the State and Central Governments as facilitators of the development process where the people (either through their elected representatives and/or local level participatory organisations) assume increasingly greater responsibilities in decision-making appertaining to their

local level development, while administrators as well as technical staff play the secondary role of providing administrative support, technical help and coordination of development activities.

5. Who should provide training for each of the target groups and coordinate training programmes for decentralised planning? In this regard what should be:

    (i) role of Central and State Government Ministries and departments in curriculum development, in implementing training programmes and in the coordination of training;
    (ii) role of academic and training institutions (like Colleges, Universities, Administrative Training Institutes, State Institutes for Rural Development and the like) in the training process;
    (iii) role of specific or specialised professional training institutions (like the I.T.I.s, I.I.T.s, and I.I.M.s) in the training process;
    (iv) impact of trainer' experience and orientation on curriculum development and on the effectiveness of training programmes; and
    (v) role of the people as trainers and the scope for learning through experience sharing between individuals and combination of individuals at the local level?

6. What training approaches/methods should be adopted from amongst the following:

    (i) on-the-job training;
    (ii) seminars and workshops, using case-study methods;
    (iii) experimental training methods, and the like;
    (iv) formal courses which combine lecturing methods with field attachment/practice;
    (v) study tours;
    (vi) mobile training modules, libraries and resource centres;
    (vii) festivals and simulation exercises;
    (viii) dramas and film shows; or
    (ix) youth and peer group meetings, and the like ?

7. What should be the resources for training; a strengthened institutional capacity, that is, increased availability of adequate and appropriate training aids/ materials, adequate funds, and legislation to ensure sufficient autonomy or other requirements.
8. What should be the sources for funding the training for decentralised planning?

   (i) Central, State and Local Government funds set aside for training;
   (ii) external technical assistance; or
   (iii) internal revenue raised through levies and fees consultancies and cost-saving measures by undertaking self-reliant projects?
9. Wherefrom would commitment and support for training for decentralised planning come, given that Government support for training is demonstrated through its budgetary allocations to training activities ? One might add here that commitment of government officials to take up decentralised planning training could be obtained by making training much more rewarding through issue of recognised diplomas: salary rise after successful completion of training of a set standard; improved prospects for promotion after completing successfully a set of specified training courses; and linking certain promotions to successful completion of specialised training courses.
10. What is the concept of Trainers and Training of Trainers for decentralised planning, given that:

    (i) any official with a subordinate is a trainer or a potential trainer, and peers can become trainers through experimental training courses,
    (ii) the term trainers includes opinion leaders, training and educational institutions, and institutional agencies for training that might exist,
    (iii) trainers require extensive training both in knowledge sought to be imparted to the trainees, and in effective communication skills and knowledge of

decentralisation planning policies, methods and guidelines, and

(iv) training capability of trainers can be enhanced through undertaking research/evaluation studies relating to operation of decentralised planning mechanism; producing case studies to be used as teaching materials; undertaking study tours in and outside the country; and through seminars, workshops, refresher courses, and the like?

11. What should be the mode of evaluation of training for Decentralised Planning ?

VII. QUALITATIVE TRAINING NEEDS IN THE INDIAN CONTEXT[8]

Let us take up the second key issue first: assessment of training needs. The point of departure, then, for assessing the training needs is the extent of decentralisation in planning proposed and the planning process envisaged and the various decentralised planning procedures associated with it which are all pre-designed for a given context. In a country of India's size with its federal structure, a decentralised system of planning is by all accounts a complex phenomenon. There would be inter-state variations in the procedures for planning at the local level and fitting in the decentralised plans with the general planning procedure that is followed today at the State and Central levels, which has a bearing on the estimation of training needs, is not an easy affair. Some commonalities may be expected to emerge in the institutionalization of the democratic framework and in the decentralisation process, which may be taken as the basis for identifying the key steps and key actors and then broadly derive the training needs.

Our assessment of training needs for decentralised planning may be based on three fairly well conceived experiments in this regard in the country, viz. West Bengal, Gujarat and Karnataka models. Against this backdrop, the key steps and the key actors in decentralised planning would be as follows:

	Key Steps	*Key Actors*
1.	Preparation of a needs statement or the most acutely felt problems of the Panchayat area.	Gram Panchayat
2.	Preparation of maps of the local area/block, outlining the existing facilities, resources and resource use.	Panchayat Samiti
3.	Technical assistance to the Gram Panchayats to projectise their "needs" (with the help of overseers and engineers).	Block level Overseers and District Engineers and other officials of the sectoral departments at the block/district level.
4.	Preparation of a statement of the on-going and proposed programme of plan outlay of different departments/authorities in each block.	Block Development Officer
5.	Collating the "needs statement" or what may appear as "Charter of demands" at first inspection of Gram Panchayats and drawing up the schemes to meet the most pressing needs of the gram panchayats.	Block Development Officer and other Block level officials.
6.	Approving the schemes for forwarding to the planning authorities at the district headquarters.	Panchayat Samiti
7.	Scrutiny of the block plans and schemes; drawing up schemes aimed at finding solution to major area problems and prioritising development schemes in accordance with the goals and strategies of District Development.	District Planning Committee through its Sub-committees
8.	Vetting of the District Plan and its final approval.	District Planning and Coordination Council (Zilla Parishad)

Clearly enough, the third key issue raised in the preceding section is answered from the foregoing in as much as the target groups needing training on different aspects of decentralised planning could be identified as follows:

(i) The Gram Panchayat Officials,
(ii) The Gram Panchayats Chairman/Vice-Chairman.
(iii) Panchayat Samiti Chairman and members.
(iv) Members of the District Planning Committee or Board,
(v) Members of other Sub-Committees of Planning Boards or Committees,
(vi) Members of the District Planning Coordination Committees or Boards,
(vii) Members of the District Planning Council (Zilla Parishads).
(viii) Heads of District Offices (Line departments),
(ix) Assistants dealing with planning matters in the district level offices of the government, and
(x) Functionaries at the Block level.

It is important to note that in-service training and the post-entry training are deemed as equally important, because decentralisation implies a transformation in attitudes on the part of the functionaries who will be manning and promoting decentralised planning at different spatial and institutional level. To enable them to imbibe the right attitudes, it is necessary to introduce training for decentralised planning as an important component of post-entry training at the Central, State and local levels.

Thus broadly the officers or functionaries for training in decentralised planning in the India context may be classified as follows:

A. For Post-Entry Training

(i) All India Level—Officers of the higher Civil Services particularly of the I.A.S. and I.F.S.
(ii) State Level—Officers recruited by the State Public Service Commissions.
(iii) Local Level—Officers recruited by the State or Local Service Commission.

B. For In-Service Training

(i) Civil Servants who supervise and coordinate district and sub-district planning activities at the district level (that is, District Magistrates, Collectors or Deputy

Commissioners; District Development Officers; Chief Secretary, Zilla Parishad).

(ii) Policy-making personnel at the State level belonging to the State Planning and Statistical Departments.

(iii) Personnel operating special and area-based programmes whose plans have to be integrated into the district and sub-district plans as the case may be.

(iv) Members of the district planning team such as the District Development Officer, District Planning Officer, the District Statistical Officer and the District Economic Officer.

(v) Heads of Departments at the District level of agriculture, animal husbandry, cooperation, industry, and such other departments.

(vi) Assistants dealing with planning matters in the district offices of line departments.

(vii) Block Development Officers and other block-level line agency officials.

(viii) Village Panchayat Officials.

(ix) Non-Officials of the Panchayats (Gram Panchayat Pradhans, Subhadipatis and so on).

(x) Non-official members of Zilla Parishad and District Planning Board and Committees (if such organisations exist) and sub-committees of such Boards and Committees.

(xi) Faculty in the training institutions (for Trainer's Training).

The above is a long illustrative list of target groups, though not an exhaustive one, for training in decentralised planning. Any attempt to quantify their number would lead to staggering figures which indicates the magnitude of the task and complexity of efforts involved in training for decentralised planning.[9]

VIII. FOCUS OF THE PRESENT DISCUSSION

This paper will deal specifically with only two vital aspects with regard to All India Level Officers, namely:

The training objectives of the target group and the

knowledge, skills and attitudes to be developed, given the major technical tasks and steps involved in Local Level Planning which would determine the qualitative content of training for decentralised planning; and

the basic training packages that are necessary to meet the training needs of the target groups.

Against the backdrop of the process of planning and at the local level (with the specification of key steps and key actors), as detailed in Section VII above, the technical tasks involved in the decentralised planning process may be set forth in terms of several specific tasks and steps. A check list of such specific tasks and steps is at Appendix A.

IX. THE TRAINING OBJECTIVES

To undertake the various tasks and steps involved in local level or decentralised planning efficiently the acquisition of certain knowledge (concepts), skills (techniques), and attitudes (behaviour) is imperative. The nature of the knowledge to be imparted and the degree of its depth will be a function of the needs of each target group and the time available for the relevant training. The new entrants into the system who will be going through a post-entry training must be enabled to acquire knowledge pertaining to:

- the decentralised or local level planning process;
- tools and techniques needed for local level planning;
- participatory techniques; and
- group dynamics.

The training programme designed for the new entrants into the system ought to equip them with the required cognitive and analytical skills in dealing with both the technical system and the system of human management, enhance their decision-making capability and stimulate critical and innovative thinking related to local level planning. For the District Officers who comprise the district planning machinery (the personnel constituting the planning team at the district level) also, the training programme must have, by and large, a similar curriculum, which explains why these two categories of personnel may be deemed as constituting a homogenous group for the purposes of training for decentralised planning.

For the group of sectoral functionaries and Heads of Departments at the district level, who are specialists, the emphasis in training ought to be on the comprehensive aspects of local level planning, where the term comprehensive connotes that planning in one sector will be conditioned by the forward and backward linkages in other sectors and that a wide range of inter-disciplinary issues are to be incorporated into the planning framework. The sectoral functionaries have to be trained to overcome their narrow departmental perspective and to obtain wider visions having a total perspective of several disciplines, and at once, upgrade their skills in planning for their particular sectors with a greater degree of precision and sophistication. Clearly enough, techniques of resources analysis project formulation, problem and project prioritization, monitoring evaluation, control and stimulation will be at the heart of their training programme.

In the case of sub-district level functionaries, the training programme would focus on imparting knowledge and skills necessary for the identification of the problems of their area and the priorities. The knowledge of physical, economic and social processes that are essential to generate (of the requisite quality). Selectivity is warranted to determine the nature of skills to be imparted in a training programme, which obviously, will be a function of target groups for whom the training programme is being designed, their responsibilities.

Training programme is also related to attitudinal change, which is a complex process and the hardest one at that ability to work and interact as a member of a planning team, responsiveness to divergent views and opinions, acquisition of multi-disciplinary visions including broadening of perspectives and changing of mind-set, capability to unlearn and learn, ability to negotiate with superiors on resource allocation and project selection, ability to motivate subordinates to economise or cut on resource use, willingness to immitate and innovate, sensitivity to the results of monitoring and public criticisms, the ability to work with the common people and their representatives and the ability to manage conflicts are, *inter alia*, important elements of attitudinal changes which are desirable for a successful local level planner. In drawing up a training programme for decentralised planning (or for that matter any training programme) one should not lose sight of the fact that knowledge, skills and attitudes are an inter-related whole and one may even hazard the hypothesis that the acquisition of certain types of knowledge and skills also induce certain kinds of attitudinal change.

X. PROBLEMS OF TRAINING INDIAN ADMINISTRATIVE SERVICE OFFICERS

The problems that one faces at the Lal Bahadur Shastri National Academy of Administration, Mussoorie, in training the officers of the civil services lie in the domain of:

(a) the techniques, and
(b) the attitude.

The imparting of knowledge is relatively easy. We take the second thing first. It has been our endeavour to inculcate in the officers we train the sense that they owe allegiance to the Constitution of India, and the pride of the civil services lies in defending, preserving and protecting the Constitution as by Law established. Because allegiance to the Constitution is projected as an article of faith, the officers are told that the creators of the Constitution, namely the half-clad half-fed people of India are the ones to be served and looked after. They are urged on to:

"Go to the people
Live with them
Serve them
Respect them
Plan with them
Start with what they know
And build on what they have."

This is an extremely difficult task because it requires considerable amount of unlearning on the part of the officers. In an age when public service is at a discount, when base motives of power, self, and the allurement of a "fast buck" are at a premium, the social fabric lionizes the new entrants *to* the civil services as having achieved whatever a man wants to achieve in life. From the word "go", it is not very uncommon that an officer enters the Academy (and with it in the civil services in India) with a bloated ego, with often misplaced pride and at times vulgar motives. To bring about attitudinal change in such officers, to serve the people, and not be their masters, is a difficult task. Our real problem figuratively speaking is tantamount to transformation of picture 1 to picture 2. That is we try to imbibe in them what a distinguished civil servant has told us, "that they have to become friends before they can advise and guide ". This is particularly difficult because the civil services in India have inherited traditions from the Indian Civil Service, where the basic orientation was of a ruler and not that of an agent of change.

It is difficult to impress upon the impressionable minds that the real power rests with the people and, therefore, the question of empowerment does not arise in the conventional sense and as used in common parlance. To drive home the point we ask them to look into space specificities of the source and the nature of power; remind them that power should never be conceived of as synonymous with political power which can be transferred and re-transferred. Every human formation has its own way of creating and exercising power; has its own long history of resistance and self-defense; has an unique experience still reflected as traditions, conventions, modes of behaviour, folklores, usage and customs. They are best adapted to each particular group's culture and opportunities, and they are not residuals which are outdated and replaceable by universal recipes.

These at first appear like "words of learned length and thundering sounds" (discharged upon the trainee officers) which lead them to repeatedly ask for the definition of the role of the administrator in decentralized planning and they seek a model, a prototype, to follow. Unfortunately, we have a "somewhat distressing conclusion that there is no clear cut rule of thumb or well-established and recognised role of the administrator in decentralized planning." Because the system is so nebulous there is no cut and dried frame in terms of which an administrator as an individual can responds: this is the central problem to which different individuals have to seek their own answers, within a framework which is largely subjective at the present time. And, therefore, as Edmund Burke had said, of his source of wisdom in relation to the British Constitution, the administrator in the Indian context has to make a reference to the basic democratic, secular and socialistic goals set forth in the constitution to identify for himself his role in the kaliedoscope of the "turmoil" through which a democratic country in its adolescence passes. "This is not escapist formulations: behind it is a strongly held belief that this is the starting point on which the fundamentals of a more sophisticated decentralized planning system need to be evolved".

At the National Academy the buck does not stop at only delineating the constitutional role of the administrator: there is considerable emphasis in the development of entrepreneurial ability amongst the officers. Our efforts at developing Administrator Entrepreneurs is not directed at producing a bunch of "profit-maximizers" or "sales-maximizers" or "whatever-maximizers" you have in business and industry. Our attempt is to develop the entrepreneurial spirit in the administrator: the urge to move on; the urge to innovate; the capacity to raise resources; given the constraints and the inclination to grow. These are most important in the context of decentralized planning as we see it now and as it is likely to shape up in the foreseeable future till the end of this century, because the freedom to plan is severely circumscribed by the inflexibility in the areas falling under the district sector, because the paucity of available resources for local level planning and the pre-emption of funds by the on going schemes is very distressing. Unless the Administrators-Planners are able to innovate, raise resources and strive to move on, within these parameters, our dreams of having good local level plans will falter on the rock of reality.

This brings us to questions of techniques. Fortunately for us, the people whose training is entrusted to our care have two things overwhelmingly weighted in their favours one, they are well educated and there is an increasing technicalisation of the services (Table 1 would reveal the situation); two, they are still among the best brains in the country. These among themselves make our task with regard to techniques difficult and at once easy. Easy because their backgrounds in mathematics, engineering and sciences, pure and applied, provide considerable leeway to the faculty to use liberal doses of mathematics. Quantitative, statistical and econometric techniques and so on in the course inputs, make the teaching of sophisticated, quantitative and qualitative techniques applicable in decentralized planning so much the easier. Difficult because they have to be satisfied with the "why of everything" and not just the how of it. It would not be surprising at all if some of the trainees turn out to be better equipped, or so they believe in terms of techniques than some of their faculty. This seriously complicates the learning process.

TABLE 1

Composition of 1990 Batch of IAS Officers

(i)	Engineers	38
(ii)	M.B.B.S.	5
(iii)	Other pure science Masters/Honours Degree Holders	22
(iv)	M.B.A's	14
(v)	Economic Science Masters/Honours Degree Holders	7
(vi)	History and Social Sciences Masters/ Honours Degree Holders	16
(vii)	Masters Degree Holders in Literature	3

We do not believe that the people whom we train would themselves ever soil their hands in actually preparing district or sub-district plans. We do believe, nevertheless, that despite the contours of the administrator's role in decentralized planning being somewhat blurred, the officers we train have to be leaders building a planning team; have to facilitate the working of the planning team; will have to harness people's participation; will have to be facilitators in implementing the plans and be a link between the development agencies or Panchayati Raj Institutions and the state administration or bureaucracy in the entire scheme of things. Given the state of art, the first thing that these officers need is a sound understanding of the theoretical underpinning of decentralizing planning; its inner logic and the binding theme, and then a first hand knowledge of the "nuts and bolts" of framing a district or sub-district plan, which is particularly critical because perhaps this is the last time in their service that they get to be taught how to draw up a plan for the district or the block or whatever other unit of planning is chosen. While the theoretical basis, logic and the binding theme that runs through decentralized planning are imparted with comparative ease, the "nuts and bolts" component, of necessity, has to be restricted to an "overall methodology", it cannot be as diverse as the methodologies adopted by the different States to which these officers are allotted. This, therefore, brings forth before us, in no uncertain terms the need for a set of manuals of which the Core Planning Manual will be the hub, appertaining to plan formulation, plan implementation and plan monitoring, for the District, Block and Village level planning, collectively called here local level planning.

In the context of decentralized planning there are certain areas, like collection of data, collation of data, storage and retrieval system of data; planning procedures; resource inventory; resource generation; problem prioritization, environment impact analysis, benefit cost analysis and the like, which maybe deemed essential and integral parts of any planning exercise. These essential elements could form the Core Planning Manual which will be "inelastic" to space and State. Such a Core Planning Manual has to be very carefully planned because it means the production of a document that is expected to have, or will have, a lasting value and that will be guiding the planning "excursions" of a large number of officers and assisting in the acquisition of certain essential expertise, slant and method by a large number of functionaries down the line at the district and sub-district levels.

The Core Planning Manual will be supplemented, supported and expanded by the existing methodology of decentralized planning already developed or are being by the relative States and by the guidelines that each State might have formulated or is in the process of formulating. While the Core Planning Manual will provide the skeleton, the guidelines and methodological debates would clothe it with flesh and blood. These taken together will greatly facilitate the preparation of plans and improve the inclination of the civil service officers to dabble in decentralized planning. The Core Planning Manual will provide the required continuity and minimum rigour, whereas the supplemental elements will prevent the entire gamut of decentralized planning exercises from being circumscribed by the inflexibility of well set norms: invariant, automatic and axiomatic.

Because we envisage at the Academy that the officers of the civil service will be leaders in building a planning team, there could hardly be any debate that these officers, at least over the rest of this century, would play the role of trainers more for their subordinates, and to a lesser extent for their peers. The issues with which these officers have to immediately struggle with appertain to training of their peers and subordinates in the realms of decentralisation, the planning process, the tools and techniques of planning. That would take them directly into the sphere of preparing training materials. Whatever model of district administration a State may have, there is no gainsaying the fact that their offices will keep them very busy. It is, therefore, essential to provide them with training materials, to which we may now presently turn.

XI. TRAINING MATERIAL : MANUAL THEREFOR

The discussion earlier relating to the various target groups and the broad content of the knowledge, skills and attitudes needed by them to effectively perform the various talks and functions demanded of them in a decentralised operational context, indicates that different training is to be provided to the officers manning various positions to deal with the individual requirements of their peers and subordinates. While some basic knowledge pertaining to decentralisation, the planning process and the tools and techniques of planning may be common to many of the training packages (with varying degrees of emphasis) to be designed for the different target groups, there will also be certain specific and special requirements to be taken into account for these different categories. Hence different training material tailored to the needs of the different target groups will be required, to avoid overlaps, eliminate gaps and facilitate the training that is imparted.

XIL. THE BASIC TRAINING MANUAL AND TARGET-GROUP-SPECIFIC TRAINING MANUAL

In the context of decentralised planning, there are certain subject areas such as concepts, methods, and techniques, general planning procedures and basic exercises which may be deemed as the 'essential knowledge and skills' as emanating from the Core Planning Manual that can form the core material of a Basic Training Manual, and which would be fairly independent of placespecific considerations, rendering it into a relevant document for adoption in diverse contexts. The Basic Training Manual should be supplemented with other target-group specific training material. This will be Target Group Specific Training Manual, which will, apart from indicating what portions of the Basic Training Manual will be applicable to each of them, would further elaborate on what other specific knowledge and skills would be relevant for each of the identified target groups, which may include some job-specific instructions, tasks and functions, tips for improving performance, some rural of thumb techniques management guidance (change management skills), attitudes to be cultivated, conflict resolution techniques to be learnt, relevant to their jobs, and the like.

Thus, once the Basic Training Manual and the. Target Group Specific Training Manual are ready, the district administration will be equipped with some standardised training materials and will be in a state to run its training to train up people with some degree of confidence and competence. Indeed, the development of training materials will be a continuous exercise. From time to time, guidelines and instructions for district and lower level planners will be issued by the Planning Commission and the State Planning Departments, which will have to be suitably incorporated into the training packages. Thus, the training materials that will have been produced will be needing constant modifications and refinements.

If the ideas on the preparation of training manuals stated above are accepted, then some directions for the future are clear. The first priority in our agenda for action would be to focus our attention on the preparation of the Core Planning Manual and the Basic Training Manual for decentralised planning. Such manuals, as we have stated earlier in respect of Core Planning Manual, should be very carefully planned, as it means the production of document—that will have a lasting value and that will be guiding the training of and assisting in the imparting of certain essential knowledge, skills and attitudes to a large number of functionaries manning different positions at the local level. These Manuals can be also used to improve the quality of training content in local level planning in other training institutions, which has been rather uneven in the past. It may be added that primary reasons for the non-existence of such a Basic Training Manual with many of these institutions focused on local level planning is the absence of a permanent core faculty in them having the relevant expertise, interest and enthusiasm to engage in a year round activity focused on local level planning, combining training with research of direct relevance to the teaching programmes, thus, helping to generate useful training materials.

We are convinced that if we are to focus on developing a good Core Planning Manual and Basic Training Manual for decentralised planning, which could be used directly by a wide range of clientele we must proceed on certain systematic lines, so that a productive as well as quality output ensues from such an exercise. For this purpose, it would be necessary to pool all the expertise available in the country and to effectively bring to bear on this exercise, the know-how and guidance from several sources. It has to be ensured that the tools and techniques of planning that are advocated in these Manuals should be simple, practical and realistic, matching the capabilities of the prevailing team of field staff, who will be really practicing it every time, projects in such a way that the desired objectives of level planning are realised; the knowledge necessary for identifying local resources, local capabilities and local constraints including constraints to the use of natural resources; the knowledge necessary to organise groups such that they participate in some or all the steps of planned development at the local level (including the formation of user groups for the maintenance of projects); the knowledge necessary to orient their attitude from that of a regulatory agency to that of development agencies and the knowledge essential for the mobilisation of local resources for local level development (at least to supplement resources received from higher level) would all have to be updated.

For the Non-Officials at the district, and sub-district levels, the focus of training will be towards increasing their understanding of the process of decentralised planning, of enabling them to delineate specific roles and to develop the ability to communicate with their superiors, peers and subordinates in a spirit of partnership particularly so with regard to local resource (including natural resource), local level capability and constraints, and to orient their attitude towards development.

Though the above discussion of the knowledge content of the training programmes for the different target groups is admittedly general, for the present purposes it may be considered sufficient.

As regards the skills that are demanded for working

effectively within a process of institutionalized planning, they may be broadly classified as falling into two categories, namely, basic skills and contributory skills. Basic Skills consist of, *inter alia,* information collection, information handling and information processing, are (both inter and intra) analysis, resource analysis, resource allocation, problem identification and prioritisation, target formulation, project identification and appraisal, project prioritization, monitoring and evaluation, control and stimulation, integration of programmes/projects, participation and effective communication.

The contributory Skills, *inter alia*, consist of demographic and manpower analysis, locational analysis, map analysis, demand analysis and forecasting techniques, land capability analysis, system analysis, environmental impact analysis, plan finalisation and social accounting, amongst others.

Basic Skills are clearly skills necessary for a local level planner to undertake the overall tasks of analysis and detailing of a local level development plan, as against Contributory Skills which are specialised in nature having bearing on the management and development of resources or having bearing on the specific sectoral aspects of planning provided by various disciplines. It would be most unrealistic to expect that a single planner can acquire all these skills. The proposed Manuals should not be seen merely as an exercise in the presentation of some existent and ongoing knowledge and experience; they .will be innovative and will serve to clarify many "grey areas" in the field of local level planning concepts, methodology and techniques. Through on-the-job working they could richly contribute towards firming up our local level planning methodologies, on which there has been so much confusion. These are the reasons why the current task of preparing the Manuals must be done in close association with a number of experts.

CONCLUSION

We have concerned ourselves with the question of issues in training and training needs for decentralised planning and the scope and content of the Manuals to be developed for this purpose. Based on the insights gained from our own experiences in an international context, we have mounted a plea for some promising directions in which training effort could be directed, so as to build up capabilities of human resources available for planning at the local level. Our success at upgrading and updating the capability of the key actors involved in decentralised planning will have a strong bearing on the success of planning at the grass-roots level, variously called local level planning and decentralised planning, in an effective manner.

NOTES AND REFERENCES

1. Adebayo Adedeji: "Administrative Adjustment and Response to Changes in Economic Environment", paper presented at the Fifth AA PAM Round table at Arusha, Tanzania, in December 1983.
2. Diana Convers: "Organization for Development", *Journal of Administration Overseas*, Vol. XII, No. 3, July 1974.
3. Justin Maeda: "Decentralised Systems of Government: Issues and Challenges", in Decentralised Administration in West Apica. Issues and Training Implications (London—Commonwealth Secretariat) 1987.
4. These Issues have been dealt with in detail in Diana Convers: Decentralisation for Development (London: Commonwealth Secretariate) 1983, and in Amitava Mukherjee: "Decentralisation: Some Conceptual Issues" in B.N. Yugandhar and Amitava Mukherjee: Readings in Decentralised Planning, Vol.11, (New Delhi: Concept Publishing Co.) 1991, Chapter 3.
5. Justin Maeda: *loc. cit.*
6. See M.J. Balogun: "Pattern and Problems of Decentralisation", paper read at the Workshop on Decentralised Planning from 1st to 8th March 1987 at Lagos.
7. *Ibid.*
8. K.V. Sundarams: "Training Needs for Decentralised District Planning", in B.N. Yugandhar and Amitava Mukherjee: Readings in Decentralised Planning, Vol. II (New Delhi: Concept Publishing Co.) 1991, pp. 205-34.
9. An assessment of training needs is contained in the Report of Working Group on Training for District Planning (New Delhi: Planning Commission) 1989.

REFERENCES

Amitava Mukherjee: Towards a Non-Static Theory of Profits (New Delhi: Abhinav Publishers) 1990, for some of these theories.

K.V. Sundaram: *loc. cit.*

Padma Ramachandran: "Attitudinal Orientation Required for Decentralised Planning and Implementation", in B.N. Yugandhar and

Amitava Mukherjee: *op. cit.*, pp. 431-38.

Proceedings of the Workshop of District Magistrates/Collectors on Responsive Administration (Coimbatore: Ministry of Personnel, Public Grievances and Pensions, Government of India), June 1988.

R.K. Dars: "Role of the Administrator in Decentralised Planning", in the Keynote Addresses and Nodal papers for the International Expert Group Meeting on Decentralised Planning held from 11th to 13th June 1990, at the L.B.S. National Academy of Administration, Mussoorie.

These are the steps needed for development promoters for large scale people's participation in China during the forties as quoted from Mass Educator by Jimmie Yen.

APPENDIX A

Scheme of Methodology

PART-I: Pre-Planning Stage

STEP-I: Assessing Environment for Decentralisation

(i) Assessment of Administrative and Organizational Environment.
(ii) Assessment of Financial Environment
(iii) Assessment of Planning Environment
(iv) Assessment of Environment for People's Participation

STEP-II: Assessing Decentralised Planning Parameters
STEP-III: Determining Planning Approach
STEP-IV: Determining Planning Process
STEP-V: Finding Implications for Step of the Planning Process Steps
STEP-VI: Reconciliation

PART-II: Planning Stage

A. Initial Planning Phase

STEP-I: Setting Goals and Objectives
STEP-II: Preparatory
STEP-III: Reconnalissance
STEP-IV: Main Field Study

B. Strategic Planning Phase

STEP-V : Current Area Analysis
(a) Aggregate Area Analysis
(b) Inter-Area Analysis
(c) Intra-Area Analysis
(d) Natural Resource Analysis
(e) Market Centre Studies

STEP-VI: Simulation of Future Scenario Analysis
(a) Labour Force
(b) Poverty

(c) Poverty and Economic Growth
(d) Consumption Pattern
(e) District Income
(f) Personal or Household Income
(g) Projection of Sectoral Income
(h) Agriculture
(i) Model for Local Area
    (i) Consumption Sub-Model
    (ii) Demography Sub-Model
    (iii) Sectoral Income Sub-Model
    (iv) Sectoral Employment Sub-Model
    (v) Agricultural Sub-Model
    (vi) Industry Sub-Model
    (vii) Macro-Model
(j) Industry

STEP-VII : Problem Prioritisation
STEP-VIII : Formulating Strategies
STEP-IX : Project Identification
STEP-X : Assessment of Projects and Strategies

C. Tactical Planning Phase

STEP-XI : Project Prioritisation
STEP-XII : Action Planning

DECENTRALISED PLANNING : CONCEPT, APPROACH, IMPLICATION AND LACUNAS

AMITABH SHUKLA AND RAHUL SINGH

Decentralisation is only means: the end is people-oriented planning. Decentralisation is only a starting point to this end in the hope that the effective organization of the prople meant to bring them in the production process can be more successful at lower points. These is a fear based on past experience that at lower levels the vested interests are more powerful. This apprehension must be proved false, if decentralization is to hold the field.

Way back in 1952, Nehru warned that though we had to start with the top down approach in first plan, soon we had to develop a procedure where by "people may feel that the plan is something that has been evolved with their cooperation so that they are responsible for the success.

This paper covers the concept, approach, implication of decentralized planning in detail. This is an holistic analysis of the above mentioned expects of approach towards Decentralized Planning in India.

DECENTRALISED PLANNING—AN EXCITING CONCEPT

India is committed to the idea of planned development in which a persist and functional relationship between national, state, districts, metropolis and urban areas exists. The preparation of the comprehensive development plan has invariably led to precedence for planning from the top-down instead of simultaneous process of planning at different levels. The national objects of planning are:

1. Increase in rate of growth.
2. Efficient use of resource and improved productivity.
3. Removal of poverty and unemployment.
4. A speedy development of indigenous sources of energy and other resources with proper emphasis on conservation and maximization of benefits.
5. Strengthening the impulses of modernization for the achievement of economic and technological self-reliance.
6. Improving the quality of life of the people, specially of the weaker sections of society through the provision of thc minimum needs.
7. Reduction in regional and urban-rural inequalities and in the diffusion of technological benefits.
8. Reduction in income in equalities.
9. Controlling the growth of population.
10. Improving the ecological and environment assets.
11. Preparing the active involvement of all sections of people in the process of development.
12. Bringing about the changes in attitudes and values of people and the like.

Achieving of these objectives is greatly constrained by the lack of clear perceptions of the various levels at which these objectives could be effectively persued. Majority of the National objectives narrated above are very significant and relevant at local level. Its no wonder that the approach of central planning adopted for long time, has led to considerable frustration. It is in this context that the concept of decentralized planning has become some what of an exciting discovery.

The concept of decentralized planning has become some

what synonymous with the concept of District Planning, but, this concept is not very appropriate. Decentralised planning connotes a better perception of the needs of local areas, makes better informed decision-making possible, gives a better voice in decision-making to the people for whom the development is meant, and serves to achieve better coordination and integration among programmes enabling to fulfil needs of the people to be taken into account. District planning is a kind of area-based sub-state planning and arises from the need to supplement national and the state plans with a more detailed examinations of the resources, problems and potential of local areas. The local area is accepted as the District and the investment programmes are tailors accordingly. It is similar to that of area planning which assumes that the District is a sub-state decision-making unit within the system of multilevel planning. Therefore, in the process of decentralized planning, one level lower than the state planning is represented by planning at the District. Whether that is most appropriate level and unit of planning and whether further turns of planning are needed to answer fully the requirements of decentralized planning are to be determined by the constraints in the administrative system, paucity of required basic data and qualified personnel to undertake planning on a systematic basis.

In broader sense, the move towards decentralized planning is the reaction of following present day procedural aspects of centralized planning:

(a) Carrying out the theoretical and applied exercise at the national level by the Planning Commission which has the overall responsibility for planning process including formulation of national plans and outlays of the state plans.
(b) Determining at the centres the share of the public and the private sector outlays in relation to the suitable objectives of the growth of the country.
(c) Procedures followed for discussing the strategies, priorities, outlay (both of the Central and state plans) financing and implementation.
(d) Approval of sectoral outlays of the state plans by the Planning Commission right up to the last insignificant head of development.

(e) Imposition of central sector and centrally-sponsored schemes without any discussions at the working group meetings with the state teams.

While broadly keeping the national objectives, the over-reliance on the sectoral planning and tailoring uniform activities and patterns are to be replaced by a simultaneous process of planning at different levels enabling harmonization and integration of one level with the other, achieving, *inter-alia*, the establishing of inter and intra-sectoral linkages and the rural-urban migration.

APPROACHES OF DECENTRALISED PLANNING

The approaches of decentralized planning are still in a formative stage. There is no doubt, many conceptual and methodological issues which are still unresolved. This is a continuous process with various dimensions.

There is the issue of conformity between national priorities and the state priorities. In so far as increased production, reducing unemployment, alleviation of poverty, bringing about better income distribution, developing rural areas and the involvement of the people in the planning process, including the determining of priorities and implementation are covered. There need to be no conflicts looking to the general nature of the problems in most of the states of this vast country.

However there is still the danger of state priorities getting jettisoned. In certain cases its honestly possible that priorities may have to differ depending upon the level of the development reached in different state regions and the special problems confronting them. Also, the planning set-up and the implementation set-up are highly vertical in their linkages and the bureaucracy in both is one which carries with it the feudal traits of controlling authority at the top-level hanging on the "Order I give" policy expecting the trickle down "to work the rest." Decentralised planning can help in substituting the uncertain trickle down hopes by the grassroots assessment.

RELIANCE ON THE GEOGRAPHICAL REGIONS IS ANOTHER DIMENSION

(a) In the process of decentralised planning, the district offers a sub-system or a sub-region. We should visualize all the feasible levels of planning within the state instead of striking a beeline to the District. In contrary this approach is advantageous, as it is a well recognized administrative boundary and offers an established frame of reference for functioning of different sectoral activities. While scientifically one may think of homogenous regions like water resources, forest resources, and mineral resources, etc. one may have to think of simple method of bringing about decentralised planning; with a good decentralised planning set-up.

(b) Where a district is found to be too large or where it is found to distort the urban-rural mix of population that is to be served by development programmes, bifurcating such a district into two can be desirable. One of the interesting examples is from Karnataka where we created two districts like Bangalore Urban District and Bangalore Rural District out of single Bangalore District for National purposes by the Planning Department; but later it was accepted on administrative ground also. It appears that a division is more suited in some states. We can't afford to be dogmatic on this issue. One way is to allow the state to choose whatever they feel is more convenient-division or district. But on balance, wisdom seems to lie in the choice of the district as third tier of planning excepting in states which are too small and do not stand in comparison with average state in the country.

(c) Removing imbalance is yet another important aspect. The approach has to take note of the characteristics of region and the level of development in different parts of the region. The sub-regions in the district are to be studied for developing the strategies for correcting any intra-district imbalances. Here again, the present state of affairs seems to suggest that the recognized sub-regions such as the block as an aggregation of certain villages with a limit on the population to be served may have to be kept rural plans only. With the introduction of the IRDP and other area-oriented schemes the need to integrate the rural activities, particularly with small and medium towns has become a crucial issue. The small and medium towns have to function as focal points for certain activities and for providing certain amenities including the marketing facilities or banking services and the like. In this context the working group on District Planning has recommended that the towns with the population of less than 10,000 should be treated as an integral part of District for the purposes of overall planning and implementation of development programmes in the district. These are also the major plan schemes of the state sector which are to get located in one or more districts. These can be the state as a whole as a unit of planning although the location of some activities do fall within district, some of them being of infrastructural nature and other of the nature of end products. The decentralised planning at the district level are not integrated with the other schemes of the district. This is all the more important when some of these activities provide the much needed linkage, supplying even infrastructure. Our endeavour should be to develop suitable integrating mechanisms for bringing about these within the ambit of the decentralised planning at the district level in view. It must be emphasized that the decentralised planning has to great extent depended upon the regions which are in some way or the other already developed instead of trying to do this exercise *de novo* in the first phase.

It is not as if the acceptance of the block as another tier in the planning process within the state is a completely satisfactory one. But the block has all the characteristics required for a planning unit. Within the block there are variations and the major test of integrating the sectoral activity with the spatial aspect requires the adoption of an area which can become convenient for optional planning of both the functions and the services.

(d) From the foregoing it will be seen that the choice and

the number of levels of planning would turn out to be very important in the developing of approach to decentralised planning. The infrastructure available, the skills available, the resources available and the awareness on the part of the people would be crucial factors. Another major but highly neglected issue is of rural-urban integration.

DETERMINATION OF ACTIVITIES AND PROGRAMMES FOR DECENTRALISATION

The concept and methodology of decentralised planning will have to take along with them the necessary approaches that would enable the formulation of the schemes/activities that are consistent with the level at which decentralised planning is supposed to take place. It is, therefore, imperative for defining the 'Local Sector' as distinct from the district sector accepting the district as one of the tiers next to the State sector. The local sector may be looked as one more level below the district level where a particular activity or a scheme/project can be formulated and implemented successfully utilizing the instruments which are available to them. A very clear-cut approach to the determination of the schemes/activities which are to be transferred from the State to the district and from the district to the local sector should be attempted. Undoubtedly, there will be resistance for giving up of control over planning and implementing the activities which have been so far handled, though not efficiently, by the line departments which are having a vertical control. Even in the case of local sector one has to appreciate the need to have a very clear idea of the level at which the local sector scheme is being handled. As said earlier, the block may be another unit of planning. Within the block, a group or cluster of villages called as the mandal, as is done in some of the experiments which have now been carried out under decentralised planning in some of the States such as Karnataka, Andhra Pradesh can be the lowest tier of planning. The size of the mandal should be such as to answer satisfactorily the criterion of population threshold, which is the minimum required for sustaining an activity and the distance threshold which connotes the area or the distance which the people are in a position to move about for getting the benefit of such activity/services required.

It must be noted that once the local sector is defined, and activities to be undertaken under multi-level planning are determined successful decentralised planning would call for a single stream of programmes assigned to them. For example, if the institutional framework provides for the Panchayati Raj institutions like the Zilla Parishad, and the Mandal Panchayat, all plan schemes and non-plan schemes which are determined as capable of being handled by these bodies must bear their full responsibility. There cannot be as in Maharashtra, two flows of schemes – one flow goes under the Zilla Parishad set-up and the other flow within the plan itself will be administered by a State agency at the district level. In the Karnataka model, this anomaly in decentralised planning has been eliminated by providing for a single stream. It is, however, too early to evaluate the efficacy or otherwise of this approach.

INTEGRATION OF ACTIVITIES/PROGRAMMES

One of the most difficult approaches under decentralised planning is one of securing integration of the schemes in a consistent planning framework. Integration has to be in terms of (a) activities which are inter-dependent within the same sector and among the different sectors; (b) materials/ products or the area considered more appropriate for sustaining the activity. The sectoral activity deals with the function and how best the function is performed depends on where they are located and how satisfactory the location is. In determining the suitability of a location for particular plans the approach of service centres, and growth poles is helpful. The growth centres have the potential for radiating the effects of the function and would lead to further developments. Several exercises have revealed that generally the mandi, towns and block headquarters or the taluk headquarters have all the characteristics of growth centres. Small towns possess the characteristic of service centres, Integration has to ensure the location of an activity at an appropriate area. It is possible that the demand for a particular activity like say employment may be high in certain areas; the integration of an employment generating programme has to be suitably located keeping the high incidence of unemployment in view in order to secure the sectoral and spatial integration. Once multi-level planning is visualized under decentralised planning, the mandal plans are to get integrated with the block plan, and again, all the block plans should get integrated with the district plan and all the district plans with the state plan. For ensuring the location and the function in a consistency model, mapping will be necessary at the different levels. It must be emphasized, at this state, that the method of having committees/boards or giving representation to the concerned departments/agencies on the institutions which are functioning at different levels has not been very successful in the past. Only detailed exercise of showing the relevant department/ agencies against each activity and with reference to its backward and forward linkages can help in a proper integration of these plans. The discussions have to focus more on these aspects.

LINKAGES

The integration of activities of the various sectors of development take us to the intra and inter-sectoral linkages which are to be established if the schemes are to result in optimum benefits. The formulation of a consistent plan and its proper timely execution requires clear-cut understanding of the inter-dependence or the linkages of the different sectors of development. Only then the demand and supplies of various sectors could be identified and precisely assessed for getting the desired results. The achievement of the targets of a sector not only depends on its own effort, but, very much owes to the quantum and content of the programmes of the related sectors because every sector of the economy is connected with several others either as supplier or as purchaser. Getting an input from the other sectors can be called the backward linkage and supplying its own output to various other sectors either raw-material or as a finished product can be called as the forward linkage. Various departments or agencies pertaining to these sectors have thus a two-way transaction. The imperative need of inter-departmental/agency co-ordination is, therefore, obvious for successful and timely execution of the programme concerned.

To complete the coverage of approaches, we have to refer to the formulation of the programme or the activity over a time span. It is ideal if a perspective of say, ten years is kept in view while analyzing the resources, the needs, the infrastructural gaps and the potential. Within such a perspective, a five year plan can be worked out and with reference to such a plan, an annual plan can be prepared for the various levels. This secures temporal harmonization of the programmes in addition to the integration of the spatial and the sectoral plans.

INSTRUMENTS

The approaches and instruments may not exist in water-tight compartments in decentralised planning. There is an inter-connection, but for purpose of our analysis we are picking out the major elements that can be presented as instruments. We visualize the following as the main instruments for decentralised planning. (i) Disaggregation of funds/allocation of funds; (ii) Credit planning and its integration with the district plan; (iii) Settlement patterns; (iv) Institutional framework/organization; (v) District Collector/Deputy Commissioner; (vi) District Planning Body/ Machinery; (vii) People Participation; (viii) Budgetary Control and Accounting; and (ix) Change of Power Structure.

DISAGGREGATION OF FUNDS/ALLOCATION OF FUNDS

Along with decentralization to different levels, there should be endowment of adequate fiscal powers or flow of funds to these levels to match their responsibilities. While one may refer to the pattern envisaged in a federal set-up like share of taxes, enhancement of grants, raising resources from new taxes, etc. the present Central-State financial relations including the spread and coverage of taxes/sources of funds obtaining in our country is such that laying down of principles for any such transfer of funds on the federal lines almost gets ruled out.

What is, therefore, happening is that under State planning, efforts are made to disaggregate the programmes district-wise, wherever possible, and on that basis, disaggregation of funds for the district plan is attempted. As the major portion of plan investment is in major irrigation and power projects, a small proportion of the plan funds come for disaggregation.

The first impediment to decnetralised planning arises at this level itself. At the national level, State plan outlays and their sectoral allocation are finalized at Delhi. This should be first undone if we are to adopt decentralised planning. State plan outlays relating only to power, major industries, major irrigation and major transport which involve inter-State coverage should be within the domain of the Planning Commission. The rest should devolve to the states in a sectorally untied manner. Identification of those activities which could be planned and implemented at the state level and those which are relevant to the district is to be attempted. With a broad demarcation between the State sector and the district sector, funds should be allocated to the district on a criterion which would fulfil the tests of equity, fairness and removing inter-district disparities. Special problems of any district or districts must also be taken into consideration. Thus, a lump sum amount should be allocated to each district. Without going into the issue of developing a criterion which is a separate issue, we reiterate the basic point here that a lump sum transfer of funds to each district is the first step in realizing the objective of decentralised planning. The perception of local needs within the district, location of production programmes in agriculture and allied activities, development of infrastructure, planning for utilization of resources available in the area, etc. will have to be handled with a strategy of development for the district worked out by the district planning machinery and discussed at the Zilla Parishad, Sectoral and sub-sectoral and sub-regional allocation of funds should then be attempted by the Zilla Parishad. While so doing, the logical relationship among the different sectors or programmes and determining of the properties and linkage among them for getting the optimum benefits are to be attempted. Thus, a major step which the administration has to handle is making available the lump sum funds and permitting the district development authorities/Zila Parishads to determine the strategy, priorities and allocations. Some exercises show that the proportion of plan funds that may come for disaggregation and lump sum allocation may not exceed 25 percent to 30 percent of the total plan funds.

Since we are not beginning afresh, decentralised planning is confronted with the conundrum of on-going schemes and this preempts the resources almost leaving nothing to plan further. We thus meet a situation of fast accompli with standardized old on-going schemes with varying interpretations that favour them. It will be argued that there is no scope for meeting the needs of the people by bringing in grass-roots programmes since all funds are consumed by the so-called on-going schemes. Therefore, the administration has to shift the emphasis to sectoral allocation from district-wise lump sum allocation. In the process, one of the basic requiem of district development planning is totally diluted. Funds are allocated sectorally to different districts and some freedom is given to change the allocation from one sector to another within the ceilings. Again, in order to provide for loose ends, where some untied resources are required, a margin of about 10 to 15 percent of the funds may be kept at the disposal of the district authorities as in Gujarat and other State models and they could use it as they consider fit. In order words, the spatial aspect is circumscribed by a little flexibility in allocation. If in a given district the strategy requires a different type of sectoral allocation and strategies are perceived at the local level, there is no scope for doing so. It is essential that sectoral allocation from the State level is not continued for district planning. The ostensible reason for sectoral deployment is that it is easy to bring about integration of a sectoral plan of a district with the sectoral plan of the State. But it must be noted that vertical integration does not form the core of decentralised planning. The greatest bane of Indian planning is sectoral outlays are protected due to vertical hierarchical bureaucratic controls. The programmes are to be integrated first horizontally in district development planning and then inter-district vertical sectoral integration is to be achieved. The latter presents little problems once the former is accomplished by taking care of production and infrastructure at the district level.

The allocation of funds so far discussed relates only to the plan. This presumes that institutional framework about which we will be discussing later is of nature which takes care of only the plan schemes or even it may cover them only partially, depending upon the pattern of decentralization.

An effective pattern is one of full decentralization. This should mean that at the district level there is "social instrument of decision-making which would be of local autonomy, administrative capability and planning expertise." It is a mini-Government and as such should deal with all development matters. If this is accepted, non-plan funds, corresponding to the activities/schemes transferred to the third tier of planning should also be transferred to them. Available experience in Karnataka shows that if both the plan and non-plan funds are disaggregated for transfer to this tier, it may amount to nearly 48 to 50 percent of the total State budget. But the Karnataka model needs a careful study over a period before coming to any firm conclusions about wielding this instrument in this manner.

INSTITUTIONAL FRAMEWORK

Along with decentralization must go institution building. The institutional framework at the third tier must be such as to ensure integration of 'political, district administration and local institution' for determining programme of development and their implementation at the district level. It should ensure interaction with the population or institutions with elected members and other organizations working for development in that area, should be capable of bringing all these under the control of a single agency, and must have adequate mechanism for the formulation of the plan based on local resources, analysis of the felt need and the requirements of the area. It should also be in a position to clearly demarcate the sphere for the execution of the development programmes included in the decentralised plan at that level.

What could be ideal instrument of institutional framework is debatable. In the initial phase, however, one can look to the experiments that have been done in a few states like Karnataka, Andhra Pradesh, Maharashtra and Gujarat. Unlike the Maharashtra model in which two streams of programmes are permitted, the Karnataka model has established a single stream in the sense that all the plan schemes identified as falling within the districts and the local sector and the non-plan items have been transferred to the newly formed Zilla Parishads and the Mandal Panchyats. Both in Karnataka and Andhra Pradesh, Mandal Panchayats are formed with a group of village though the population size varies from 8,000 to 12,000 in Karnataka as against 35,000 to 50,000 in Andhra Pradesh. At the grassroots level, the village panchayat has been retained in Andhra Pradesh while in Karnataka, it is replaced by Gram Sabha. As for the block and taluk set-up, Panchayat Samithi has been abolished in Andhra Pradesh while in Karnataka, it has been returned with no powers.

One major point which is often commended is the role of the District Collector. Some argue that in view of the inter-dependence of the law and order function and the development function, the task of formulation and implementing development plan at the district will fail to take-off without the active participation of the District Collector. It is argued that Collector must play a role of the chief co-ordinator in the district planning bodies. This is in total contrast to the Karnataka model where law and order function is vested with the District Collector exclusively and he is outside the Zilla Parishad for which a senior officer is appointed as the Chief Secretary. Whether this is desirable has been discussed at great length at the various meetings/conferences of the Collectors organized by the Government of India at which the then Prime Minister Mr. Rajiv Gandhi himself had personally participated in the discussions to assess the final validity of any model. According to these discussions District Collector should be the chief co-ordinator and he should combine both the development and the law and order functions. I understand that in a separate session, you are discussing the role of the collector and perhaps in another key-note address this point is bound to get full attention. I would, therefore, only summarise my stand here looking at him as an instrument.

The District Collector has to attend to a large number of activities. This leaves him little time to provide initiative and the guidance in the formulation of the plan, its integration into a consistent district plan and implementation. In a sense the chief-co-ordinator should not be like just a chairman to take a meeting or to preside over the deliberations. He should be in a position to find adequate time for detailed discussions, taking fresh initiatives, giving guidance to officers for carrying out the work of planning and implementation. It is not easy to get convinced about efficacy of continuing the amalgam of development with law enforcement. Development has become more complex and with the democratic process enforced with full public participation, it is in a way better to keep the law and order enforcing authority independent and somewhat insulated from the new decentralised democratic institutions like Zila Parishads and the Mandal Panchayats.

DISTRICT PLANNING MACHINERY

In the framework of multi-level planning, it is necessary to analyse the local needs and objectives *vis-a-vis* National and State objectives, analyse the natural and human resources, review the present level of development attained, list out and map amenities available at village, block and the district levels, examine the district needs in their social, economic, temporal and spatial dimensions work out linkages with the different sectors and the different areas, formulate policies and programmes, prepare manpower plans, determine priorities relevant for the district, monitor the implementation of the plan schemes and evaluate the whole process and the end result.

This, undoubtedly, calls for expertise and therefore, the district planning machinery should comprise of functionaries who are specialists in such tasks. Also it should be remembered that the preparation of the plan should be the responsibility of one single agency at the district level. Often, there is a tendency for the District Collectors to say that they have the line department personnel with skills and therefore, a separate planning machinery of experts may not be required. This is too much a simplification of the decentralised planning process. That is why the Report of the Working Group on District Planning has argued that the Chief Planning Officer, who heads the District Planning machinery being assisted by an able team of experts drawn from disciplines like economics, statistics, agronomy, cartography, economic geography, sociology, banking, agriculture animal husbandry and so on should be next to the District Collector in rank. These specialists must have proper orientation in the actual preparation of the decentralised plans. In fact, it would be ideal to prepare an approach paper to the District-Zila Parishad plan which should be fully discussed before the plan work is undertaken. It may be recalled here that this approach was tried in Karnataka in 1974 when the State initiated the process of district planning. Again, the district planning machinery has to cater to both the third and fourth tiers of decentralised planning. This means that for the fourth tier like mandal, there must be available some officers of the planning machinery. It may be desirable to locate one officer with auxiliary planning staff at the block to cover mandals which are sub-regions of a block.

It is not enough if planning machinery is provided. The present plan calendar should first of all undergo a change. Instead of waiting for the approval of the Planning Commission of the

State Plan somewhere in November, in early June itself the districts should be told of their resources that will be available for their plans. This can be based on Five-year plan of the district and the previous year's plan size, allowing for a step up outlay of 10 to 15 percent. Similary, the mandal's share is to be indicated. On this basis, the district plan with the plans of mandals intergrated into it must be prepared, well before the State Plan is prepared. The state plan must emerge on the basis of all district plans. It should not be difficult to make marginal adjustments in the total outlays in case resources fall short of what was originally indicated. A new calendar suited for this purpose must be prepared and enforced rigourously. If these procedures are not adopted, there is very little chance of decentralised plan being meaningfully implemented through multi-level planning.

PEOPLE'S PARTICIPATION

One of the strong features of the decentralised planning is that it enables the full involvement of the people in the process of plan formulation and implementation. Everything cannot be done by the government alone. Energies of the people will have to be released especially, in the rural areas so that they will participate in the development of their area. Therefore, public participation is an essential instrument and this would help in assessing the felt needs of the people mobilizing local resources for plan implementation, carrying out people's sector, reducing resistance to plan formulation and implementation, stepping up the speed of implementation by mobilizing popular support and co-operation. Thus, there must be people's participation in decision-making, in implementation, in the delivery of benefits and in the assessment or evaluation of the results. In the planning cycle it is not enough if participation is limited to just some kind of representation on some planning bodies. The involvement should be there at the pre-plan stage, plan formation stage, at the level of implementation and finally at the level of evaluation. That is why, it is now aptly said that the people's participation is a missing ingredient in the present method of planning. Decentralised planning not only makes up the missing ingredient, but, it would also contribute to the developing of a distinct style of development responsive to the needs of the people. The manner of participation should be such as to provide a forum for discussions and negotiations. Mere representation on the planning bodies whatever is the model will not serve the needs of decentralised planning. While the Panchayat Raj Institutions provide for representation of the people, effective use should be made of the voluntary organizations and also associations of the poor and the unorganized even though there can be some formal representation to them on the panchayat raj bodies. The success of decentralised planning very much depends upon the extent to which effective and non-frictional people's participation is secured.

There are bound to be conflicts between officials and non-officials and also between the officials and the people who approach them for facilities. No one should underestimate the sabotaging effects of such conflicts. Harmonising of these relations poses the greatest challenge as well as an opportunity for ushering a new order.

Keeping the District Draft Plan or a set of proposals before a Board or a committee at the district level/Zilla Parishad will not in itself elicit the kind of involvement and participation from the people which we expect. Popular participation of this type will not help the process of planning to any considerable extent and it might even distort planning as rational locational decisions cannot be taken because of the pressures of the dominant individuals or their whimsical attitudes. If the purpose of peoples' participation is to improve the planning process, it is necessary to secure enlightened participation of not only political leaders but also other knowledgeable people like progressive farmers' social workers, agricultural labourers, entrepreneurs, etc. whose practical suggestions would be of invaluable significance to the planners.

Obviously this is a function of education of the local leadership and its consciousness of the real meaning of national socio-economic objectives. From the view point of possible variation in the coverage and depth of local interest, it is necessary to recognize the importance of the national frame and the State frame. The need to allow more resources for backward areas, for weaker sections, for generating employment for the landless labourerts, etc. should be properly understood. It must be noted that no real social transformation could come about unless there is full understanding and cooperation from local elements in this regard. Therefore, while in the initial stages, the national frame may serve a useful purpose, the full and meaningful pursuit of national objectives requires an educational effort in relation to local leadership which must be considered as extremely important and essential. In part, the process of decentralised planning must be understood as that of communicating to local leadership and population aspirations and ideologies with which the National Plan is informed. On the other hand, the realism and the effectiveness of the national and State plans, depend essentially on an understanding at the national and State levels of the possibilities and difficulties of local planning.

IMPLICATION OF DECENTRALISED PLANNING

- Decentralised planning can help in substituting the uncertain trickle down hopes by the grassroots assessment.
- Earlier spatial planning and sectoral planning are running parallel, without much coordination. This has resulted in uneconomic utilization of scarce investible resources, regional disparities in the level of development and social inequalities. Due to introduction of decentralised planning this piecemeal approach will be substituted by comprehensive and organized approach leading to planned and comprehensive development. Moreover for optimum utilization of scarce investible resources regional dimentions of planning should be taken into consideration.
- In decentralised planning, the Region as a planning unit establishes a link between the national, state and local level planning unit.
- Decentralised planning helps to highlight the constraints and potentials of area as well as identification of critical stresses which affect the population.
- Decentralised planning is an holistic approach toward analysis of land utilization pattern, water resources availability. Demographic profiles, economic characteristics, economic engagement of social characteristics of an area, so that a (cowabe) comprehensive and analysis shall be made for the

preparation of detailed proposals in order to identify the problems of the area.

- Decentralised planning helps in analyzing the various sector such as—Agriculture, Sector, Irrigation Sector, Animal Husbandary Sector, Industrial Sector, Health Sector, Education Sector, Transport Marketing and Communication Sector. This analysis may lead to analysis as well as linking various sectors with each other to achieve a comprehensive results.
- Decentralised Planning System/arrangement which is visible, distinguishable, which has transparency, and at the same time if we can integrate all the apparatus, all the resources available, then perhaps it would be easier to implement things.

RECOMMENDATION

When we talk of decentralised planning, it does not merely imply that planning decisions are taken at below district or below block level. And usually if block plan is worked out by block development officer or mukhia who has been elected 10 or 15 years ago and is no longer accountable to the people, that does not constitute decentralised planning. I do not believe that merely no transferring the decision-making process to a lower level, the local, we can achieve the object of decentralization. Effective decentralization requires the necessary institutional arrangements at various levels.

REFERENCES

Chandra Sekhar, B.K. (1984), "Panchayat Law in Karnataka: Janta Initiative in Decentralisation," *Economic and Political Weekly*, Bombay, April 21.

Ghosh, Arun (1988), "Decentralised Planning: West Bengal Experience," *Economic and Political Weekly*, Bombay, March 26.

G.O.I. (1984), Report of the Working Group on District Planning, Vols. I & II, New Delhi.

G.O.I. (1988), Report of the National Commission of Urbanisation, Vols. I to VII, New Delhi.

Midha, R.K. (1989), "Note on Natural Resources: Data Management System" in Report of the Committee on Information Gap, New Delhi.

Rao, C.H.H. (1989), "Decentalised Planning: An Overview of Experience and Prospects," *Economic and Political Weekly*, Bombay.

Sinha, Arun (1990), "Panchayat Raj Legislation and Development, District Planning and Management: Emerging Roles," in Course Materials, School of Planning and Architecture, New Delhi.

Venkatachalam, P. (1990), "Development of District Information System—A Case Study Under NRDMS Project", in Course Materials, School of Planning and Architecture, New Delhi.

Vinod Kumar T.M. and Mahavir (1990), District Planning and Management—A State of the Art Survey, District Planning and Management, School of Planning and Architecture, New Delhi.

Vinod Kumar T.M. and Mahavir (1990), District Planning and Management, District Planning Case Studies, School of Planning and Architecture, New Delhi.

ANNEXURE

Some more Elaboration of the Approach of the Integration of Schemes/Programmes: Integration of Special Scheme Funds and Schemes of Autonomous Bodies

There are a few other issues which must be touched upon. With increased centralization in planning, *ad hoc* efforts are made to tackle some specific problems on a district-wise basis. The result is multiplication of production-oriented district schemes whichever supposed to be an integral part of the district plan and yet get implemented in a totally isolated manner. For example, NREP, IRDP, DPAP, Anthyodaya, Rehabilitation of Bonded Labour, Child Welfare Development Schemes, Landless Rural Labourer Employment Guarantee Programme, etc. are Centrally-sponsored schemes. The latest in the series is the Jawahar Rozgar Yojana. Because of the funding principle, namely, the total cost being shared between central and the State Governments in the ratio of 50 : 50/80 : 20 all these schemes has separate organizational patterns although placed under the overall control of the Deputy Commissioner (Special) at the district level. The result is their implementation in an isolated manner. For each one of the schemes, there is separate staff. This very composition has built within it anti-intergration barriers. It would appear that accounting needs coordinated development of planning. As these schemes do not get integrated with plan schemes which provide infrastructure, complaints are heard that the special programmes are poorly implemented since infrastructural backup is lacking. That is why individual beneficiaries programmes are not becoming very effective. If district development planning is to proceed in an integrated manner, it requires a total loss of separate identity of the schemes in the present form. The totality of the plan effort should take note of the requirement of the locations and bring about a synchronization of individual beneficiary schemes with area development schemes. If this is done, there can be considerable saving of manpower as well as reducing frustration in implementation. The department incharges of certain sectors have a tendency not to treat these special schemes as their own. Thus, the conflict between their own department schemes and schemes of other departments in ruining the task of rural development. If one is to overcome this problem, the Planning Commission or the concerned Central Ministries should have to agree for pooling of those funds at the district level. This need not, in any way, prevent accounting responsibility scheme-wise in respect of expenditures. The crucial test should, therefore, be one of how far an arrangement is conducive for the total development of a given area like a district. On the basis of the strategy of development thoughout for the district, the priorities and schemes determined should get implemented within the overall geo-physical plan. The tragedy is that there is greater concern for the sponsoring ministry's and controlling authorities privileges than for systematic planning and implementation for achieving success in area development.

Similarly, there are implications for the State level planning in respect of a series of activities like warehousing, dairy, agricultural research, agricultural implements, industrial development, electricity generation and distribution, road transport, etc., which are implemented by certain autonomous bodies. There are also the major plan schemes of the State sector which are to get located in one or more districts. They have kept the State, as a whole, as a unit of planning although the locations of some of their activities do fall within the district. Some of them are of an infrastructural nature and some are in the nature of an end product. District development planning will be incomplete if all these development programmes that are to take place within the district are not integrated with the other schemes of the district. This is all the more important when some of these activities provide the much required linkages, and supplies, even infrastructure. Unfortunately, these are also now getting implemented in isolation.

There was a stage when some of the State level organizations did not recognize the regional dimension in their operations and this continues even now in certain areas. They have to reorganize their administrative structures to suit the needs of district development planning.

Democratic Decentralisation Through Panchayati Raj Administration: A Study of its Prospects in Mizoram

R.N. Prasad

CONCEPTUAL FRAMEWORK OF DEMOCRATIC DECENTRALISATION

The democratisation of the political process has brought the concept of decentralisation and political participation into sharp focus. So there is now the Question what is this democratic decentralisation? To know democratic decentralisation, firstly, it is better to understand what is decentralisation? The word "decentralisation" refers to the "transfer of authority away from the national capital whether by decentralisation, that is delegation, to field officers or by devolution to local authorities or other local bodies." It is specifically "the transference of authority, legislative, judicial or administrative, from a higher level of government to a lower level." Further, decentralisation is a method "embracing both processes of deconcentration and devolution." Deconcentration stands for the "delegation of authority adequate for the discharge of specified functions to staff of a central department who are situated outside the headquarters while devolution is the legal conferring of powers to discharge specified or residual functions upon formally constituted local authorities." In the organisational context it refers to delegation of decision-making. The concept of decentralisation is, thus, one of power-sharing.[1]

Why is decentralisation needed ? Because decentralisation symbolises democratic values being a process of power-sharing in decision-making and based on the principle that most decisions are taken by the people who are affected by them. But the institutional machinery of democratic decentralisation should be elective. The decentralised authority should not become the monopoly of an individual but it should vest in a committee. Decentralisation of power aims at better and faster communication, involvement and commitment of people in development, mobilisation of support and utilisation of resources in a better manner for national development, reduction in delay in decision-making, greater equity in allocation of resources and investments, reduction in apathy of administration to clientele.

Devolution is thus, a more profound form of decentralisation under which both decision-making and operations are in the hands of local institutions in which locally accountable persons manage activities and will be more responsive to local conditions. Dennis A. Rondinelli has given the main features of devolution as under:

(1) giving of autonomy and independence to local government and clearly perceiving it as a separate level over which central authorities exercise little or no direct control;
(2) provision to have clear and legally recognised geographical boundaries of the local units over which they exercise authority and within which they perform functions;
(3) giving of corporate status and power to the local government to raise sufficient resources to perform specified functions;

(4) implying the need to develop local governments as institutions in the sense that they are perceived of by local citizens as organisations providing services to satisfy their needs and as governmental units over which they have some influence; and

(5) as an arrangement in which there exists reciprocal, mutually benefiting and coordinated relationship between central and local governments.[2] Thus devolution of power from the District to Panchayat has created three-tier system of democracy which has given enough scope for creating a participatory democracy. So the government of the day in order to ensure political stability should be farsighted to decentralise.
In the Indian context, it was realised that with transfer of functions and vesting of necessary powers, the Panchayati Raj Institutions would be better equipped to undertake development programme. These would become projection and foundation of over all political set-up of the country. As it is rightly said, a grass-roots democracy is, thus, essentially decentralised democracy in which the management of public affairs does not begin and end at the top but operates through a wide net-work of people's participating units in local area which form more or less a miniature government in themselves and are thus real centres of power and therefore, of democratic thought and action. Briefly, grass-roots democracy is not just a window-dressing but an effort at sowing the democratic seed deep into the soil of a country.[3] Decentralisation is a prime mechanism through which democracy becomes truly representative and responsive.

The Panchayati Raj as a process of democratic decentralisation aims at:

(i) providing a broad base to democracy by striving to achieve the cherished ideal of village self-government;
(ii) affording the much needed training ground for future leadership;
(iii) creating an awareness and initiative in the rural people about the community development programme;

(iv) proper utilization of the available man power and other rural resources which have mostly remained under exploited and unutilised;

(v) developing a sense of community feeling and self-reliance in the village;

(vi) helping the weaker sections of the community to participate in the management of rural affairs;

(vii) bringing rural consciousness among the officials and impressing upon them the utility of a coordinated and inter-related approach to various development programmes;

(viii) ensuring quicker acceptance of the new ideas in the country-side; and

(ix) planning an overall balanced development of the rural areas and thereby raising the standard of living of the rural people.[4]

LIMITATIONS/WEAKNESSES IN THE FUNCTIONING OF PANCHAYATI RAJ SYSTEM

The provision of the Panchayati Raj Institution a framework of rural local government which has inbuilt decentralising tendencies, was incorporated in the non-justiciable part (iv) of the Directive Principles of State Policy of the Constitution of India. Article 40 which is a directive to the state, stipulates: "The state shall take steps to organise village Panchayats and endow them with such powers and authority as may be necessary to enable them to function as units of self-government." Thus the Panchayat system is nothing but a set, an institution placed at a different levels that function to accomplish the multiple goals/tasks assigned to the rural local self-government.

Since the Balwantray Mehta Committee recommended the Panchayati Raj system in India way back in 1954, several attempts have been made, at the national as well as state levels to strengthen the Panchayati Raj system in the country. There are certain limitations/ills such as domination of the PRIs by bureaucracy and the upper and richer strata of the rural community, absence of scientific basis of the planning process at the Panchayat level and programme implementation, devolution of financial and administrative powers; apathy of citizens towards local problems ; factions, partisan groups, and lack of intergroup adjustments, lack of technical competence, of people's orientation/ participation and of inter-departmental coordination and structural overlapping of functions underlying the Panchayati Raj system. Besides, traditional leadership entrenched in caste and landownership is still in dominance. Functional leadership has not yet emerged. Vested interests, corruption, inefficiency, groupism, unhealthy rivalry, misuse of powers, and motivated decisions and actions have already affected the functioning and limited the utility of Panchayati Raj to an average villager.[5] However, the potential of Panchayati Raj in a country like ours cannot be denied. The Panchayat system has to play a very important role in the overall development of the economy, policy and development administration of the country. But being denied of the constitutional status and due to lack of political will on the part of political masters and public apathy and indifference, the Panchayati Raj Institutions have failed to deliver goods. These bodies suffered from lack of resources and had to function in a state of perpetual neglect.

THE 73RD CONSTITUTIONAL AMENDMENT ACT, 1992

So with a view to improving the participation of the rural people in the process of their development and also the involvement of people in the process of decision-making directly affecting their life, the government of India has provided a constitutional status for the village Panchayats under the Constitution (73rd Amendment) Act, 1992 which after having been ratified by Seventeen State Assemblies, has been passed by the Lok Sabha on 6 December, 1992. After it was passed by the Parliament, the President assented this Bill on 20 April 1993 which later became an Act. This Act was brought into force by a notification with effect from April 24, 1993 on which date, all provisions in various state acts which were repugnant to the provisions of the constitutional amendment ceased to remain in force. Many states had, by then, amended their acts. So this amendment act is the culmination of various proposals made by the earlier committees or sub-committees on Panchayati Raj bodies and thus giving PRIs a viable shape.

The Salient provisions of the Act are as follows:

1. There shall be Panchayats at the village level in each state.
2. At the village level, Gram Sabha will be constituted comprising persons registered in the electoral roll of the village. The Gram Sabha will exercise such powers and perform such functions as the legislature of the state may by law provide.
3. Panchayats shall be constituted in every state at the village, intermediate and district levels, thus bringing about uniformity in the Panchayat Raj structure. However, the states having a population not exceeding 20 lakh have been given the option of not having any Panchayat at the intermediate level.
4. The elections of all the members of Panchayats at all levels will be direct. The elections for the post of chairmen of the intermediate and district levels will be indirect. The mode of elections of chairmen to the village level has been left to the state government to decide. The Chairmen of the Village Panchayats can be made members of the Panchayats at the intermediate and the chairmen of Panchayats at intermediate level can be members of Panchayats at the district level; MPs, MLAs and MLCs can also be members of Panchayats at the intermediate and district levels. Apart from some individuals, who occupy responsible position in one institution do play a different role in other higher level institutions of Panchayati Raj system.
5. Reservation of seats for SCs/STs have been provided in proportion to their population at each level. Not less than one-third of the total membership has been reserved for women and these seats may be allotted to different constituencies in a Panchayat. Similar reservations have been made in respect of the office of the chairman also.
6. Legislature of the state shall be at liberty to provide reservation of seats and offices of chairman in Panchayats in respect of backward class of citizens.
7. An uniform term of 5 years has been provided for the PRIs and in the event of supersession, elections to constitute the new body should be completed before

expiry of 6 months from the date of dissolution. The reconstituted Panchayat will function for the remaining period of the five year term.

8. There shall be an independent Election Commission set-up in the state to superintend, direct and control the electoral process and preparation of electoral rolls.
9. The legislature of a state may by law endow the Panchayats with such powers and authority as may be necessary to enable them to function as institutions of self-governrnent and such law may contain provisions for the devolution of powers and responsibilities upon Panchayats at the appropriate levels, subject to such conditions as may be specified therein with respect to preparation of plans for economic development and social justice and implementation of schemes for economic development and social justice as may be entrusted to them including those in relation to the matters listed in the Eleventh Schedule.
10. The state legislatures have been given to authorise the Panchayats to levy, collect, and appropriate suitable local taxes and also provide for making grants-in-aid to the Panchayats from the consolidated fund of the concerned state.
11. In each state a Finance Commission has to be constituted once in every five years to review the financial position of the Panchayats and to make suitable recommendation to the state on the distribution of funds between the state and local bodies.
12. With a view to ensuring continuity, it has been provided in the Act that all the Panchayats existing immediately before the commencement of this amendment act will continue till the expiry of their duration unless dissolved by a resolution to that effect passed by the state legislature concerned.
13. The state legislature should bring the necessary amendments to their Panchayat acts within a maximum period of one year from the commencement of this amendment act so as to conform to the provisions contained in the Constitution.[6]

So far the Constitution (73rd Amendment) Act, 1992 has only provided the general guidelines for the effective and efficient PRIs in the country. It has granted the PRIs a constitutional status, some sort of a uniformity by making three-tier system a permanent feature, regularity by making election an imperative after the termination of the PRIs after every five years and the State Election Commission to conduct and supervise the elections, more financial autonomy with the constitution of the State Finance Commission. It can be said that India is on the threshold of a historic transition of political power to grass-roots with all the states completing the process of enacting fresh legislation on April 23, 1994 to strengthen the PRIs, the day, the Panchayats became a part of the Constitution of India. But mere legislative enactments do not ensure effectiveness and viability of the PRIs in the states. What is more important is their operationalisation.[7]

MIZORAM AND THE 73RD AMENDMENT ACT

However, the 73rd Constitutional Amendment Act is not applicable to Jammu & Kashmir, Meghalaya, Nagaland and Mizoram and certain Scheduled Areas of the country. The governments of Meghalaya and Nagaland denied the application of the constitutional provisions relating to Panchayats to their respective states on the ground that the Traditional Self-Governing Institutions to carry on the village administration have already been in operation in these states since pre- and post-independent India. The government of Mizoram also refused the application of the constitutional provisions concerning Panchayati Raj system mainly owing to the operation of democratically elected village councils since 1954 which have been set-up under sub-clause (e) of clause (3) of the Sixth Schedule to the Constitution of India with a very limited functions and powers mostly administrative and Judicial of petty nature under the Lushai Hills District (Village Councils) Act, 1953 and the Pawi-Lakher Autonomous Region (Village Councils) Act, 1954. These Acts have been adapted by the government of Mizoram and the District Councils since 1972. But it appears from the analysis of the Village Council Acts that the councils have been denied to the devolution of financial resources, administrative responsibilities and political powers. Briefly, the councils lack both political decentralisation and economic decentralisation whereas the essential pre-requisites for the new Panchayati Raj system to function as institutions of self-government are: (i) Clearly demarcated operational areas, (ii) Adequate power and authority commensurate with responsibilities, (iii) Necessary human and Financial resources to manage their affairs, and (iv) Functional autonomy and non-interference from outside agencies. The new Panchayats must be seen as "Third Tier of Government" as the constitutional amendment act opens possibilities for fulfilling these conditions. In other words, the Panchayats have to play some vital roles in the country such as decentralisation of administrative, financial, and political powers, contribution towards strengthening the planning process at the micro-level and over all rural development and improvement of the access of the rural poor masses to the highest level of decision-making bodies. These development roles have been incorporated in the Eleventh Schedule (Article 243-G) of the Constitution (73rd Amendment) Act, 1992 which may be categorised in terms of twenty-nine operative subjects such as agriculture, land reforms, minor irrigation, animal husbandry, fisheries, social forestry, small scale industries, rural housing, drinking water, roads, rural electrification, poverty alleviation programme, primary and secondary education, technical training/ vocational education, cultural activities, health and sanitation, family welfare, women and child development, social welfare, welfare of the weaker sections, public distribution system and maintenance of community assest, etc. Briefly, these operative subjects create and maintain social service, productive infrastructure in rural areas and promote productive and development activities and implement social service programmes.[8]

The Panchayati Raj Institutions are the creation of the Constitution of India whereas the Village Councils are created by enactments of the District Councils and their provisions are amended by an executive administrative order of the councils/ government (Mizoram). So they differ structurally and operationally. What I want to point out is that the Panchayati Raj Institutions have larger scopes to accelerate socio-economic development in the rural areas whereas the socio-cultural and econo-political transformation of the poor tribesmen is beyond the scope of the village councils. The councils have not been given greater autonomy in administrative, political, financial, judicial, planning and developmental sphere. So the councils have neither created a significant impact at the village level nor have provided leadership to local community due to lack of financial resources and devolution of powers and responsibilities. The councils, thus, stand no comparison with the 73rd constitutional amendment act whose ethos is devolution of power. Briefly, the councils have failed to evoke the local initiative and people's participation in the development activities as well as to bring about social and economic changes in the rural areas mainly owing to a strong tendency towards centralisation in the state, though there is a talk of decentralisation of power to district and lower level bodies. Such a process of centralisation is just not compatible with the talk of decentralisation of planning.[9]

Reservation of one-third seats and chairpersons for women, SCs/STs and OBCs is a step towards silent revolution. A social transformation aimed at women, SCs/STs and OBCs can be achieved by the Panchayats. The Panchayat will ensure their participation and effectiveness in decision-making. But the Village Council does not provide for reservation of seats for women. So women cannot usher in an effective participatory grass-root democracy. It only provides decision-making power/responsibility for male tribesmen whereas women are relegated to a position of perpetual power-addressee: can we call it worthy enough to be equated with self-governing institution? It does not stipulate any devolution of power.

SIXTH SCHEDULE

The recommendations of the Bardoloi Sub-Committee for the carry-out of the simple and inexpensive administration of the tribesmen of certain hills districts of the then state of Assam were incorporated in the Sixth Schedule to the Constitution of India. This provided for the Constitution of the Autonomous District Councils (ADCs) for the major tribesmen and the Autonomous Regional Councils (ARCs) for the minor tribesmen other than the major tribal people within a district. Accordingly, the Autonomous Hills District Councils in some of the hills districts (except Nagaland) such as Khasi and Jaintia Hills, Garo Hills, Mikir Hills, (Now Karbi Anglong District), North-Cachar Hills and Lushai Hills of the then composite Assam state were first set-up in 1952, and 1953, the Pawi-Lakher Regional Council for the three tribesmen (Pawi-Lakher and Chakma) was also set-up in the then Lushai Hills District (now MIZORAM). The Mizo Hills District according to the provisions of the North-Eastern Areas (Re-Organisation) Act, 1971 was elevated to the status of the Union Territory of Mizoram in 1972. It was envisaged in the Act that the Mizo Hills District Council would cease to exist from the date on which the Legislative Assembly of the Union Territory of Mizoram was constituted. The Pawi-Lakher Regional Council was also trifurcated into three District Councils such as the Mara District Council, the Lai District Council and the Chakma District Council. In February 1987, Mizoram was inaugurated as the 23rd state of the Indian Union.

For the last forty years, these Autonomous District Councils have functioned in their respective autonomous areas. Many of these ADCs have passed from time to time a number of laws, acts, rules and regulations, etc. dealing with the people of their respective areas in diverse ways—relating to such pertinent issues like land, forest, primary school education, planning processes, markets, trade, developmental activities, etc. to mention a few of them, some such legislations have direct effects on the other traditional institutions like the chiefs, tribal councils, etc. Many changes have taken place since 1952. The role, functions and working of these constitutional bodies from time to time have been studied by many scholars of the region. A number of criticisms have also been levelled against the effective functioning of these councils. The relevance of the ADCs today has been questioned from time to time especially after the creation of full-fledged states where the District Councils are in existence. On the part of the District Councils, they have been demanding more autonomy and direct funding from the government of India to strengthen their powers and functions. They have been persistently voicing their grievances against the treatments meted out to them by the different state governments in the matters of provision of grants, according of approval of the legislative proposals of the ADCs, supersession of the ADCs, etc. since their set-up in the sixth scheduled areas of North-East India. Such grievances were directed against the then composite state of Assam before 1972. The situation is not so different today even after the re-organisation of Assam which has resulted into the creation of full-fledged states like Meghalaya, Mizoram, Manipur and Tripura. For example, today, a tug-of-war is still continuing between the government of Meghalaya, Mizoram, and Assam, Tripura and the ADCs over a particular paragraph 12-A of the Sixth Schedule to the Constitution of India which gives overriding power to the state legislation over the legislations made by the ADCs. Besides, the autonomy of the ADCs has been greatly affected in the area of financial independence. The ACDs in the matter of financial allotments have to depend on their respective state governments. The Sixth Schedule confers few developmental functions on the ADCs, though there is a enabling clause whereby the state governments can entrust such functions with them. Lacking in statutory support, the ADCs have to depend on the changing political relations with the state leadership. Therefore, the developmental functions of the ACDs depend very much on the political party or parties which run the state administration. If the same political party is in power both at the state and the District Council levels, the latter may have a smooth sailing in its programme of developmental activities. If it is otherwise, a number of obstacles and hurdles may be created by the party in power in the state to jeopardise the plan of action that might be chalked out by the District Council for the development of the autonomous districts.[10]

A comparative study of the Sixth Schedule to the Constitution of India and the Constitution (73rd Amendment) Act, 1992 relating to the Panchayati Raj Institutions has now become necessary for certain reasons. The PRIs cover as many as 29 subjects within their jurisdiction. When all these provisions of the 73rd Constitutional Amendment about the power, scope of function and financial support for the exercise of power and discharge of the responsibilities by the Panchayati Raj bodies are compared with those attached to the ADCs under the Sixth Schedule, it is found that while the ADCs have many regulatory powers subject to state control, the PRIs are in a more advantageous position in respect of developmental functions. The ADCs have no development and welfare functions as their mandatory functions. They can take up such activities only on being assigned by the state. The 73rd Constitutional Amendment has enabled the PRIs to take up some development and social service activities of higher order. For instance, the ADCs can only establish and manage primary schools and dispensaries whereas the PRIs can establish and manage even secondary schools and hospitals.

The 73rd Amendment ensures the establishment of elected Panchayats at the village level, incase of the Sixth Schedule, this is not mandatory. Though the ADCs can set-up Village Councils and Town Committees, some of them have not devolved power at this level and have not constituted these councils/committees.

It seems that the ADCs are in situations of higher order, in terms of actual function, they enjoy less power in some cases, and in some other cases, they are hedged so much by the political whims of the state level political elite that their effective functioning becomes problematic.

On in-depth analysis, it appears that while the 5th Schedule overtly treats the tribal peoples as political wards, the Sixth Schedule covertly treats them so and only provides the concerned tribal peoples political toys to play with.[11]

Therefore, it is suggested that the application of constitutional provisions relating to the Panchayats by the political structures of the states and the Sixth Schedule areas to their respective jurisdictions seems to be an imperative need and thereby such states will definitely join the national mainstream deriving a lot of benefits from the democratically, politically and economically viable systems to better the socio-economic conditions of the poor tribesmen. As Gassah aptly puts it, "if the Panchayati Raj bodies under the 73rd Amendment are not introduced in the Sixth Schedule areas, these areas will enjoy less power of self-government than the rest of the country." B.K. Roy Burman has further added, "the exceptions made in respect of the Fifth and Sixth Schedule areas in the 73rd Amendment should not be an executes not to introduce democratic apparatuses and to initiate democratic process at the grass-root level with immediate effect."[12] While accepting the systems, there should be no fear that the powers of the political structures would be curtailed, once the Panchayats are constituted. Undoubtedly, their authoritative superiority would remain intact. Because the state government/the District Council and the Panchayats are two separate independent bodies, they cannot be linked without making constitutional amendment. In fact, suitable nomenclature and terminologies with which the tribesmen are familiar, may be adopted. It is left to the legislatures of different states to make the necessary enactments on the Panchayats.

CONCLUDING RELEVANT OBSERVATIONS

It may be also mentioned that to the constitutional provisions relating to the Panchayats, the state, which has a population of more than twenty lakhs, can have three-tier of Panchayati Raj Institutions—Panchayats at the village, intermediate and district levels.

The Panchayats at the Intermediate level may not be constituted in a state having a population not exceeding twenty lakhs. Such a state may have two-tier of Panchayati Raj Institutions—Panchayats at the village and district levels. However, these constitutional provisions relating to Panchayats have been mentioned for the consideration of the political masters because they should be ready to decentralise powers to grass-root institutions keeping in view the constitutional directive under article 40 of the Constitution. This is also true that the application of the 73rd Amendment to the state of Mizoram entirely depends on the political will of the state leaders and their willingness to share power with lower elected bodies. They should have a faith in lower governance and not in central planning.

What is required is that the legislators should cut across party lines and implement laws in true spirit with the implicit of purpose of transferring power to the people, and to plug the loopholes in the existing system. Only when the tiers of the Constitution the centre, the states and the local bodies will function with regularity and efficiency, the federal nature of the Constitution, the democratic nature of the Constitution, the democratic nature of polity will be preserved. Otherwise, the Constitution will become very much distorted in its contents as well as implementation. What is required is the "will" to make the PRIs a viable democratic institution on which real democracy will thrive on. Thus, the concept of Panchayati Raj has come to be accepted as an extension of democracy up to the village.

The PRIs are the primary institutions of democracy where people from village, block and district can participate. Except for them, none of the other institutions can have direct participation of the local people. The concept of participation of the people should be considered as an ideological commitment and therefore what is needed is legislative and structural measures to give legitimacy to people's participation. Devolution of power has to start here, and this is also where people at local levels get into the mainstream of development as well as public affairs. The PRIs especially the "Gram Sabha" make the concept of "direct democracy" like that of Greek city-states of Plato and Aristotle days feasible at the present and centuries to come. The Gram Sabha's have been designed to be the place where development issues should be discussed, development programmes initiated and beneficiaries of development schemes selected.

Thus, the Panchayati Raj system provides an alternative institutional framework for accelerating the tempo of the rural development as well as marginalising the role of bureaucracy in the areas of rural development which carries the imprint of Gandhian philosophy. Alternative form of government is necessary for rural India including rural Mizoram which can allow miximum participation of the people in the developmental works. That helps the maximum utilization of resources flowing to the Panchayats in various anti-poverty projects like the JRY; the poverty alleviation and special programmes like the IRDP, TRYSEM and Area development programmes like DPAP, DPP, etc. All schemes falling under MNP and programmes of the nature of local development work. Infact, the PRIs would become watchdog bodies to ensure proper implementation of the employment generation programmes and thereby play an important role in accelerating the socio-economic development in the rural areas. But for the proper implementation of these programmes, the activities and functioning of the PRIs will have to be closely watched and monitored so that they do not overstep their limits and cause irreparable damage to those living in their jurisdiction. What is needed is a consensual and uniform approach of regular auditing of all expenditures incurred by the Panchayats. It is also insisted that the accounts should be shown in a public place. Besides this, display of the written accounts, verbal direct communication to the common people in an open meetings is also considered essential. These are the ultimate democratic checks on the entire system.

Panchayati Raj Institutions are model parliaments. They are not only taking decision to solve the socio-economic problems, but also a training ground for the people in the art of decision-making which help the nation to have more trained legislators for democratic government. Ethnic eruptions in the country and the demand for self-governance within the Indian Constitution demonstrate the fact that the human collectivities are in need of organisational power. Democratic decentralisation of powers to grass-root institutions would reduce tension at higher level with the centre and states. It helps intergating the various human segments and unity can be preserved. Thus, the PRIs would maintain Unity and integrity of the nation. But the democratisation of our pluralistic society cannot be ensured merely by legislative and administrative actions of the state. These enabling provisions will require a massive work on the part of intellectuals, non-governmental organisations, professional bodies and political parties to exert pressure to restore power to place where it belongs. They should create awareness among the people about the value of the new role the PRIs have to play in the rural society. As public vigilance is the price of democracy, people have to organise themselves to demand more powers to PRIs.

The 73rd Constitutional Amendment Act provides for periodic elections which will give to local community an ample opportunity to throw young energetic and action-oriented leadership. The district and decentralised planning will also emphasise the need-based planning reflecting the hopes and aspirations of the people. People's aspirations include equity, i.e. Social Justice, people's participation in decision-making, implementation, monitoring and evaluation and sharing the benefit of change and development, representative character of grass-root democratic institutions, protection of the interest of SCs, STs and socially deprived sections including women, maintenance of social harmony, removal of feuds and factions, sense of freedom and equality. It is also hoped that the Panchayats will directly and effectively implement the centrally sponsored developmental and employment generating programmes for the benefit of the local community. Even identification of beneficiaries is also to be done by the Panchayats. The Act further aims at reducing political and bureaucratic interference in rural development programmes. For this, many states have redefined and redesigned the role of state bureaucracy in order to facilitate effective functioning of PRIs. Briefly, this Act seeks to enshrine democracy at the grass-roots. It also intends to give power to the people. Thus, the greater is the power of the Panchayats, the better it is for the people. It will end corruption and fight and finish power brokers and middlemen in politics.

It can be further added that if the problems, both at macro and micro-levels are not solved, if the 'vested interest' and the power-brokers/middlemen are not knocked out of the system; if a half-hearted unplanned exercise is being done for the democratic decentralisation; if the financial autonomy conferred with accountability is not improved, all this will affect the people's participation adversely. If the policy of the government in giving impetus to the Panchayati Raj movement is implemented faithfully and fully, it will indeed bring about the political, social and economic changes, which will not only strengthen the democratic character of the Indian society, but will also prove a perennial source of throwing up energetic leadership.[13]

It is better to conclude with Rajiv Gandhi who has said, "We trust the people. We have faith in the people. It is the people who must determine their own destinies and the destiny of the nation. To the people of India, let us ensure maximum democracy and maximum devolution. Let the people be empowered."

Notes and References

1. Hoshiar Singh: Decentralised governance and participatory Democracy Below State Level (in) C.P. Barthwal (ed.) *Public Administration in India*, New Delhi, Ashish Publishing House, 1993, p. 299.
2. Mohinder Singh: Democratic Decentralisation Through Panchayati Raj: Problems and Prospects (in) C.P. Barthwal (ed.) *Public Administration in India*, New Delhi, Ashish Publishing House, 1993, p. 309.
3. *Ibid.*, p. 310.
4. *Ibid.*, pp. 310-11.
5. Ramesh K. Arora and Rajni Goyal: Indian Public Administration: Institutions and Issues, New Delhi, Wishwa Prakashan (2nd edition) 1995, p. 308.
6. R.N. Prasad: New Panchayat system in India and its Relevance in Mizoram (in) R.N. Prasad and A.K. Agarwal (eds.) *Landmarks: A Study of Public Administration in Mizoram*, Aizawl Lengchhawn Press, 1995, pp. 332-36.
7. *Ibid.*, p. 336.
8. *Ibid.*, pp. 338-39.

9. *Ibid.*, p. 339.
10. L.S. Gassah: The Sixth Schedule and the 73rd Amendment: An Analysis, (this paper was presented at the Rajiv Gandhi Foundation Sponsored Sub-Regional workshop on 'Panchayats' and organised by ICSSR-NERC, Shillong in October 1995.
11. B.K. Roy Burman: Self-government in Tribal Areas and 73rd Amendment (in) State Panchayat Acts—A Critical Review (Annexure-V) 1995, published by Vani-Voluntary Action Network, New Delhi.
12. *Ibid.*, Annexure V.
13. R.N. Prasad: *op cit.*, pp. 340-48.

Index